cultural
icons

Auto Opium

The automobile continues to be the privileged product of the culture of mass consumption, yet there has been little scholarly attention to what concerns consumers most – the appearance of cars. *Auto Opium* is the first comprehensive history of the profession and aesthetics of American automobile design. The author reveals how the appearance of vehicles became an integral part of the system of mass production and mass consumption forged in the struggles of American society.

The book traces the development of automobile design, from the first utilitarian cars around the turn of the century to the most modern of symbol-laden cultural icons. The author shows that the aesthetic qualities of vehicles were shaped by the social conflicts generated by the process of mass production. These conflicts became channeled into the realm of mass consumption, where working Americans demanded beautiful, stylish, and constantly improving cars to compensate them for the deprivations of mass production. Creating a unique blend of business, social, and cultural history, *Auto Opium* connects the social struggles of America to the organizational struggles of designers and the marketplace struggles of firms.

David Gartman is Associate Professor of Sociology, Department of Sociology and Anthropology, University of South Alabama.

Auto Opium

A social history of American
automobile design

David Gartman

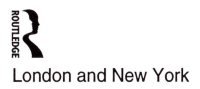

London and New York

First published 1994
by Routledge
11 New Fetter Lane, London EC4P 4EE

Simultaneously published in the USA and Canada
by Routledge
29 West 35th Street, New York, NY 10001

© 1994 David Gartman

Typeset in Times by LaserScript, Mitcham, Surrey
Printed and bound in Great Britain by
Biddles Ltd, Guildford and King's Lynn

British Library Cataloguing in Publication Data
A catalogue record for this book is available from the British Library

Library of Congress Cataloging in Publication Data
A catalog record for this book has been requested

ISBN 0–415–10571–4 (hbk)
ISBN 0–415–10572–2 (pbk)

Religion is, in fact, the self-consciousness and self-esteem of man who has either not yet gained himself or has lost himself again. . . . It is the fantastic realization of the human being because the human being has attained no true reality. . . . The wretchedness of religion is at once an expression of and a protest against real wretchedness. Religion is the sigh of the oppressed creature, the heart of a heartless world and the soul of soulless conditions. It is the opium of the people.

Karl Marx

The fact is that the automobile became a hypnosis. The automobile became the opium of the American people.

Fortune

To Betty Gartman
A woman who holds up more than half my sky

Contents

Illustrations

Preface

When researching this book in Detroit, I was given a tour of the General Motors design studios by the vice-president for design, Charles Jordan. I was whisked through the impressive facilities, experiencing an exhilarating rush of enticing images that can only be compared to a visual rollercoaster ride. Catching my breath before entering yet another room on my ride, I asked Jordan about a slick, futuristic scale-model car on a pedestal outside the door. "This," he pronounced proudly, "is our latest design religion." "Design *religion*?" I queried, my curiosity piqued by this intriguing terminology. "Yes," he replied. "We like to give people something to believe in."

This analogy between automotive style and sacred beliefs immediately evoked in me two associations, one intellectual, the other emotional. At the intellectual level, Marx's famous characterization of religion as the "opium of the people" flashed through my mind. Could stylish consumer products like cars function as a similarly narcotizing ideology, the false consciousness of contemporary capitalism?

But this bit of intellectualizing, conditioned by my theoretical allegiances, was quickly overwhelmed by an emotional reminiscence of more primordial origins. While growing up in a working-class family in a Houston suburb, automobiles had given my family, especially my father and me, something to believe in, a meaning and focus for our lives. Some of my earliest and fondest memories are of automobiles – washing, repairing, riding, and vacationing in them. My father's identity depended fundamentally on cars – "I'm a Chevy man," he resolutely declared, and never bought anything else. The workaday world of the oil refinery brought him few gratifications and numerous indignities, many of which I remember being heartfully recounted at supper time. But these wounds were soon soothed by the comforting salve of automotive consumerism. Regardless of the indignities of the workday, my father found upon returning home his shiny green 1955 Chevrolet with its powerful V–8 engine and rumbling dual exhausts waiting in the garage of our working-class suburban home ready to provide empowerment and escape. In it our family could leave the work world behind and take our place among the amorphous mass of "middle-class Americans" on the road, at the park, in the shopping mall.

Like so many working-class kids, I was soon infatuated with cars. At age ten I could identify every make and model from the distance of a suburban block. In school I filled reams of paper with drawings of cars, and at home I built model cars and pored over the pages of *Hot Rod Magazine*. My main aspiration in life was to get a job – any job – that paid enough to buy a big suburban house and allow me to build hot rods with my dad.

Were my dad and I simply dupes suffering under the delusions of false consciousness, oblivious to the inequities and indignities of America's class system due to the obscuring ideology of automotive consumerism? In confrontation with one another, both my intellectually hostile and emotionally pleasurable images of automobiles seemed simplistic. Autos and other consumer goods did not delude us about the existence of social inequities in postwar America. They merely made them more tolerable and painless. My family was daily made aware of class inequities but felt unable to do anything about them. We, like most working Americans, were merely trying to make the best life we could with the limited opportunities provided us. And participating in America's automobile culture was part of that limited but tolerable life we constructed.

Perhaps the opium of ideology – whether religious or consumerist – operates more like an actual analgesic than most Marxists suspect. People take painkillers to alleviate the symptoms of their affliction, not to fool themselves about its existence. They continue to be aware of its presence and hope for a cure, but in the meantime seek to make a bad situation at least tolerable. Working Americans struggled throughout this century for a better life for themselves and their families. But when social cures for their ills seemed remote, they were often forced to settle for the individual palliative of consumer goods like autos. They actively struck the best deal possible and were not deluded dupes.

This more subtle approach to the consumer ideology of automobility informs my study of automobile design in the United States. It complements and extends the analysis of my first book on the American auto industry, *Auto Slavery*. There I examined the development of the automotive mass-production process, arguing that its repressive technology and organization was determined by a complex, dialectical process of class struggle between managers and workers. Here I extend this argument from the production to the design and consumption of automobiles. I hope to demonstrate in what follows that the aesthetic qualities of cars were shaped by a contradictory process of class conflict in American society as a whole. Americans blocked by class power from realizing their aspirations in production were forced to turn to beautiful, stylish goods in consumption for a semblance of power, progress, and sociality. For a relatively brief period in American history, the substitute satisfactions of auto consumerism were sufficient to induce acceptance of the indignities of mass production. But ultimately America's mode of mass consumption came into contradiction with its mode of mass production, generating the social struggles of the 1960s that led to the demise of this ill-fated coupling pioneered by the auto industry.

In the long and winding road traveled by this project to its final destination, I have received a great deal of roadside assistance from fellow travelers. Funds for parts of this journey were provided by the University of South Alabama Research Committee, College of Arts and Sciences, and Department of Sociology and Anthropology. In addition, the College of Arts and Sciences provided release time and a sabbatical leave for research and writing. Early into my journey two cheerful graduate assistants, Gina Kristl and Gunn-Bente Olsen, provided bibliographic research. Mimi Hill, Linda Burcham, and Dana Linderer helped with clerical tasks. And my colleagues in the Department of Sociology and Anthropology – especially Mark Moberg and Marvin Smith, themselves knowledgeable auto enthusiasts – tolerated, encouraged, and participated in my auto obsession.

Numerous people helped fuel my research journey by providing or assisting me in obtaining data. The Interlibrary Loan staff at the University of South Alabama Library provided timely and good-humored help in tracking down a mountain of often obscure sources. Ron Grantz of the National Automotive History Collection at the Detroit Public Library offered guidance through the extensive holdings. David Crippen of the Ford Motor Company Archives provided not only access to the invaluable oral histories collected in the Edsel B. Ford Design History Center but also shared with me his extensive knowledge and enthusiasm for automobile design. And Billy Delevich gave me unlimited access to and guidance through the collections of the General Motors Design Staff Library.

For illustrations I am indebted to the Design Library of the GM Design Staff, GM Photographic, the National Automotive History Collection of the Detroit Public Library, the Chrysler Historical

Collection, and the Archives and Library of the Henry Ford Museum and Greenfield Village.

Automobile designers in Detroit's Big Three automakers generously set aside time from their pressure-packed duties to be interviewed by this unimportant academic. Open, good-natured, and tolerant to a person, they provided invaluable confirmations and, more often, refutations of my inchoate ideas on design. Special thanks go to Charles Jordan of GM, David Turner of Ford, and Jeffrey Godshall of Chrysler, who not only agreed to be interviewed themselves but also arranged interviews with their colleagues. I hope that these designers recognize that although my book is often critical of their industry, I attribute no malice or ill will to them personally. They are, like most other Americans, caught up in a system not wholly of their own making.

Numerous colleagues, known and anonymous, furthered my journey with comments and criticisms at various stages. Norbert Wiley and Randy Collins are foremost among them, but reviewers for several journals and commentators at numerous conferences and colloquia also helped steer me back on the track when I lost my way. I hope they recognize their directions in the final destination.

My editor at Routledge, Chris Rojek, provided guidance through the last perilous miles along the road to publication. Knowledgeable not only about the twists and turns of publishing but also about the subject area itself, Chris was a welcome traveling companion as I became road-weary.

Finally, my family gave me the moral and emotional support without which I never would have dared to embark on this trip. My wife Betty and daughters Greta and Hanna provided the tolerance, love, encouragement, and gentle goading – "Still working on that car book, Daddy?" – that hastened the journey and made it enjoyable.

If, despite all this exemplary roadside assistance, my vehicle has occasionally lost its way, swerved off the road, and run out of gas, this is attributable solely to the frailties of the scholar at the wheel.

Chapter 1

The aesthetics of Fordism

FORDISM: THE MARRIAGE OF MASS PRODUCTION AND MASS CONSUMPTION

Henry Ford's revolutionary mass-production process for manufacturing automobiles stands as an almost universal symbol for modern industrial capitalism. Both its hitherto unimagined material productivity and its similarly unprecedented impoverishment of the human spirit are simultaneously captured by the contradictory image of the automobile assembly line. Along such lines and in other mechanized processes pioneered by Ford, degraded and dehumanized workers toil to produce the very products that enrich their leisure lives. The incredible productivity of Fordist mass production makes possible, perhaps even necessary, mass consumption. Historians remind us that not only did Henry Ford innovate production methods that steadily lowered the price of a complex, mechanical consumer good, but he also pioneered the transformation of the toiling masses into consumers by raising his workers' wages to an incredible five dollars a day. In liberal ideology, the sins of Fordist mass production against the human spirit are more than atoned for by this rise in the material prosperity of the masses that is its corollary within industrial capitalism.

Recently, however, the positive nature of this coupling of mass production and mass consumption under the rubric of Fordism has been challenged by a generally critical school of thought known as the Regulation School. This group of French economists heavily influenced by Marx conceptualizes the rise of mass consumption from the base of mass production not as just compensation for but the consolidation of a basically exploitative system of production. No humanitarian impulse but the sheer requirements of reproducing the capitalist economic system as such motivated the extension of the capacity to consume mass-produced products to the working class. These French theorists build their analysis on the insights of an Italian thinker, Antonio Gramsci. In his seminal essay, "Americanism and Fordism," Gramsci uses the latter term to refer not merely to revolutionary production methods pioneered by Ford but also to the new mode and standard of living which necessarily accompanies them. Ford's revolution in production requires a similarly revolutionary transformation in the consumption of the working class, which Ford also initiated with his Five Dollar Day and cajoling investigations into workers' private lives.[1]

Generalizing on Gramsci's insights, the Regulation School theorists postulate that every form of capitalist production requires a complementary form of consumption. Each such stable, equilibrious system of production and consumption within capitalism is called a regime of accumulation. However, they hold that this equilibrium between production and consumption is not established automatically through the autonomous workings of the economic market, but requires a set of noneconomic institutions to regulate the behavior of individuals and ensure their conformity to economic requirements. This set of noneconomic institutions is called a mode of regulation.[2]

Fordism is a regime of accumulation based upon specialized machines and the semiautomatic assembly line. These production processes separated workers from any skill or control over their work, and consequently increased the intensity and productivity of their labor. This new mass-production process required a new mass-consumption process for its completion and realization. In order to absorb the masses of products streaming out of Fordist factories, workers' means of consumption had to be commodified, that is, they had to become consumers of the products they produced. It was necessary to increase the workers' level of consumption and the wages that supported it to ensure not only the macroeconomic reproduction of capitalism as a whole but also the microeconomic reproduction of labor power within the firm. Fordism intensified work pace to such an extent that the recuperation of labor power could be accomplished solely in nonworking hours by the time-saving consumption of commodities purchased on the market.[3]

This balancing of mass production and mass consumption was not, however, accomplished automatically by the self-reproducing mechanisms of the market, but required the construction of a set of social institutions regulating individual actions to system needs. Large, stable markets for standardized goods were required to justify the large fixed investments in mass-production technology. The modern, bureaucratic corporation emerged as the institution that created such markets through coordinated means of advertising, product design, and mass distribution. A collective-bargaining system focused on wages and benefits and conceding managerial control of production emerged as the institution ensuring the stability of consumer demand and worker effort required of Fordism. And finally, an interventionist state was gradually constituted to guarantee adequate levels of aggregate demand with countercyclical policies and social insurance programs.[4]

CRITIQUE OF THE REGULATION THEORY OF FORDISM

For the Regulation School, then, the system of mass consumption, which brings some of the fruits of mass production to the working class, is not the humanistic end and ultimate justification of advanced capitalism. Mass consumption is merely the functional requirement of a fundamentally exploitative system which takes as its end the production of profit, not the needs of human beings. But despite its insights into the rise of mass consumption from mass production, regulation theory seems inadequate in at least two areas. First, the explanations of this school are marred by the fallacious logic of functionalism, which takes the causes of things as their consequences. In accounting for the emergence of the institutions of mass consumption, regulation theorists deem it sufficient merely to demonstrate that they are required for the continued functioning of the capitalist system. But the mere fact that an institution is needed by the system does not explain how and why it emerges through the concrete, historical actions of socially situated people. Systems are abstractions – they do not act, only people do. Socioeconomic systems meet their requirements of reproduction only through the actions of individuals, who feel these requirements as personal needs.[5] To explain why mass consumption followed on the historical heels of mass production, we must know why concrete people felt the need to consume larger and larger quantities of commodities. Stuck at the macro level of system requirements, regulation theorists never get down to this micro level of individuals and their felt needs. Individuals appear in their analyses as mere supports of the system, who are effortlessly molded to want what the system requires.[6]

This functionalist reduction of individual needs to system needs leads to another typically functionalist problem in regulation theory – the underestimation of the importance of class conflict. Focus on functional needs diverts attention from the fact that individuals in different social positions have different interests in the system's functioning. Some have their needs met by the smooth functioning of the system, but others do not. These different socioeconomic positions with their distinct interests are generally called classes. Attempts by the dominant class to reproduce the system from which it generously benefits often run up against the opposition of the dominated class. Class conflict is an inevitable part of any class-divided system of production, and not only creates problems for its smooth functioning but also shapes attempts to solve these problems.

Regulation theorists largely ignore the role of class conflict in the rise of mass consumption. They conceptualize its emergence as a simple social engineering project implemented unproblematically by the dominant class to solve the economic problems of mass production. But mass consumption is more validly seen as a contingent and historically evolving result of the class conflict created by capitalist mass production. It emerged not as an economic solution to abstract problems of reproduction but as an ideological solution to the concrete problems of conflict within mass-production factories. To quell the eruption of worker discontent with the dehumanizing conditions of mass production, capitalists and managers found it necessary to compensate workplace repression with consumption freedoms. But this extension of increasing levels of consumption to workers was not a simple, conscious strategy of capitalists foisted on easily duped workers but the complex, unintended outcome of a process of class struggle in which the actions of each class were limited by those of its opponents.

A second inadequacy of the regulation theory of Fordism is its nearly complete inattention to the aesthetics of mass-produced consumer goods. Because these theorists conceptualize mass consumption from the standpoint of system needs alone, they pay little attention to how these goods appeal to individuals, beyond fulfilling their physical needs. The appearance of mass-produced goods is naively assumed to be dictated by the necessities of mass production alone. To allow for mass production on inflexible, automatic machines, it is argued, products like Ford's Model T adopted a functionalist aesthetic, i.e., were reduced to stark, standardized designs eschewing any superfluous style changes or decoration. Through advertising and other manipulative techniques, corporations standardized consumer wants to render them satisfiable by these standardized products.[7]

But this simplistic causal connection between mass production and functionalist aesthetics is clearly mistaken. Due to their myopic focus on Ford, regulation theorists neglect the real pioneer in product aesthetics who forged a design idiom joining mass production and mass consumption – General Motors's Alfred Sloan. In order to compete in an automobile market in which demand for basic transportation was becoming saturated, Sloan decided in the mid-1920s to offer customers "style," cars with superficially distinctive and diversified ornamentation. This style changed annually to aesthetically depreciate models with years of functional service remaining and to whet consumer appetites for the new. And GM arranged its different models in a stylistic hierarchy, stimulating consumers to upgrade their autos and achieve consumer mobility. Sloan's pioneering work in planned obsolescence and product hierarchies provided the model for other mass-production industries faced with competing in markets in which demand for functional goods was saturated.

So contrary to the regulation theorists, consumer goods eschewed a standardized, functionalist aesthetic shortly after the onset of mass production. The foundation of mass consumption became an aesthetic of change and diversity, which was required to stimulate consumer demand sufficient to sustain high-volume mass production. But the new aesthetic of Fordism was not the simple result of capitalist schemes to expand markets for mass production. It was the complex result of an interaction of this economic requirement with the needs of consumers themselves. And these needs were not unilaterally shaped by marketplace manipulation but had their origins in the complex struggles of the Fordist workplace.

COMPLETING THE FORDIST FRAMEWORK: THE CONTRIBUTION OF CRITICAL THEORY

The inadequacies of the Fordist framework may be overcome by appending to it the insights into mass consumption made by critical theory or the Frankfurt School. Like regulation theory, this school of social thought finds its theoretical foundation in Marx's historical materialism. But unlike the former, critical theory focuses not solely on the economic but also the cultural function of mass consumption, the way it channels individual needs into forms which legitimate capitalist mass production. Critical theory's conception of the culture of mass consumption begins at the level of individuals and their needs.

Historically, culture has served as a repository for all the human needs that are not realized within a given form of society. Art, music, literature, and crafts have provided an outlet for the free, self-determining activity that human beings need but are denied in most areas of their lives by the class structure of society. Such culture can serve a critical function in society, reminding people of the needs unjustly denied them and holding out the promise of a future fulfillment. However, critical theorists contend that this utopian function is eliminated in advanced capitalism with the rise of a mass culture, which serves not as a repository of repressed needs but as an ideological adaptation of human needs to the requirements of capitalist mass production.[8]

This ideological legitimation of mass production by mass consumption is best analyzed in Max Horkheimer and Theodor Adorno's seminal text, "The culture industry: enlightenment as mass deception." Here the authors argue that capitalist mass production is governed by a dehumanizing technological rationality or logic of reification. For the sake of profit, human beings are reduced to things, stripped of any freedom and reduced to heteronomous cogs in a productive machinery designed and controlled by the agents of capital. In an attempt to find refuge from the dehumanizing realm of production, its victims flee into the privatized realm of consumption in the home. In their leisure lives, workers seek to recoup some of the autonomy and individuality lost in the work world. But the logic of reification pursues them there in the form of consumer products and prevents this culture from providing a critical negation of capitalist work. A culture industry emerges to provide people with leisure commodities with which to escape dehumanized mass production. But since the production of these cultural goods is governed by the same logic of reification found in the other forms of mass production, the culture industry turns out similarly standardized, dehumanized products whose consumption serves to reinforce the demands of work. As in mass production, in mass consumption real human needs are reduced to formal properties for the sake of manipulation. Consumers are reduced to market segments whose needs may be classified and standardized for the sake of profit. Consequently, mass consumption becomes merely a prolongation and ideological reinforcement of capitalist mass production. As Horkheimer and Adorno write:

> Amusement under late capitalism . . . is sought after as an escape from the mechanized work process, and to recruit strength in order to be able to cope with it again. But at the same time mechanization has such power over a man's leisure and happiness, and so profoundly determines the manufacture of amusement goods, that his experiences are inevitably after-images of the work process itself. The ostensible content is merely a faded background; what sinks in is the automatic succession of standardized operations. What happens at work, in the factory, or in the office can only be escaped from by approximation to it in one's leisure time.[9]

The Frankfurt School's focus on the way mass consumption ideologically integrates an individual's needs with the requirements of Fordist mass production necessarily lends greater attention to product aesthetics. Since the purpose of consumption is to compensate people for and consequently reconcile them to the dehumanizing process of mass production, then the aesthetic form of products is just as or more important than their utilitarian content, for people seek through these goods satisfaction not merely of material needs but also of needs of the human spirit. Critical theory's central insight into mass-consumption aesthetics is that, to offer ersatz satisfactions for needs repressed by mass production, consumer goods must not appear to be mass-produced, must not bear the visible marks of the standardized, deskilled process of production from which they issue. If consumer products displayed their true nature as homogenized assemblages of parts produced by heteronomous, degraded labor, they would be constant reminders of the dehumanization suffered by people at work and consequently incapable of providing the forgetting of these maladies in leisure that compensates for them. The things of mass consumption must obscure the social relations of production from which they originate – they must themselves be "thingified" or reified.

The aesthetic reification of products required to integrate them into the amnestic world of mass consumption is accomplished primarily by sealing over the fissures and tensions that the socially antagonistic and fragmented production process inevitably produces. Forgetting the inhuman domination of the workplace is possible only if the products consumed in leisure conceal the scars, lacerations, and cleavages inflicted on nature – both human and nonhuman – in the process of their production. The culture industry accomplishes this through the artificial imposition of a smooth, organic appearance on the technological essence of products. Adorno argues that people prefer in their cultural commodities the appearance of nature to the appearance of technology, for while the latter's ugliness is reminiscent of the domination of capitalist mass production, the former's beauty does not bear the stigma of capitalism. Images of nature appended to technological products provide temporary relief from the capitalist production process by referring to a world beyond or before the domination of things and people by the logic of exchange value. Within a society of continuing class antagonisms, the peaceful, seamless world of nature serves as a pseudo-reconciliation which leaves social cleavages untouched and reinforced. Adorno writes that, when the image of nature is "falsely claimed to be a state of real reconcilation, then natural beauty would be reduced to a means for justifying and disguising antagonisms in a society. . . ."[10] In the music of mass culture, for example, all forms that might bear witness to the social antagonisms of capitalist production are exorcised and replaced by a sweet, superficial glossiness. Musical dissonance and complex melodic developments are replaced by simplistic harmonies and superficial gaiety so popular tunes may be consumed without disturbing the mental relaxation of listeners.[11]

Having glossed over the marks left on products by the antagonisms of their mass production, the culture industry is then free to manipulate their appearance in order to offer ersatz satisfactions of needs denied in this alienating production process. To obscure product standardization and compensate people for their similar reduction to standardized things at work, producers offer the illusion of diversity and individuality. Popular music, for example, offers this pseudoindividuality through instrumental improvisations, which appear spontaneous but in reality conform to strict formulas.[12] And to compensate people for the timeless repetition of the same operations at work, leisure products make a fetish of the latest and the new. The culture industry focuses on the latest hit tune, the newest film star, the hottest trend in art. But, as Adorno reminds us: "What parades as progress in the culture industry, as the incessantly new which it offers up, remains the disguise for an eternal sameness; everywhere the changes mask a skeleton which has changed just as little as the profit motive itself since the time it first gained its predominance over culture."[13]

Through such aesthetic manipulations, critical theorists contend, the products of alienating mass production cover the telltale marks of their social origins and enter harmlessly into the realm of mass consumption to serve as substitute satisfactions for needs denied at work. People are ideologically adjusted and integrated into the oppressive system of Fordist production by a propaganda of manipulated things. The culture industry turns material products into powerful tools of persuasion, screaming "you've never had it so good" so loudly in leisure that the repressive cadence of the production line fades into the background of consciousness. In the process, the very nature of human needs is changed. The true needs for love, freedom, and self-determining activity rooted deeply in the human body and mind are purged of their explosive potential and perverted into false needs for commodities which support the Fordist system.[14]

THE LIMITATIONS OF CRITICAL THEORY

Unlike regulation theory, the critical theory of mass consumption calls attention to the needs of individuals and the way that they are integrated into mass production through the aesthetics of consumer products. And it also reveals this integration of mass consumption and mass production to be the result of concrete human action, not some functional requirement of the system. But the action in critical theory's portrayal of mass consumption is unilateral – the conscious manipulation of the masses by the culture industry. The Frankfurt School gives us culture czars constructing consumer products with the explicit intent of supplying superficial satisfactions that ideologically reconcile people to capitalist mass production. Through the propaganda of mass consumption, the masses are easily persuaded to abandon their true needs for false needs satisfied by commodities. And to this unilateral manipulation of their lives, both at work and play, the masses offer little or no resistance. Critical theory's use of "masses" instead of "working class" to refer to the dominated populace of advanced capitalism conveys its conception of these people as completely disorganized and atomized by the complex structures of production and consumption. Resistance to the class domination of Fordist production is precluded by the ideological integration engineered by mass consumption. The needs of the working class are so thoroughly transformed into the false needs for commodities that people no longer feel the need for social change but are perfectly satisfied with their state of domination, even complicit with it. Consumer complacency has so thoroughly gripped the masses that the traditional Marxist idea of class struggle is rendered a conceptual relic.[15]

Critical theory's limitation of the action shaping mass consumption to the manipulation of the passive masses by conspiratorial elites distorts the historical process by which mass consumption arose and became adjusted to mass production. As critics of the Frankfurt School have pointed out, the working classes of capitalist society have not been as supinely passive nor the capitalist classes as omnisciently manipulative as portrayed in these works.[16] The historical record reveals that the coupling of mass consumption with mass production to form the Fordist regime of accumulation was the result of a contingent process of class struggle and capitalist competition, in which employers groped to find strategies that not only contained resistance at the workplace but also competed successfully for consumers in the marketplace. The aesthetics of mass-produced products are better conceptualized as the result of this historically situated, contingent process of class struggle.

The cultural theory of Georg Lukács better grasps the centrality of class struggle in shaping the aesthetic forms of cultural productions. Although critical theorists have been heavily influenced by Lukács's work, especially his concept of cultural reification, they do not recognize the importance of historically situated class conflict in bringing this reification into existence. Lukács conceptualizes cultural works as active interventions in the class struggles of historically concrete societies. In their productions, cultural producers seek to resolve in formal, imaginary ways the problems and dilemmas created by the antagonisms of a class-divided society. These interventions are always political – they legitimate the interests of one class or another in the struggle for power – although most often not consciously or intentionally so. Cultural resolutions of social conflicts are inevitably political because their producers are limited in their conceptual horizons, first, by the interests of their class position, and second, by the relation of that class to the historical struggles of humanity for freedom. For example, Lukács argues that the productions of the bourgeois writers became reified, thus obscuring the social relations of class, only after capitalist society was consolidated and the bourgeoisie was no longer itself involved in active conflict with the feudal ruling class. No longer having the interest of an ascendant class in active conflict but now possessing the interest of a ruling class in consolidating its rule against the rising class of workers, bourgeois writers unintentionally began to depict social reality as an established, static thing, thus hiding the reality of dynamic class relations behind the facade of unchanging nature.[17]

Lukács's cultural theory implies that the rise of mass consumption and its reified aesthetics are driven by the motor of historical class struggle. In such a formulation, working-class people would appear not as passive objects of capitalist cultural manipulation but as active subjects struggling to realize their needs against the opposition of their class enemies. This more active conception of the origins of mass consumption requires a modification not only of critical theory's conception of culture but also its idea of human needs, upon which culture is based. Critical theorists hold that the true human needs for conscious, free activity, which provide the foundation for liberating class struggle, are easily displaced by the false needs for commodities inculcated by the propaganda of the culture industry. A more active, class-struggle conception of culture requires for its foundation a conception of human needs as more intransigent and less malleable than suggested by critical theory, rooted in a human nature that may be developed, diverted, and channeled by societal forms but not fundamentally transformed. Such a conception is found in Marx's 1844 *Economic and Philosophical Manuscripts*, where he postulates a set of inherent human capacities and needs – a "species-being." Humans are by nature, Marx argues, active, social creatures whose consciousness gives them the potential for self-determination, activity free from necessity. The historical mode of production may constrain and limit the realization of this potential, but it cannot suppress the natural desire for freedom. This desire remains intransigent and provides for Marx the potential for overturning capitalist alienation and building a society of freely associated producers which realizes human nature. Only because Marx holds to the inalterable character of basic species-needs can he assert that the historical class most deprived of their fulfillment by total alienation and reification can be the agent of their ultimate historical realization.[18]

The Frankfurt School, particularly Herbert Marcuse, originally sought to integrate these Marxist insights about human needs with Freudian psychology. Marcuse holds that the need for free activity linking people to other humans and nature has a somatic basis, is built into the body as instinct. But he goes on to argue that the manipulations of the culture industry are so powerful that they reach down to this somatic level and displace true needs with false needs for commodities.[19] This conception of the total malleability of human needs is incompatible not only with Marx but also with Freud, who holds that although they may be repressed, channeled, and sublimated, the instincts themselves are intransigent. Rather than see the needs appealed to by consumer goods as false needs engineered by the culture industry, my formulation conceptualizes them as true needs for self-determining activity channeled by class conflict into the only path compatible with capitalism – commodity consumption. This conception portrays working-class consumers not as passive dupes unaware of their true needs but as active people consciously struggling to realize their needs in the best way possible. It implies that the forms of consumer products are not open to total manipulation but are constrained by the necessity of appealing, however obliquely and perversely, to the desires blocked by the alienating organization of capitalist mass production. The aesthetics of Fordist commodities becomes an arena of conflict, in which class struggle and capitalist competition force producers to superficially adjust their inhumanly produced goods to the real human needs displaced into consumption.

EMPIRICAL APPLICATION OF MODIFIED FORDIST THEORY: THE AMERICAN AUTOMOBILE

There is no more crucial case for testing the validity of this modified theory of Fordism than the American automobile. The theory takes as its paradigm of twentieth-century capitalist development the revolutionary changes in the production and consumption of goods introduced by the American auto industry. This industry pioneered mass-production technology that fantastically increased output at the cost of degrading and alienating the labor of its millions of workers. And automotive corporations similarly pioneered the techniques of marketing and distributing mass-produced consumer goods to the working masses, whose revolt against the degradation of factory work raised wages and created mass markets. Planned obsolescence, annual model changes, and product hierarchies were all policies originating in the auto industry to stimulate the sales of its product. And at the heart of these marketing strategies was an overriding concern for the aesthetic design of the automobile. American automobile corporations were the first mass-production firms to employ a full staff of in-house designers whose sole concern was the appearance of the product. Their experiences of integrating product styling into large, mass-production corporations created the model for other firms to follow.

The following study examines the history of the American automobile industry's pioneering efforts in the design of mass-produced goods in light of the theory of Fordist aesthetics outlined above. I hope to show that automobile design was fundamentally shaped by the dual exigencies of capitalist competition and class conflict within American society. Class conflict produced an insulated realm of mass consumption that ideologically legitimated the degradation of mass-production work. And capitalist competition drove auto firms to expand their sales into mass markets, which could be accomplished only by obscuring the auto's connection to this degrading work and offering ersatz satisfactions for it. My focus throughout is thus predominantly on class conflict, with gender and racial struggles downplayed. Consequently, my history of auto design is necessarily incomplete, and requires supplementation by the research of scholars more knowledgeable about gender and racial divisions and antagonisms than I. However, I hope that my study can provide a foundation for such research, for I believe that the class structure and conflicts of America have conditioned how these separate structures of oppression have come into play historically.

To demonstrate these theses, I examine historical evidence at several overlapping and interpenetrating levels of American society. Much of the subsequent analysis is preoccupied with the evidence of business history. I focus on the design of automobiles in the context of organizational struggles within firms for power and competitive struggles between firms for markets. Particularly important data at this level are the purposes and intentions of automotive managers and designers in instituting specific design policies. However, to understand the real as opposed to the intended effects of design on consumers, the public perception and reception of automobiles is also examined. Evidence of the received effects and meanings are culled from American cultural history. And finally, all of this evidence is placed in the broader context of the social history of the United States, that is, the social conflicts and antagonisms of differentially placed groups, especially classes, that molded the development of both American business and culture.

This evidence is used to trace the development of American automobile design, beginning with the first manufactured automobiles around the turn of the century. The detailed historical narrative ends around 1970, although I do bring the story up to the present with a more sketchy epilogue. This cutoff date roughly marks the beginning of Fordism's decline and the onset of a protracted period of crisis and restructuring. This period deserves the specific scholarly scrutiny it is now beginning to get. But its details fall beyond the scope of this study, which is concerned mainly with the growth and consolidation of the Fordist system of production and consumption and how it molded automobile design.

My examination of these concerns begins in Chapter 2, which treats the early and largely utilitarian development of the basic automotive form. During this period the basic configuration of the automobile was worked out without much conscious attention to aesthetics as such. The rise of stylistic concerns around 1910 and their diverging paths of development are the topics of Chapter 3. During the period extending to about 1925, automotive design was bifurcated into mass and craft vehicles. While the latter cars developed integrated and coordinated shapes produced by a laborious craft process, the mass-produced vehicles developed a disjointed, rectilinear form adjusted to the requirements of the deskilled production process. This growing aesthetic gap in vehicles testified to the growing class cleavages produced by Fordist mass production. Chapter 4 treats the way in which class struggles precipitated by these cleavages, as well as competitive and organizational struggles, gave rise to the "styling" of mass-produced automobiles in the 1920s. The struggles of American workers against the degradations of Fordist production forced up wages and allowed them to construct a world of insulated mass consumption. But in order to sell cars to this growing market, companies found that they had to cover over the telltale marks of mass production and its class differences. So beginning in the 1920s, GM began to offer mass-produced cars that resembled handcrafted vehicles and to employ a staff of stylists to accomplish this camouflage. The flowering of these design trends came in the 1930s and is treated in Chapter 5. The exacerbation of competitive and class struggles by the Great Depression placed a premium on stimulating sales through designs that obscured the tainted factory origins of autos. The result was the streamlining craze of the period.

But as the United States emerged from the Second World War as the undisputed world leader in mass production, it became clear that more was required to sell autos to the increasingly prosperous and suburbanized working class than a smooth organic shell to hide the fragmented, mechanical reality. In the 1950s, the period covered in Chapter 6, cars began to offer fantastic fulfillments of desires denied at work, culminating in the bizarre, finned dream machines of the era. But as the finned illusions of the 1950s turned into standardized clichés, raising public skepticism about the superiority of American technology, the automakers appealed to America's frustrated desire for individuality with a bewildering proliferation of models in the 1960s. Chapter 7 treats this segmentation of the market into narrow niches, which appealed to a people seeking to define their fragmented identities with consumer goods. This decade also contained the stirrings of revolt that shook the Fordist system of production and consumption to its very foundations in the 1970s. The epilogue sketches the demise of Fordist design and the rise of increasingly bifurcated design idioms that testify to the polarized class structure emerging on the ashes of Fordism.

Together, these chapters trace the development of the automobile and its design from a useful machine of transport to an ideological dream of transportation from the ills of capitalist production. In modern America, consumer products, and above all the automobile, became the major vehicle of ideology, legitimating and justifying the system to its millions of victims. The car provided to twentieth-century capitalism what religion had to its nineteenth-century predecessor – a world of narcotizing illusion in which the repressed desires of real life could be sublimated and superficially satisfied. This study traces the cultivation of this auto opium.

Chapter 2

Early development of the automotive form

In 1906 Woodrow Wilson, while president of Princeton University, offered an opinion of the automobile that was common during its infancy. "Nothing has spread Socialistic feeling in this country more than the use of automobiles. To the countryman they are a picture of arrogance of wealth with all its independence and carelessness." Just over a quarter-century later Adolf Hitler reflected the judgment of his age in pronouncing Wilson's verdict on the auto wrong. Hitler, an ardent disciple of Henry Ford, announced: "I have come to the conclusion that the motorcar, instead of being a class dividing element, can be the instrument for uniting the different classes, just as it has done in America, thanks to Mr Ford's genius." In emulation of his hero, Hitler tried to bring automobility to his nation's masses by launching a massive highway construction project and beginning production of the "people's car," the Volkswagen.[1]

Hitler's forced, fascist scheme to bring cars to the masses was different from America's road to mass automobility through free-market entrepreneurs like Ford. Yet these different means should not obscure the similar ends. In both countries, the spread of this consummate consumer good united classes not in reality, by narrowing the gap of economic and political power, but merely in appearance, by obscuring class differences behind a facade of mass consumption. And this auto- motive ideology required more for its accomplishment than cheapening vehicles and spreading their ownership. The aesthetics of automobiles also had to be transformed. In the days of Wilson's pronouncement, the new horseless carriages connoted class and power through their very appearance. But by the mid-1930s, these class connotations were being displaced by an aesthetic of democracy that seemed to unite opposing classes.

AMERICA, 1893–1911: CRISIS, CONFLICT, CONSOLIDATION, CULTURE

Wilson's fear of the automobile inciting socialist feelings reflected his tumultuous times. The auto burst onto the American scene in a period of capitalist crisis and class conflict, and was inevitably associated with these struggles. In 1893, the year in which Charles and Frank Duryea drove the first exploding, 1-cylinder American car along the streets of Springfield, Massachusetts, the stock market crashed, sending the nation into a depression that lasted through 1897. Just one year earlier in Homestead, Pennsylvania, the streets had been filled with the more ominous explosions of gunfire and dynamite as workers locked out of Andrew Carnegie's steel mills battled Pinkerton detectives in one of the bitterest labor disputes in American history.

These social explosions that coincided with the technological explosion of the automobile were the culmination of a period of crisis in American capitalism dating back some twenty years.[2] By the mid-1870s, the long swing of economic growth that had begun around 1850 had reached its peak and given way to decline. During the stage of initial capitalist accumulation, industrial production had grown largely by drawing more Americans into wage labor. But by 1874, larger inputs of labor failed to generate increases in industrial growth. Employers responded to increased competition by cutting wages and intensifying labor, touching off such monumental labor struggles as Homestead, Haymarket, and Pullman. The industrial workers of this period were by and large craftworkers, whose skills gave them a great deal of control over the immediate production process. And they jealously guarded this workplace control through strong craft unions and an ethical code of conduct. So when employers facing sagging profits sought to impose lower wages, longer hours, and intensified work, factories exploded in bitter class conflict.

These labor battles of the late nineteenth century led many employers to conclude that nothing short of a wholesale reorganization of the factory and society could solve the crisis. The first step in capitalist reorganization was the consolidation of competing firms into giant industrial oligopolies. The great wave of mergers in the last two decades of the century reduced competition and gave rise to large joint stock companies backed by bank financing. In a second step to address the crisis, the owners and managers of these newborn industrial giants focused on their own production processes, which still utilized traditional technologies controlled largely by skilled workers. They realized that increasing the productivity and profitability of their firms required a revolution in the production process itself, transferring the power to control production from skilled craftworkers to capital. The battle plan for such a revolution was offered by Frederick Taylor's program of scientific management, which began to attract the attention of industrial managers during this period. Taylor's techniques of time study, centralized planning, division of labor, and incentive wages launched the revolutionary war to wrest skill and knowledge away from craftworkers and consolidate these into the hands of white-collar technicians and professionals. But the battle would not be won until Henry Ford entered the fray with his powerful new weapons of mass production.

The workers of emerging industrial giants did not, however, take managerial efforts to deskill and debase their labor lying down. The capitalist reorganization of the labor process was met with often-bitter opposition by workers and their unions. And corporate capitalists faced opposition not only from workers but also from small capitalists, farmers, and middle-class reformers, who rightly feared that their own interests were threatened by the growing power of the industrial giants. To contain and suppress this outpouring of social discontent, corporate capitalists subtly shaped and steered it into forms compatible with their interests. In many of their activities they found ready allies in the new middle class of professionals and specialists. Both groups championed the Progressive movement, which sought to rationalize the social order through efficient, bureaucratic administration that displaced the partisan political struggles in which the working class was beginning to exert influence. Such a rationalized, cooperative, bureaucratic political framework provided the stability and predictability that monopoly capitalism required.

These monumental economic, social, and political changes had a profound influence on the cultures of American society, particularly that of the propertied class or bourgeoisie. Adjusted to the demands of competitive capitalism, the traditional bourgeois ethos emphasized individual autonomy and salvation through self-denying work. But the rise of large-scale monopoly capitalism undermined the ideal of the autonomous self by making the average bourgeois dependent upon the organized market and hierarchical corporation. Increasingly, businessmen and professionals sought to recoup a sense of autonomy and selfhood in private, leisure activities. In the late nineteenth and early twentieth centuries, the bourgeois work ethic was gradually replaced by a therapeutic ethic, stressing self-realization through healthy recreation and consumption that provided relief from the bureaucratic routines of business and politics.[3]

The American working class of the turn of the century stood largely outside of the changing bourgeois culture, with an alternative, if not oppositional, culture of its own. Native-born craftworkers carried into this period a mutualistic code of ethics which restrained the individualistic pursuit of gain in the name of the collective interest of the craft. Their defensive struggles with corporate employers generated an even broader ideology of mutualism that clashed with the acquisitive individualism that justified capitalist society. The influx of unskilled immigrant workers created cultural divisions within the working class that prevented a unity of ideology and action. Yet, as Roy Rosenzweig has noted, within each insular ethnic community there existed a similar culture of mutuality, reciprocity, and collectivity that differed from bourgeois individualism and often provided the basis for parochial working-class struggles.[4]

Realizing that workplace struggles against new production methods often had their basis in these solidarities of working-class communities, corporate capitalists and their middle-class allies resolved to rationalize the lives of workers outside the factories, as well as within. In the first decade of the twentieth century, corporations and community reformers intervened to control and stabilize workers' leisure activities in order to support their rationalized workplace activities. Through corporate welfare work, community social work, and Americanization programs, bourgeois crusaders attacked working-class saloons, rowdy holiday celebrations, unorganized play, ethnic traditions and customs, and other manifestations of the alternative working-class culture. In their place they sought to inculcate workers with the bourgeois cultural traits of individualism, privatism, and acquisitiveness, all founded on the insular, stable nuclear family. In many communities these bourgeois intrusions into working-class culture were unwelcome, and class struggle raged on the cultural as well as the economic and political fronts.[5]

This intense class conflict in American society around the turn of the century inevitably shaped the reception and development of the automobile, which emerged during this period. At first expensive and unreliable, this technological innovation was immediately associated with the idle sport and conspicuous consumption of the wealthy. Its very appearance attested to the command of the labor of scores of skilled craftworkers who produced, drove, and maintained it. And the automobile's unwelcome intrusion into farm and working-class communities symbolized the threatening grasp of arrogant corporate capital.

THE INDUSTRY AND AESTHETICS OF THE EARLY AUTOMOBILE

The early pioneers of the automobile were very little concerned with the aesthetics or social connotations of their crude self-propelled vehicles. They were practical mechanics and engineers preoccupied with the mechanical problems of adapting an engine to a personal means of transportation. In fact, most of the early inventors paid scant attention to vehicle design, being content to merely mount a motor on a light carriage or a bicycle. In Germany, Carl Benz placed his 1-cylinder gas engine on a tricycle with a conventional tubular-steel frame. In the United States, Charles and Frank Duryea, two bicycle mechanics, built the first gasoline-engined American car from a ladies' phaeton carriage, fortified with steel bicycle tubing. And Henry Ford's first car, built in 1896, was a "quadricycle," a light-weight buggy frame with four bicycle wheels and a 2-cylinder gasoline engine mounted on the rear.[6]

The bicycle and carriage industries of the United States contributed not only their products but also their capital and manufacturing facilities to the upstart motorized contraption. While other investors were leery of the new contraption, manufacturers of bicycles and carriages proved willing to divert existing plant facilities and labor to the production of automobiles in attempts to diversify their product lines. It was relatively easy for bicycle companies like Pope, Rambler, and Willys to turn to auto manufacturing due to similarities in production and construction. Both vehicles were constructed of steel parts like chain-and-sprocket drives, wire wheels, and ball bearings, which were produced by skilled machinists on machine tools and assembled by skilled mechanics. Many of the machine tools and metallurgical processes pioneered for bicycle manufacture were quickly adapted to auto production. The main contribution of the carriage industry was the overall layout and appearance of the first automobiles. Unlike the bicycle frame, the light buggy proved a good platform for automotive components – strong enough to bear the weight, yet not so heavy as to strain the power of the still-primitive gasoline engines. Manufacturers of horse-drawn vehicles like Nash and Studebaker took up production of motor vehicles in the industry's infant stage. Between about 1897 and 1900, the vast majority of cars manufactured in the United States were modeled on light buggies and called "runabouts." They had an engine under the seat, chain drive to the rear axle, a simple box body, equal-sized carriage wheels, and tiller steering. Aesthetically, they lived up to their name of "horseless carriages."[7]

Figure 1 1898 Winton, an example of the early runabout design. These cars revealed little concern for automobile design as such, merely adopting the form of horse-drawn carriages. (Courtesy National Automotive History Collection, Detroit Public Library)

Even more influenced by carriage design than these first gasoline-engined autos were the electric vehicles. Early vehicles with electric motors had the advantages of being silent, free of objectionable emission odors, and easy to operate, making them popular with the upper class, especially the women. Electric autos quickly became part of the bourgeois social scene and were consequently fitted with the elegant, handcrafted coachwork to which this class was accustomed in horse-drawn vehicles. But these electric vehicles had distinct disadvantages which proved their ultimate demise in competition with gasoline-powered autos. The main mechanical problem was the short range of operation on a battery charge – usually less than 50 miles. But the cultural connotation of femininity that the electrics acquired was also a handicap in an industry with a pronounced masculine bias.[8]

The conservatism of many Americans toward mechanical innovations may have also steered the primitive auto toward carriage styles. Such innovations often disrupt established lifestyles and traditions, creating a resistance that has often been overcome by casting the new technology in an older, familiar form. Most early autos were costly and thus available mainly to the wealthy bourgeoisie. But many in this genteel group seemed put off by the rude, mechanical contraptions. So early manufacturers sought to increase their acceptability by concealing all the machinery and making them look like the horse-drawn vehicles with which this group was familiar. As an early automobile journal, *The Horseless Age*, stated on May 3, 1899: "Most designers struggle to make the self-propelled carriage as innocent of machinery and as short as though a horse were to be attached at any time."[9]

DEVELOPMENT OF A UNIQUE AUTOMOTIVE FORM

The anachronistic carriage aesthetic of early automobiles was displaced in the middle of the first decade of the century by a more appropriate mechanical aesthetic. A major reason for this shift was the technical deficiencies of the buggy-inspired vehicles. These cheap, light cars were weakly constructed and lacked power, and consequently could not stand up to the stresses of daily use on rough roads. One buggy car, the 1-cylinder, $500 Brush Runabout, was popularly described as "wooden body, wooden axles, wooden wheels, wooden run." But an aesthetic deficiency also handicapped the carriage design – it had a "horse-wanted look." Without the horse, which lent a sense of power and horizontal direction to the vehicle, the motorized buggy seemed uneasily high and lacking a sense of propulsion.[10]

Although the buggy-type auto made a brief resurgence in popularity between 1907 and 1910, the trend among American manufacturers from the early years of the century was toward the European design known as the Système Panhard. Invented by the French manufacturer Emile Levassor in 1891, this innovative layout placed the engine under a hood at the front of the chassis, and followed it with a friction clutch, a sliding-pinion gearbox, and a final drive to the rear wheels. This configuration not only allowed for larger engines and better weight distribution, but it also marked a radical aesthetic departure from the carriage silhouette. European cars adopting the Système Panhard were longer, lower, and heavier, with their means of locomotion visually registered by the long, prominent engine hoods and the exposed drive chains. They were obviously machines, not horse-drawn vehicles, and initiated the development of a mechanical aesthetic which celebrated technical innovations.[11]

Initially this European design was poorly received by America's equine upper class. But by 1905, a writer in a popular journal remarked that America's "horsey people" were being "unconsciously educated away from shapes that remind one of things not mechanical, toward shapes that are not only mechanical but typical of standard automobile construction." By mid-decade, the proudly mechanical Système Panhard had become so popular among American manufacturers that autos which clung to the outmoded carriage layout had to disguise the fact. The 1905 Buick Model C, for example, had a fashionably long hood after the French design, but the engine was still under the seat.[12]

While the Europeans developed this layout on the heavy, luxurious touring car for the grand bourgeoisie, American automakers produced more moderately priced autos of the French design. By 1905 the American market for high-priced cars (over $2,000) was reaching saturation. So in an attempt to generate sales among the growing professional and managerial class and newly prosperous Midwestern farmers, manufacturers began to offer moderately priced cars ($800 to $1,000) which had a Panhard layout but were lighter, higher, and more powerful than most European cars. Most of these American cars weighed between 1,500 and 2,000 pounds, had wheelbases between 100 and 115 inches, and were equipped with pneumatic tires, a pressed-steel, riveted frame, semielliptic or elliptic springs, a steering wheel, an open side-entrance body seating four passengers, and a 4-cylinder engine mounted under a hood in front of the driver.[13]

Once the automobile was accepted as a machine in its own right, the aesthetic focus fell on the mechanics, which were no longer hidden but prominently displayed. Manufacturers began to compete with one another on the basis of technical advances, so they wanted every new and exciting feature visible. Automobile advertisements of the day followed a technical, "nuts-and-bolts" approach. A small, crude illustration of the car was overwhelmed with columns of fine print detailing its technical features. This stress on technical innovations also led early on to the practice of annual models. The automobile industry was from the beginning highly seasonal, for the use of its open vehicles was generally confined to the warm, dry months. Sales reflected this seasonality, being brisk in spring and summer, then trailing off in the fall. Manufacturers incorporated technical innovations into their products during the fall production hiatus, then introduced these new and improved models in January at the all-important New York Automobile Show. By 1905 some companies were marking their cars with model years to register their technical progress.[14]

AN AESTHETICS OF FRAGMENTATION

Although in the first years of the twentieth century the automobile was acquiring a distinct, mechanical form all its own, these vehicles were far from aesthetically harmonious and pleasing. The early cars were precariously high for their length, especially the closed cars, which required high roofs to accommodate silk top hats and other *haute* millinery gear. Even on open cars conventional methods of mounting axles and springs on frames resulted in great height. And weakly constructed frames, made of wood or steel tubes, prevented elongation of the cars to produce more pleasing proportions. Consequently, their overall appearance was clumsy and stumpy.[15]

These early automobiles also had a disjointed and discontinuous look, lacking any aesthetic unity between their elements. As one knowledgeable commentator stated: "The cars of the 1885–1905 period had a generally untidy look. Each part seemed determined to live its own separate life – bonnet or hood, dashboard, front seats, rear seats or tonneau, mudguards, frame, wheels, axles and so on all grouped together in an arrangement that was seldom properly organized." They were conglomerations of unrelated shapes, with little evidence of effort to aesthetically ease the transition between the parts. Directing his or her eyes along the side elevation of a typical 1905 open touring car, the observer experienced a series of abrupt visual transitions or shocks. The horizontal line of the low hood abutted abruptly against the dashboard at a right angle. Then the eye leaped up the dash to the top line of the body, whose lack of doors quickly led the eye back down and around the cut-out entry to the front seat. Then the line of sight took a series of jumps up and down over the protruding seat backs before falling abruptly to the ground at the body's rear. And along this visual roller-coaster ride the observer also encountered a clutter of equipment and accessories – hand brakes, bulb horns, wicker baskets, tool boxes – casually scattered over every square inch of surface area. The overall effect was a rather thrown-together look that could be disturbing and perplexing.[16]

The fragmented appearance of the early autos was the consequence of a number of intersecting social factors. Popular fascination with the technical innovations of this new machine led manufacturers to expose its functional parts, which were usually aesthetically incongruous due to the circumstances of their production. The earliest manufacturers of autos usually assembled their cars from components purchased from separate companies – a body from a carriagemaker, engine and transmission from a machine shop, wheels from a wheel manufacturer. Although these parts were often of the highest quality, they were visually incompatible, for the workers of different firms could not consciously coordinate their work. Even after some of the larger automobile manufacturers began to produce their own mechanical parts, they still purchased bodies from an outside supplier. The chassisbuilder designed and built the chassis as a separate unit, complete with radiator, hood, cowl, fenders, and running boards. The bodybuilder received from the chassis firm only dimensional specifications, from which workers constructed a body with seats and upholstery. When installed on the completed chassis this body often joined it in an incongruous clash of color and style. Thus, the fragmented appearance of these cars resulted from this unplanned coordination of early production through the economic market, which threw together an ill-assorted melange of parts into auto plants.[17]

Another social factor responsible for the lack of aesthetic unity in the early autos was the lack of class unity between their occupants. Many of these automobiles were designed to be driven by a chauffeur and were consequently composed of two distinct units whose discontinuity attested to the class barriers between servant and master. In the chauffeur's cab accommodations were primitive and functional, lacking windows, doors, and sometimes a roof. The seat was made of durable leather, and the compartment was crowded with the unclean controls necessary for operation. By contrast, the passenger section was totally enclosed against the elements and appointed with the finest cloth and wood. The two compartments were often marked by a visual

Figure 2 1908 Buick Model 10, with the European-initiated Panhard layout. The car evidences a self-consciously mechanical form, albeit one with a fragmented, disjointed appearance. (Courtesy National Automotive History Collection, Detroit Public Library)

disjuncture. The delicately curved roof of the passenger section often abruptly intersected the rectilinear roof of the cab. Or sometimes the roofs of the cab and the passenger compartment were marked by separate curves, giving the roof line a two-humped configuration. In the opinion of one commentator, this "broken appearance" made these cars "positively ugly," resembling "two independent carriage bodies stuck together as a sort of afterthought." But the social chasm of class separating driver and passengers prevented these cars from being designed as aesthetic unities.[18]

Despite their clumsy proportions and disjointed appearance, these early automobiles often had a certain visual appeal. The very complexity of shapes and textures could be entertaining. And although their components lacked aesthetic integration, when produced with high standards of workmanship these autos could attain a visual distinction. This was especially true of their bodies, which were often built by carriagemakers with the same painstaking care and attention to detail traditionally employed on exclusive horse-drawn vehicles.

EARLY BODY STYLES AND CONSTRUCTION

The bodies of these early automobiles dominated their appearance. And most were produced by the careful craftsmanship of coachbuilders that had been cultivated over several centuries. For their supply of bodies, the early automobile manufacturers usually turned to the established coachbuilders, who merely adapted popular carriage body styles to autos. The bodies of the most expensive makes were usually custom-built on the supplied chassis to the tastes and specifications of the customer. Volume automakers ordered large batches of several body types from carriage companies, some of which were beginning to use mass-production methods. But at this time carriagebuilding was mainly the province of craftworkers imbued with time-honored skills and traditions, some of which were clearly incompatible with auto manufacture. For example, carriagebuilders traditionally achieved comfort and stability by adding weight, but heavy bodies severely strained early auto engines. And craftworkers were used to departing from written specifications, introducing changes as they saw fit to improve appearance and construction. Automakers complained that such deviations necessitated costly alterations in fitting the body to the chassis. For their part, the carriagebuilders complained that the short wheelbases and high chassis of the early cars made it impossible to provide the flowing lines and spaciousness traditionally incorporated in carriages.[19]

Adapting carriage-inspired bodies to automobiles created a problem-solving process that ultimately resulted in styles unique to the motor vehicle. Bodybuilders found it easy to fit early autos with two seats, but furnishing additional forward-facing seats behind these proved difficult. The large rear wheels and driving chains interfered with the entrance to the rear seats. The first solution to the problem, introduced about 1897, was the rear-entrance tonneau, a rounded, tublike body added behind the driver's seat. Its seats were forward-facing, located in the rear corners, and accessed through a rear entrance door. Introduced in America around 1901, this style had its own problems. Not only was the body difficult to fit with a top, but the rear door let out the passengers into the muddy roads.

When pressed-steel frames were introduced circa 1901, a better solution to the rear-seating problem was found. These stronger frames allowed the construction of cars long enough to place side doors in front of the rear wheels. This side-entrance tonneau body, introduced on the European chassis in 1902, spread to America around 1905. And with it came the popular Roi-des-Belges or tulip phaeton style. Initially commissioned by King Leopold of Belgium, this elegant body had wide, bulging sides and a rear of double-reversed curves reminiscent of a tulip. This spacious body was popular on the expensive makes on both sides of the Atlantic, while the simple side-entrance tonneau or double phaeton was placed on less costly cars.

Most of the early bodies were open – enclosed bodies were too heavy for small auto engines – and fitted with retractable canopies of cloth or leather. But people seeking shelter from the weather demanded closed bodies almost from the outset. The first ones, emerging around 1900, were simple, two-seated enclosures known as coupes. To carry more passengers in enclosed comfort, the limousine emerged, designed to be driven by a chauffeur. This was essentially a closed tonneau mounted behind an open driver's seat. To give rear passengers some air and sunshine in pleasant weather, the landaulet was built, a closed body on which the rear part of the roof could be folded down.[20]

Whether closed or open, however, the bodywork on these early autos generally evidenced a style and grace that spoke of careful, refined craftsmanship. The automobile emerged just as the Art Nouveau movement was sweeping both Europe and America, and the bodies reflected its emphasis on curvilinear, organic motifs. The flowing double-reversed curves of the tulip phaeton clearly revealed this influence. But traces of this aesthetic could also be found on less expensive automobiles like the 1901 curved-dash Oldsmobile. On this car the curved footboard or dash swept gently down the front across the open entrance, then up to the seat without once assuming a straight line. The seat-cushion base carried the line up, across, and back down in a convex curve, which then quickly flattened to the largely rectangular box that was the body's rear. These graceful curves were accented with red molding and yellow pinstriping. These early bodies generally had little superficial decoration to detract from the carefully developed lines and surfaces. The striping and molding was designed merely to emphasize the contours of the body. These organic, curvilinear bodies often clashed with the severe, rectilinear lines of the mechanical parts exposed beneath them, thus contributing to the disjointed appearance of these early cars.[21]

The production of these early automobile bodies was a slow, laborious process requiring highly skilled craftworkers. First, the drafts-man took the sketch and dimensions of the proposed body and prepared full-scale orthographic projections, complete with detailed measurements of component parts. He worked carefully within the craftworkers' traditions, which specified general dimensions and forms. Using the orthographic drawings, skilled woodworkers then constructed templates to guide the manufacture of parts. The next step was the difficult and complex job of constructing the wooden frame, usually of cured white ash members cut to dimension with hand tools and simple machines and glued together with carpenter joints. Building one frame could occupy a gang of skilled bodybuilders for the better part of a week. The frame was then covered with panels, typically of hard mahogany, which were fitted into slots and fixed with white lead. Single-curvature panels were made by steaming and bending the wood to templates. The more difficult compound curves had to be produced by building up panels in sections by gluing together small ribs of soft wood, then dressing them to shape. Because this process was slow, bodybuilders began to use hand-beaten aluminum panels for compound curves beginning around 1900. These were welded together over the wooden frame with an oxy-acetylene torch. Although lighter and more ductile than wood, aluminum panels were much more expensive and used mainly on high-priced cars. Less costly cars continued to use wooden panels until about 1907, when pressed-steel panels came into popular use. These were stamped out on machines and then welded together over a wooden frame to yield what was known as the composite body. Because of its durability and cheapness, the composite body had replaced the all-wood body among volume producers by 1912.[22]

No less a skilled, time-consuming, process was the painting and finishing of these bodies. Using slow-drying varnish paints, a crew of workers finished a body by the hand-application of up to twenty coats of filler, paint, and varnish, which could occupy them for a month. After the body was completely sanded, several coats of roughstuff and then patent filling were brushed on, each of which was rubbed down with pumice and water. Then several color coats went on, followed by a coat each of color varnish and body varnish, then two coats of undercoating varnish. At this stage the striping was applied, thin lines of contrasting color around the borders of panels and other parts which emphasized their contours. Finally, craftworkers applied as many as three additional coats of clear varnish. Some volume automakers hurried this process by eliminating coats, but a quicker, cheaper alternative to the hand-application of slow-drying varnish paints would not be found until the second decade of the century. Even a large-volume manufacturer like Overland, producing over 20,000 cars in 1911, employed over two hundred artisans in the application of ten coats of paint, varnish, and filler, which required two weeks' time.

The final stage of bodybuilding was the addition of upholstery. In the trimming shops, highly skilled trimmers and leatherworkers fitted seats and panels to finish the interior. On open cars, durability generally dictated the use of leather, which was dyed, hand-buffed, and tufted. Closed cars allowed the use of fine cloth for upholstering, which was also tufted. And the more expensive of these autos were often fitted with silk upholstery, exquisite wood paneling (often inlaid), cloth curtains, and carpet.[23]

Although at this early stage the aesthetics of the entire automobile were fragmented and disjointed, these carefully constructed bodies gave the impression of great unity and cohesion. There were no abrupt transitions or disjunctures. The gaps and seams between the separate parts were carefully filled or at least covered by moldings. And the gently flowing curves and deep, lustrous finish that enveloped the body also contributed to the sense of unity that was created out of its hundreds of different parts.

This aesthetic unity was the direct consequence of the productive unity of the labor process under the conscious control of the workers themselves. These coachbuilding craftworkers controlled the entire process of construction, with little division of labor or detailed managerial supervision. While some specialized in one or another step of the process, workers had to learn all the bodybuilding crafts to earn the title of master. These workers communicated often with each other to coordinate the different steps of production, and had the discretion to depart from planned specifications when their experience and aesthetic sense dictated. As one historian of the craft has written: "Much of the subtlety of shape of a good body was contributed by the men who worked on the shaping of its panels and framing; many had a highly developed sense of proportion and a natural feeling for what was visually good. . . ." To own an automobile with such careful body craftsmanship bore direct testimony to the wealth required to appropriate the expensive labor of these workers. These cars were immediate symbols of class position.[24]

The labor processes responsible for producing the other, less visible parts of these automobiles were also skilled and discretionary, yielding results that were often separately coherent and visually appealing. Consequently, most of the work in the early auto shops left a great deal of power and control in the hands of workers. Because of the highly variant nature of this work, it was impossible for owners or their agents to issue detailed production commands. The uncertain elements necessarily remained within the discretion of workers, who jealously guarded their control of production against encroachment by managers. Early trade journals of the industry were filled with complaints that these skilled workers would not labor with the speed and methods that capitalists desired. While early auto workers often defended their work standards through union organization, after the successful open-shop drive of 1903, the industry's work force was largely unorganized. But their short supply and indispensable discretion on the shop floor gave these skilled workers the power to informally enforce their control of production.[25]

THE BEGINNINGS OF AESTHETIC INTEGRATION

As the first decade of the twentieth century drew to a close, the aesthetic integrity that was originally confined to the separate parts like the body began to encompass the entire automobile, which began to lose its fragmented, disjointed look. Several factors initiated this aesthetic trend, which came to fruition in subsequent decades. First, chauffeur-driven cars declined, leading to the predominance of owner-driven vehicles. This trend was due both to the spread of ownership down to the petite bourgeoisie or middle class, which could not afford chauffeurs, and the discovery by the very wealthy of the joys of driving. With the chauffeur gone, the class difference between driver and passengers evaporated, leading builders to conceive of the body as a unit rather than two class-specific modes of accommodation. There was now more concern for the comfort of the driver, spawning front doors, windshields, and front enclosures integral with the rear.

A second factor favoring aesthetic integration was the vertical integration of automotive firms. As early as 1903 American automakers began to turn from the simple assembly of purchased parts to the manufacture of their own components, largely in order to ensure their quality. But a corollary of this integration was better coordination of the appearance of parts. The manufacture of components in one location allowed workers to coordinate their tasks through communication. This was especially true of chassis and body manufacture. As chassis producers began to add body and trim shops to their firms, the crude disjuncture between the body and the rest of the car began to fade. Automobiles were now designed as integral units, not as assemblages of separate bodies and chassis, and their appearance began to reflect this.[26]

The aesthetic result of these factors was horizontal integration of the lines and forms of the automobile. The roller-coaster lines of the early open cars were gradually replaced by horizontal lines flowing straight from the radiator through to the rear. Between 1908 and 1911, structural changes induced by pressed-steel frames combined with aesthetic changes to emphasize the horizontal lines and bring previously disjunctive elements into a flowing linear continuity. The hood was raised, and its previously abrupt, right-angle juncture with the dash was eased by the addition of a taper dash or cowl, which sloped down to merge with the hood top and sides. And beginning about 1908, front doors were added, eliminating the U-shaped front entrances and raising these lines to the top of the body. Doors were usually mounted flush with the body surface, giving it a smooth, continuous contour. Further, the sides were gradually raised so the seats no longer protruded so far above the top of the open body. Passengers now appeared to be enveloped within rather than sitting on top of the car. The compound curves of the Roi-des-Belges open body gave way to flatter, simpler panels. And body sides and running boards were cleaned up by removing the clutter of accessories that previously broke up the continuity of horizontal lines.

Automobiles with these changes first originated in Europe around 1908 and were labeled torpedo or flush-sided bodies. The style spread to American manufacturers about 1911, with the all-important fore doors appearing on such popular makes as Oakland, Buick, and Cadillac in this year. Some automotive historians have suggested that these changes were introduced to cheapen the manufacture of cars, especially the bodies. These smoother, flatter body surfaces were probably easier to produce, paint, and finish than the elaborately curved panels of early touring cars. But their integration into a cohesive, pleasing whole was no simple task and required the skill of craftworkers, whose labor was rather dear.[27]

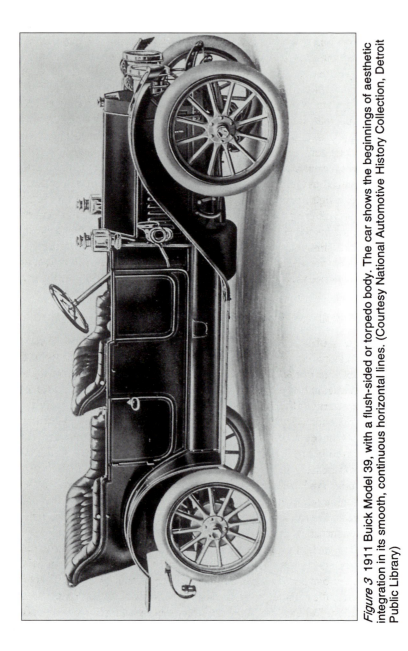

Figure 3 1911 Buick Model 39, with a flush-sided or torpedo body. The car shows the beginnings of aesthetic integration in its smooth, continuous horizontal lines. (Courtesy National Automotive History Collection, Detroit Public Library)

While some American automakers were moving toward greater aesthetic integration, other producers were introducing mass-production innovations that led to aesthetic fragmentation. In 1908 Henry Ford introduced the Model T, a low-priced, reliable automobile that proved so popular that he was forced to find ways to speed production. The result of these efforts was a series of production innovations that coalesced into the system of mass production. Fordist mass production spread to all volume automakers and shattered the organic unity of the labor process that was beginning to yield aesthetic integration. The newly divided, mechanized, and intensified labor carried out by largely unskilled workers exercising little discretion over their activities produced cars that appeared fragmented, disjointed, thrown-together. Only the shops producing high-priced luxury vehicles, where skilled workers controlled a unified labor process, continued the trend toward aesthetic integration into the second decade of the century. So the end of this first decade saw the beginnings of bifurcated automobile design that testified to the growing class chasm – luxurious, handcrafted, integrated automobiles for the upper class, and cheap, mass-produced, ugly cars for the masses.

CULTURAL MEANINGS OF EARLY AUTOS

In most of this early period, the automobile was the almost exclusive possession of the grande bourgeoisie, both in Europe and the United States. The prices of 1905 cars ranged from $600 to $7,500, making them extravagant expenditures for the vast majority of Americans, who in this year averaged $450 in annual income. Had the early autos been means of economical, reliable transportation, perhaps less affluent Americans would have stretched their budgets to buy one. But the vehicles manufactured before 1906 were far from reliable and efficient. Poor protection from the weather usually confined their operation to the warm, dry months. And their rudimentary mechanics rendered very rare indeed a trip of any distance over a few blocks that did not require at least minor repairs. These early autos were suited for those searching for sport and adventure, not for efficient transportation.[28]

The earliest motorized vehicles were defined in American culture as playthings of the wealthy, another trapping of their life of leisure. Robber-baron capitalists like the Vanderbilts and the Rockefellers were among the first auto enthusiasts and known to keep well-stocked garages. William K. Vanderbilt's Long Island villa had a 100-car garage, where he kept a fleet of some of the most expensive makes in the world. To drive and maintain his cars Vanderbilt had a crew of twenty chauffeurs and mechanics. Most of the early clubs, like the New York-based Automobile Club of America, were dominated by wealthy enthusiasts and promoted the unrestricted enjoyment of their vehicles. The automobile shows these clubs sponsored were high social occasions comparable to horse shows. The first New York Automobile Show, held in 1903 in Madison Square Garden, attracted, reported the *New York Times*, a "crowd of particular brilliance and animation," including William Rockefeller, Mr and Mrs William K. Vanderbilt, and Mr and Mrs John Jacob Astor.[29]

For many a social season around the turn of the century, automobiles competed with yachts as the focus of sport and display in the fashionable resorts frequented by the grand bourgeoisie. At Newport and on Long Island, the leisure class organized automobile gymkhanas, in which blue bloods proved their driving skills by negotiating obstacle courses, knocking over tenpins, picking up parasols on the run, and spearing dummy pigs. Some of the first auto races were also organized by this motoring elite. Often these well-heeled auto enthusiasts contented themselves by merely parading along fashionable avenues in their vehicles, which were sometimes lavishly festooned with flowers. In 1901 *Automobile Topics* reported that in Atlantic City "the automobile parade on the Pacific Avenue driveway is becoming a daily feature of society."[30]

By about 1906, however, automobiles were more practical and reliable, and ownership began to spread down the class structure. With the gradual saturation of the luxury market, American automakers began to target the growing professional and managerial class with moderately priced cars of sound design and construction. For this class an auto could be a smart business or professional investment, facilitating the rapid, economical movement of people around the city. Appealing to this motive, the manufacturer of the 1908 Maxwell Model LD, selling for $825, advertised it as the "ideal motor car for the man who desires to travel inexpensively, either alone or with another passenger, and it recommends itself to the doctor, lawyer, contractor, city and suburban salesman, builder, businessman; in fact, to everyone whose needs do not exceed economical, safe and speedy transportation for two."[31]

But cultural motives beyond mere utility also influenced this class to buy cars. Certainly they sought to symbolize their new prosperity with a vehicle traditionally associated with great wealth. But the car was more than a simple status symbol. It was intricately tied to the emerging therapeutic ethos of the American bourgeoisie. Losing a sense of autonomy in increasingly bureaucratized industrial corporations, this class sought to recoup personal efficacy in privatized leisure activities focused on consumption.

The automobile became associated with this new bourgeois ethic of therapeutic leisure. It was seen by many as the means of escaping the urban atmosphere of routine and regimentation to the restoring air of the suburbs or country. One enthusiastic endorser touted the car as "the greatest health giving invention of a thousand years. The cubic feet of fresh air that are literally forced into one while automobiling rehabilitate worn-out nerves and drive out worry, insomnia, and indigestion. It will renew the life and youth of the overworked man or woman, and will make the thin fat and the fat – but I forebear."[32]

The upper classes had always been more mobile than the lower classes, having greater access to transportation by carriage and railway. But the former was slow, and the latter subjected the individual to the dreaded collective regimentation of timetable and itinerary characteristic of emerging bureaucracies. The automobile gave the bourgeoisie a means of escaping urban industrialism that maximized individual freedom. In 1909 a writer in *Harper's Weekly* thus proclaimed that one of the greatest attractions of the auto was

> the feeling of independence – the freedom from timetables, from fixed and inflexible routes, from the proximity of other human beings than one's chosen companions; the ability to go where and when one wills, to linger and stop where the country is beautiful and the way pleasant, or to rush through unattractive surroundings, to select the best places to eat and sleep; and the satisfaction that comes from a knowledge that one need ask favors or accommodation from no one nor trespass on anybody's property or privacy.[33]

A popular pastime of the bourgeoisie that consolidated the association between the automobile and individual escapism through consumption was auto touring. In the latter years of the first decade of the century, an increasing number of affluent, urban car owners took to the roads for their vacations. They camped each night in different spots along the road, sleeping in cars or tents, and cooking over smoky campfires. Likening themselves to gypsies and homesteaders, these early auto-campers saw themselves as rebels against the routinized, monopolistic industrial establishment symbolized by the railroads. Vacation travel by car represented for them a new freedom, the ability "to break away from the hectic work routines and bureaucratic institutions of an urban industrial civilization." But this "revolt" against organized, rationalized capitalism was temporary and individual, ultimately strengthening the system by returning tourists to urban bureaucracies refreshed and re-invigorated for another round of routine.[34]

Classes in the United States for whom ownership was impossible often viewed the automobile resentfully, as a symbol of the mobility and wealth denied them by corporate capitalism. This image of the auto was prominent in the popular culture of the day. In early documentary films, like Edison's *Automobile Parade* (1900), moviegoers were treated to the spectacle of blue-blooded auto enthusiasts parading their expensive horseless carriages along the boulevards or racing them up mountains. Popular films also drove home the theme of the auto as a means of emotional transport or escape. But usually those escaping were the upper classes, as in Edison's *Boarding School Girls* (1905), in which the auto transports these students to the Coney Island amusement park. The largely working-class audience could, of course, vicariously participate in the pleasures of automobiling through such films. This was the idea behind the Tim Hurst Tours, in which moviegoers sat in a theater that looked like a touring car and watched films taken along the main thoroughfares of famous cities. But the knowledge that actual auto ownership and its escapist pleasures lay beyond the reach of the vast majority of Americans also served to stimulate the kind of class envy that Woodrow Wilson feared. This theme was present in images of the automobile like *Gray and Brass* (1907) by John Sloan, an American painter and newspaper illustrator with socialist sympathies. In this painting, as one critic described it, an "overfed, plumed, primped, and dull-witted bunch chug along in an auto barely capable of supporting their overweight." Similarly, cartoons in popular newspapers often depicted automobilists as the arrogant, idle rich whose reckless operation of their high-powered toys endangered common citizens in horse-drawn vehicles, on bicycles, and on foot.[35]

Both farmers and urban workers seemed to harbor such a class-conscious resentment of early automobiles and their drivers. Rural resentment of the intrusion of motor vehicles into farm communities had a practical basis. The loud, smelly contraptions which swarmed out of cities onto rural roads stirred up clouds of dust, frightened horses, endangered their riders and drivers, killed farm animals, trespassed on private property, and reduced roads to quagmires. But there was also a socio-cultural reason for the hostility of farmers. For them automobiles symbolized the wealth and arrogance of urban big-business interests, whose abuses of farmers gave rise to radical agrarian protests during this period. Populist resentment of these urban representatives of oligopolies led rural residents to shamelessly overcharge automobilists for overnight accommodations, repairs, and other services. They justified these practices, in the words of one historian, by "the belief that because big-city interests had cheated them out of a large portion of their hard-earned profits, they were entitled to get even in a small way." Some rural communities sought to ban autos altogether from their roads, or to severely restrict their operation with speed limits and warning requirements. And a few farmers took extralegal actions like shooting at cars, strewing tacks and glass on roads, and stretching barbed wire across roads.[36]

But rural hostility to the car declined as farm prices and prosperity rose in the first decade of the century. Higher farm incomes combined with lower automobile prices to produce a rapid adoption of the auto by farmers beginning about 1905. By 1908 the major market for motor vehicles had shifted from the big city to the country town. Farmers found a vast array of uses for the car which undoubtedly improved their lives: numerous work applications, transportation of produce to market, social visits to distant neighbors, trips to and from rural schools, frequent trips to town for business and entertainment, and sheer pleasure driving.[37]

The story was different for urban workers, who would have to wait two more decades for automobility. Their hostility to the automobile, which also had both utilitarian and symbolic motives, continued unabated throughout this period. Noisy, smelly automobiles driving in working-class neighborhoods disrupted everyday life and culture. In these neighborhoods streets were often the only open spaces, and were usually crowded with push-cart vendors, produce stalls, street entertainers, playing children, and socializing adults. The automobiles that disrupted this rich street life were resented. *Horseless Age* reported that during the summer of 1904 stone-throwing attacks on autos in some working-class neighborhoods of New York became so numerous that motorists required special police protection. But apart from this practical concern, urban workers surely noticed that these automobiles were driven by the same well-to-do capitalists and managers with which they often conflicted in the workplace. Automobiles thus came to symbolize this class's arrogant disregard for workers' lives and livelihoods in the factories as well as the streets. This class-conscious hostility noted by Woodrow Wilson was not confined to the United States. It was present in Britain also, where Walter Long, president of the Local Government Board, which enforced speed limits, wrote: "There is an embittered feeling in the general public against all persons who use motor-cars, which, as a dangerous class feeling, is, perhaps, without parallel in modern times."[38]

In the next two decades, the falling prices of mass-produced cars and the rising incomes of workers brought auto ownership within the means of many of this class. But the automobile did not cease to serve as an antagonizing reminder of class differences as a result. The growing aesthetic gap between high-priced vehicles and mass-produced cars continued to symbolize the social distinctions and antagonisms between working people and their bourgeois bosses.

Chapter 3

Diverging paths of design
Mass and class production

On March 18, 1908, the Ford Motor Company sent advance catalogs to its dealers describing its new model, designated by the letter T, to be available for sale on October 1. The realization of Henry Ford's dream of a motorcar for the masses, the Model T evoked an immediate and enthusiastic response. Praise was heaped on the car by dealers and the press. Advance orders flooded in from individuals as well as agents. By May 1, 1909 sales were running so far ahead of production that Ford stopped taking orders for nine weeks. The tough, reliable, powerful, easy-to-drive and -maintain car was an incredible value at $825, a price which fell throughout its history. Combined with generally rising earnings of employees through the 1910s, these prices brought automobility within the reach of Americans of even modest means, including many industrial workers.

But to join the ranks of auto owners, workers paid a heavy price at work. To speed up production and continually lower prices, Ford revolutionized auto manufacturing, transforming it from a skilled craft process controlled by craftworkers to a largely unskilled process manned by detail workers and controlled by technicians and engineers. In compensation for the inhumanities of his new production process, Ford paid workers the incredible wage of five dollars a day, which many used to purchase commodities for their leisure lives with which to recuperate from and forget their working lives. But the ugliness of the mass-produced products they bought to fill their refuges from the Fordist factory did not allow workers to totally forget the oppressive workplace. When compared to the "classy" consumer goods of their employers, products like the Model T were immediate reminders in consumption of the class gap between labor and capital in production. The demand of consumers for autos and other mass-produced goods that completely insulated their consumption from production led to an imperative for class-obscuring style which would prove the demise of Ford's simple motorcar for the masses.

AMERICA, 1912–1924: MASS PRODUCTION, MASS REVOLT, MASS CONSUMPTION

The story of industrial America between the early 1910s and the mid-1920s is dominated by Ford's innovations in mass production and mass consumption. Fordist factory methods were the culmination of the revolution in production launched by Taylorism around the turn of the century to resolve the capitalist crisis. The initial successes of Taylor's campaign revitalized American capitalism, creating the prosperity that fueled the growth of industries manufacturing durable consumer goods like the automobile. Between 1900 and 1912 American annual auto sales leaped from 4,192 to 378,000, stimulating efforts to quicken production that surpassed Taylorism and ultimately revolutionized American culture and consumption.[1]

Fordist methods shared Taylor's goal of speeding and cheapening production through wresting its control from powerful craftworkers. But while Taylorism merely forced workers to increase the output of existing machines, Fordism transformed the machines themselves to achieve managerial control over workers. Beginning around 1910, Ford and others replaced their universal machine tools operated by skilled machinists with specialized machines that required only semiskilled workers. Automakers also introduced mechanisms like power conveyors that allowed them to control the flow and pace of the increasingly deskilled operations. The introduction of power conveyors in final assembly at the Ford Motor Company in 1913 created the infamous assembly line, whose furious, manager-set pace reduced assembly time for the Model T from 12.5 to 1.5 worker-hours. By 1915 such mechanical innovations had reduced the proportion of skilled workers in auto factories from 60 percent to about 13 percent.

Fordist mass-production methods quickly spread to other industries, along with the mass revolt of workers they touched off. The very success of Fordism in transforming work and workers ensured that the protests that began in the earlier era of reorganization were larger and more widespread than ever before. Even though the new methods weakened the power of individual workers, they inadvertently strengthened the working class as a whole by eroding the divisions within it, reducing the vast majority to semiskilled machine tenders with similar wages and working conditions. And the large scale of production demanded by

Fordist machinery concentrated multitudes of these homogenized workers at a few huge industrial sites, facilitating communication and organization. For example, at its peak of activity, Ford's River Rouge complex employed nearly 100,000 workers.

Around 1910, these homogenized, concentrated factory workers subjected to the intensified labor of Fordism launched a wave of working-class revolt which took many forms. Some of it was channeled into overt, collective clashes between labor and capital, as when in 1913 Ford fought off an effort to organize his workers by the Industrial Workers of the World. But much of the revolt against Fordism was covert and individualistic, taking the forms of turnover and absenteeism. These struggles were motivated not solely by economic goals like increased wages and benefits but also by workers' attempts to gain greater autonomy and control over their labor. During and immediately after the First World War, demands for workers' control went beyond shop-floor autonomy to include a radical reorganization of the entire political economy, including government ownership and social administration of some industries.

Corporate capitalists searched furiously for methods to repress and contain this labor revolt, and out of the conflict they gradually devised a solution – culturally integrating the working masses into the realm of privatistic consumption pioneered by the bourgeoisie. Workers gradually surrendered any claims for control over Fordist production in exchange for a larger share of consumer goods, with which they insulated themselves from its inhumanities. As pioneers of mass-production methods, Ford and other auto manufacturers were forced to lead this mass-consumption solution to contain the revolt against them. Unwilling to concede to workers any control over production, Henry Ford made innovative concessions in wages, announcing in 1913 that his company would pay workers the unbelievable wage of five dollars a day. Although he portrayed this program as a humanitarian act, his main motive was increasing production by decreasing worker resistance. Ford saw the high wage as an incentive to "better living," that is, a bourgeois lifestyle of rationalized, privatized consumption that compensated for and supported Fordist production. The Five Dollar Day was an inducement to cajole workers to substitute such a commodified leisure life for their collective, mutualistic cultures.

Ford's offensive dramatized the general cultural program of middle-class reformers and corporate capitalists that originated in the late nineteenth century but took on a new urgency around the First World War as class conflict flared. By the early 1920s, the offensive was showing success, as the bourgeois model of privatized, home-based consumption as refuge from alienating work gained a hold among more privileged workers. American workers did not just passively adopt this leisure lifestyle at the insistence of cajoling reformers but to a large extent actively chose it from the available alternatives. But these alternatives were severely limited by the strength of corporate capital. Large employers used their economic strength to adamantly defend their control of the workplace, while simultaneously wielding political influence to defeat the working-class challenge to their state power. Under these circumstances, American workers settled for what they could realistically achieve – home-based consumption that allowed them to momentarily forget workplace dehumanization.[2]

More important than crusading progressives and cajoling employers for the spread of consumerism to the working class were cultural entrepreneurs whose main interest was not controlling class conflict but increasing their profits. In workers' rising incomes these capitalists saw the demand to support integrated empires of mass consumption modeled on the empires of mass production. In many cities commercialized amusement parks, catering to all classes, arose to displace exclusive ethnic games and celebrations. And by the 1920s, the opulent movie palace, a center of interclass, nationally distributed entertainment, was replacing the saloon as the most popular form of recreation among workers. The films they saw there created a new consumer consciousness by exaggerating the sensuous properties of objects and using material commodities as vehicles of plot and character development. Similar dream worlds of objects were created by department and speciality stores, which transformed their establishments from informative displays to visual feasts that whetted consumer appetites starved in drab, standardized factories. Advertising, a crucial part of this consumer revolution, also experienced an explosion during this period, turning routine announcements of product prices and characteristics into evocations of consumer desires for modernity, status, and autonomy.[3]

Two commodities that loomed large in this new realm of mass consumption were the single-family home and the automobile. Both offered working-class people a temporary sense of autonomy and a refuge from the heteronomy of the Fordist factory or, increasingly, the rationalized office, where white-collar proletarians were on the rise. With the car workers could go wherever they pleased, giving them a sense of autonomy rarely experienced at work. And for the working-class family home ownership meant freedom from landlords and the independence to live as they liked.[4]

So with the help of the merchants of mass consumption and leisure, workers, like other Americans, began to define themselves by the commodities they purchased. The Lynds observed in their 1925 study of Muncie, Indiana, an industrial town dominated by auto-parts plants, that because changes in the production process deprived work of its "intrinsic satisfactions," workers increasingly defined their lives in terms of consumption. "Frustrated in this [work] sector of their lives, many workers seek compensations elsewhere, . . . if no longer in the saloon, in such compensatory devices as hooking up the radio or driving the 'old bus'. . . ."[5]

The personal autonomy lost at work was recuperated in the realm of consumption, where the proliferation of product brands, models, and styles offered consumers a wide array of choices. And as mass production and mass consumption undermined the bonds of occupation, class, and ethnicity, "consumption communities" defined by these choices appeared to fill the social void. "Idols of consumption," leaders in the leisure worlds of sports and entertainment, emerged to set the fashions for the masses. Because anyone, regardless of class, race, or ethnicity, could for the purchase price participate in the good life defined by these idols, the realm of mass-consumption presented the appearance of freedom and equality, obscuring its basis in the inequality of Fordist production.[6]

Initially, however, the stark simplicity of mass-produced products prevented them from functioning in consumption to facilitate a forgetting of the inhumanities of production. Mass production so transformed the aesthetics of consumer products like the automobile that they served as constant reminders of this labor process and the class position of their owners in it. By the mid-1920s, it became clear that to perform the amnestic and compensatory functions that consumers demanded the aesthetics of autos and other products would have to be transformed to erase all reminders of Fordist production.

MASS PRODUCTION AND THE TRANSFORMATION OF AUTOMOBILE AESTHETICS

In order to use Fordist technology automobile manufacturers were forced to alter the design of their products. Specialized, automatic machines were not capable of duplicating all the complicated and discretionary tasks previously accomplished by skilled workers, so design features requiring such labor were eliminated. This policy led to product standardization – that is, the elimination of model variety and concentration of production on a few auto designs. Since specialized machinery was inflexible and economically feasible only if production was high enough to keep it continuously occupied, firms were forced to eliminate all models but one or two to achieve requisite volume. Thus, in 1910 the Ford Motor Company dropped production of its two other models and produced only the low-priced Model T. Product standardization led to the increasingly homogenized appearance of automobiles – variety and uniqueness were sacrificed for the sake of deskilling Fordist technology.[7]

In addition to general standardization, Fordist technology exerted design constraints on specific parts of the automobile. Because the body dominated the auto's appearance, design changes necessitated by deskilling and mechanizing its production were central to the evolving aesthetics of mass-produced cars. Between 1912 and 1925, the construction of auto bodies was transformed from a woodworking craft controlled by highly skilled workers to a metalworking mass-production process controlled by engineers and executed by semiskilled workers operating automatic machines. By 1912 most mass producers had replaced the hand-shaped wooden and aluminum body panels with machine-pressed steel panels formed on huge, expensive presses. The production of the wooden frame, over which these panels were assembled, was also substantially standardized and mechanized during this period. Frame members were produced on specialized wood-cutting machines and assembled in framing bucks, metal frames which ensured proper alignment. Assembly of pressed-steel panels over the wooden frame was also controlled by an assembly buck, which eliminated most hand-fitting. The panels were nailed or bolted to the frame, then welded together at the joints, a process that was mechanized and deskilled by the introduction of electric resistance machines. These were assembly bucks with electrodes that fused panels at points of contact. As production volumes and specialization increased, bodybuilding machines and assembly operations were arranged in progressive lines and connected by conveyors. Because these mass-production body plants were so expensive – over $10 million – many automakers relied on outside body suppliers like Fisher, Budd, and Murray.[8]

Beginning about 1912, the composite steel-over-wood body was replaced by the all-steel body, which was not only lighter and stronger but also cheaper to produce. Introduced to the mass market by the Dodge brothers in 1914, the first all-steel bodies were rather complex affairs, requiring the skilled assembly of over 1,200 small parts. By the late 1920s, however, advances in press technology had reduced the number of components to as few as five, whose quick assembly in welding machines eliminated most skilled labor. Although some major manufacturers, notably General Motors, delayed adoption of all-steel bodies until their construction was thus cheapened, by the early 1920s the trend toward steel was irreversible.[9]

During this period, most cars had open bodies, with closed cars or sedans confined largely to the luxury market due to their added expense. Much of this expense came from the large amount of skilled labor required to hand-hammer metal panels into the curved forms found on sedans. Curved panels could not be stamped on the primitive presses of the period. In the early 1920s, however, the sales of sedans rose, for consumers began demanding the comfort and year-round drivability that only the totally enclosed car could offer. Consequently, medium-priced producers like Hudson, Dodge, and Chandler began to make closed cars, which comprised 30 percent of the market by 1922. In this year, the sedan also broke into the low-priced field with the introduction of Hudson's Essex coach, priced at $1,495. Hudson cut the cost of the car's closed composite body largely by eliminating the curves. The flat panels facilitated their mechanical production and assembly but also yielded an extremely boxy car. In 1923 the Dodge brothers pioneered the all-steel closed car, but the limitations of press technology also made this a rigidly rectilinear affair.[10]

The cheap, employer-controlled production of automobile bodies further required that automakers eliminate the skilled labor from painting, which was traditionally done by hand-application of varnish paints. Between 1911 and 1915 they introduced two mechanical processes to eliminate skill and speed painting: spray painting, which sprayed paint from a nozzled gun by air pressure, and flow or gravity painting, which squirted paint in a stream from hoses under the pressure of gravity. To speed the drying of paint between applications, mass producers introduced drying ovens or "force rooms," where air was heated to 175°F to 200°F. By 1915, these mechanical techniques had allowed manufacturers to place nearly all painting, drying, and finishing operations on moving lines, and reduced painting time from weeks to several days.

To speed painting even further Ford turned to the use of oven-baked enamel. Long used on many accessory parts of the bodywork, enamel posed problems for the main body. The high baking temperatures often warped the wooden frame and changed color pigments. The first problem was solved by the all-steel body; the second, by eliminating all colors but black on low-cost cars. In 1914 Ford discontinued all color finishes on the Model T, announcing that "any customer can have a car painted any color he wants as long as it is black." By the early 1920s other mass producers like Dodge, Overland, and GM were similarly using only black enamel on high-volume models, whose bodies could be coated and baked in ovens in a matter of a few hours.[11]

The division, mechanization, and deskilling of these manufacturing tasks eliminated the contribution of bodybuilding craftworkers to basic design. The skill and taste which once allowed bodybuilders to make design decisions during production were destroyed as they were replaced by semiskilled machine minders and detail workers. Now design was rigidly set prior to production by managers and technicians, who alone possessed the requisite knowledge. One automotive historian wrote that previously the drawings left skilled bodybuilders some freedom of interpretation, "and it was not unknown for a good deal of 'improving' to take place." But under the mechanized and deskilled production system "this could no longer happen; what the drawing said had to be obeyed because now both design and construction were detailed on paper with an exactness not previously necessary. . . ."[12]

The technicians who produced the detailed designs of mass-produced bodies were known as body engineers, and their primary criteria for body design were strength, durability, and adaptability to the newly mechanized production process. These body engineers were hard-boiled, no-nonsense production men who thought it unmanly to have aesthetic sensibilities. Bill Mitchell, a pioneering auto stylist at GM, described them as looking like house detectives, "wearing their hats all the time, suspenders and belts, button shoes, with pencils in their pockets and their taste in their mouths." Some had received training in traditional coachbuilding methods, while others came directly from other mass-produced metal goods industries. But regardless of their backgrounds, these engineers quickly became committed to mass-production methods.[13]

This imperative of cheap, machine production took its aesthetic toll on autos. The typical mass-produced car of the mid- to late 1910s was a drab, dreary machine devoid of decoration to relieve the monotonous expanses of metal. It was starkly rectilinear, with straight, horizontal lines extending from hood to rear. The hood line was lower than the body, and the transition between the two boxes was handled clumsily with a steeply angled cowl. The dominant vertical lines of the radiator, windshield, and rear were also straight. And on closed bodies, the high, flat roof with straight pillars made the short car look particularly clumsy. This rigid rectilinearity was a direct result of the metal presses of the day, which were not large or powerful enough to cleanly stamp rounded

Figure 4 1914 Ford Model T touring. The drab, monotonous, rigidly rectilinear car became a symbol of the dehumanized, deskilled mass-production process that turned it out in droves. (Courtesy Henry Ford Museum and Greenfield Village)

surfaces. Further, complexly curved panels were difficult to weld in electric resistance machines due to alignment problems. In order to use this skill-displacing technology, most mass-producers simply eliminated the curves and other problematic forms from their designs.[14]

Another aesthetic consequence of deskilling mass-production technology was the appearance of fragmentation. Around 1910 the fragmented early cars had begun to take on a more unified look as firms became integrated, allowing craftworkers to coordinate the aesthetic details of their tasks. But mass production eliminated these skilled workers and crushed this budding integration. The detail workers who replaced them could not undertake the discretionary adjustment and coordination of their work, for they were isolated by the division of labor and largely unskilled. Engineers and technicians centralized the control of the entire process of design and production, but they could not plan for all the contingencies of production with imperfect machines, materials, and people. Consequently, parts often did not align properly nor fit tightly, to say nothing of matching in appearance.

The design as well as the production process prevented mass-produced cars from achieving a more unified appearance. Following standard coachbuilding practices, the body engineers laid out autos in two-dimensional orthographic drawings made from front, back, side, and plan views. They made no attempt to check the overall appearance by integrating the different views into a three-dimensional model. This was not a problem when craftworkers used their skills to interpret and integrate the drawings. But when detail workers took over, the result was often a car that appeared to have been designed in parts.[15]

Also contributing to the fragmented look of these cars was the visibility of uncoordinated functional parts. While the exposed parts of craft-built cars were skillfully finished to integrate them into the aesthetic whole, mass producers held finishing work on functional parts to a bare minimum. When Walter Chrysler was hired as works manager at Buick late in 1912, for example, he ordered an end to the careful finishing of functional parts, asking "what is the use of finishing up the hidden parts of a chassis as if you were going to put it in the parlor?" But these "hidden parts" were often visible, exposing the coarse and incongruous mass-production methods that produced them. This mattered little, however, to the hard-driving mass-production men, who believed that beauty belonged in the parlor, not on a machine.[16]

For all of these reasons, then, the mass-produced cars of the era looked, in the words of later designers, as if they "had been assembled from a variety of pieces, all designed independently of each other and then put together without much thought to their interrelationships." The body parts were not closely fitted, leaving large and irregular seams between doors, hood, and fenders. And due to the difficulties of producing accurate stampings, the planes in the bodies did not match well. Consequently, the light reflected from the bodies of passing cars jumped up and down over incongruent forms. If the main bodies evidenced any color, this did not match the fenders, hood, and radiator frame, which were finished separately in cost-cutting black enamel. And beneath and around the disjointed bodies were visible crudely formed and finished functional parts.[17]

The impression that these cars were fragmented, loosely joined assemblages was also conveyed by their aural characteristics – they were loud, clattering contraptions. Although much of the noise came from the rough-running engines, a considerable portion of this automotive cacophony emanated from the ill-fitting parts of the body and frame. The nails, bolts, and rivets holding together mass-produced bodies eventually worked loose, giving voice to many a raucous rattle. And the large, flat panels often "drummed" or "oil-canned" on rough roads, making these bodies sound just as loosely joined as they looked.[18]

Because all producers competing in the low-priced market were subject to these same technological constraints, mass-produced automobiles of this period also appeared remarkably homogeneous. They all had straight sides, square fronts and rears, round fenders, black enamel, and an assembled look. And the appearance of these cars changed little if any from year to year, since changing the dies and machinery for the all-steel body entailed a huge expense. While the technology of automotive mass production changed rapidly, the appearance of the cars was rather static and undistinguished.[19]

CLASS PRODUCTION AND THE AESTHETICS OF LUXURY

The initial rise of automotive mass production did not undermine but actually stimulated the demand for expensive, handcrafted vehicles. Those black contraptions pouring off assembly lines became so common among the middle class and even more privileged workers that the earlier distinction of auto ownership became diluted. Upper-class individuals began to demand vehicles that recaptured their lost automotive distinction and raised them above the horde of mass-produced, monotonous motorcars.

At first this demand was supplied by prestigious European makes like Rolls Royce, Mercedes, Hispano–Suiza, and Isotta–Fraschini, which became very fashionable among America's most conspicuously successful citizens just before the First World War. But as the demand for luxury cars continued to grow in the 1920s, stimulated by an economic expansion that bred a nouveau riche seeking to display its status, domestic manufacturers began to enter the market. In 1920, Fred Duesenberg introduced his Model A, an advanced, luxurious car making the first domestic use of 4-wheel hydraulic brakes and an 8-cylinder, in-line engine with an overhead camshaft. In the same year Henry Leland, another pursuer of engineering perfection, introduced his Model L Lincoln. Other American producers like Cadillac and Packard soon moved into this market for powerful, high-priced vehicles.[20]

To achieve distinction in engineering as well as aesthetics, the great luxury classics were built in a different manner than the mass-produced cars. Like the early shops of the industry, their factories were crowded with skilled craftworkers who lavished careful, unhurried handwork on these autos. A visitor to the Packard plant noted a "slower tempo more consistent with the building of fine, high-priced automobiles," and also observed that "the responsibility for quality falls on the skilled crafts-man rather than on a specialized machine." Production in these luxury shops was also more holistic and less fragmented. While Ford's mass-production factory divided engine assembly among eighty-four detail workers, Cadillac assigned the job to one skilled worker, for managers found that "with one assembler the interrelationship between the various engine parts is more closely studied than when a man pays attention to a single part without regard to other operations. . . ."[21]

These carefully crafted luxury classics were usually sent to separate coachbuilding firms to be fitted with custom-built bodies. Traditionally these coachbuilding houses subordinated the draftsmen to craftsmen, attributing greater importance to the artistry of construction than to the harmony of initial design. But this priority began to change in the spring of 1920, when Raymond Dietrich and Thomas Hibbard opened Le Baron Carrossiers. Unlike other coachbuilders, they undertook to design the entire car in detail on paper so as to achieve a harmonious, unified appearance. Their carefully proportioned designs integrated the pre-viously unrelated parts of the car, like the hood and body. By 1923 other coachbuilding firms were giving their own young draftsmen more aesthetic control over the entire design, resulting in luxury cars that were as balanced and integrated in appearance as they were in engineering.[22]

These powerful, magnificent machines, which could cost over $20,000, became an integral part of the lifestyle of the fabulously wealthy of the 1920s' economic boom. Prominent among these conspicuous consumers of automotive extravagance were entertainers and entrepreneurs who had made fortunes in the emerging industries of mass consumption and amusement. Some of the most outrageous automotive indulgences could be found in the capital of consumer dreams, Hollywood, where uninhibited coachbuilders like Harley Earl catered to the spectacular off-screen lifestyles of America's on-screen idols. Earl designed custom cars for the stars distinguished by their integration of elements into a unified theme. For Western star Tom Mix he attached a saddle to the roof and painted the star's "TM" logotype all over the car. More subtle in thematic unity was a $28,000 creation for Fatty Arbuckle – a long, low automobile with softly sculptural forms from radiator to rear.[23]

These custom-bodied luxury giants were beyond the economic reach of all but the grandest bourgeoisie of America. But their petite class compatriots could also find automotive distinction on a budget with production luxury cars. These cars carried the same carefully engineered and constructed chassis as their grand cousins, but their bodies were produced in volume by bodybuilding factories. However, they were distinguished from mass-production bodies by being designed as aesthetic wholes and carefully constructed by craftworkers who lavished on them large amounts of skilled handwork.[24]

Regardless of whether their bodies were custom jobs or factory-produced, these great luxury makes were aesthetically distinct from the hordes of mass-produced cars rolling off the assembly lines of this period. Those who sat behind the wheel of one of these automobiles had an entirely different motoring experience than those whose class position consigned them to the operation of the clattering, dreary, black boxes. Their superior engineering and skilled, unhurried production created a refined, relaxed driving experience. The large, powerful, hand-assembled engines ran smoothly, devoid of vibration. The close, hand-fitting of body parts and extensive insulation also ensured the noticeable absence of rattles and clattering. And the spare-no-expense engineering and production of mechanical parts produced an ostentatious ease of steering, braking, and shifting.

One did not have to drive these luxury cars to discern their distinction, for a quick look testified to the differences in engineering and construction that separated them from the mass-produced autos of the day. First, these cars were generally longer and lower than the short, stubby cheap cars. While the 1915 Model T measured 135 inches in overall length, many luxury classics measured over 200 inches. And the sweeping winglike fenders on these cars helped to visually exaggerate their length. Also prominent by comparison to mass-produced cars were

Figure 5 1924 Lincoln touring, the look of luxury. Such large, long, powerful cars with carefully integrated designs came to symbolize a life of power and discretion, far removed from the fragmented heteronomy of assembly lines. (Courtesy Henry Ford Museum and Greenfield Village)

the long hoods on the expensive makes. Originally required to house the large engines with in-line cylinders, these hoods became symbolic of power and speed and were maintained even after the V–8 engine reduced actual hood length requirements. Complementing the elongated proportions of these cars were their abbreviated heights, achieved by sacrificing headroom and lowering bodies close to the ground.

These luxury cars were also distinctive in the quality of their design and construction. They had an appearance of wholeness that sharply contrasted with the fragmented, mechanical look of mass-produced cars. The soft curves and smooth transitions on the classics lent them an organic appearance, as if they were grown, not assembled. The gaps between body panels were narrow and uniform, while seams and joints were generally invisible. The planes of the body were congruent, and the panels were devoid of ripples and wrinkles. The color finishes were lustruous and flawless. And when functional parts were visible, they were polished and painted in ways that blended with the body and fenders. In the vernacular of the day, these smooth, integrated, rounded cars with flowing horizontal lines had "streamlines."[25]

These streamlines could be rendered in metal only by a production process similarly organic and whole, whose parts were encompassed by the discretion of skilled workers. Softly rounded panels required hand-beating, and close-fittings demanded slow, skilled assembly. The lustrous paint jobs could be achieved only by the hand-finishing of numerous coats of varnish paints. These results could not be produced by unskilled, fragmented labor that merely performed a standardized, mechanical procedure in the short time allowed by the stopwatch or assembly line.

CULTURAL CONNOTATIONS OF DIVERGING AUTOMOBILE DESIGNS

Automobile design during this period thus became increasingly bifurcated. Under the rigors of mass production, low-priced vehicles grew more rectilinear, fragmented, and homogeneous, while high-priced cars produced by craft methods became increasingly curvilinear, integrated, and distinctive. And these aesthetic differences assumed cultural meanings, symbolizing in consumption the differences between people in production. Cars bore testimony to class position, with luxury cars marking a commanding position removed from the necessities of degrading production and mass-produced vehicles marking a subjection to this deskilled, homogeneous production process. The class distinctions of work followed Americans home in their cars, exacerbating class conflict and preventing leisure from compensating for the dehumanizing demands of labor.

The hope of mass automobility as democratization

Initially the spread of auto ownership made possible by mass production was perceived by many Americans as democratic, not divisive. The individual mobility once monopolized by the grand bourgeoisie was now available to the masses, giving them greater freedom and opportunities. Americans had always conflated geographic and social mobility, both in popular culture and in intellectual theories like Frederick Jackson Turner's frontier thesis. They saw class betterment as furthered by movement to geographic areas with more open opportunities. Because the automobile was the most advanced and individual means of physical movement, it immediately became associated with social mobility and freedom in American culture. As mass production lowered prices and popularized ownership, the car was championed as an instrument of democracy, equalizing among all classes the opportunities of geographic mobility.[26]

The movies of this period carried this popular theme of the auto as a vehicle of social mobility and a leveller of class barriers. In many popular films the car was the mechanism through which poor, hard-working young men rose in the class system, as well as a symbol of their success. In *The Girl and the Chauffeur* (1911), a rich young woman elopes with the family chauffeur who, by using his automotive skills, becomes a rich garage owner and saves his father-in-law from economic ruin. In *The Apple Tree Girl* (1917), an ambitious but poor country boy becomes a successful doctor through the use of a Model T to make his rounds. He then buys an expensive roadster, with which he saves the life and wins the heart of the rich woman of his dreams.[27]

By the time auto ownership had spread sufficiently to be seen as an equalizing force, however, the meaning of geographic mobility was subtly shifting. The same system of mass production that brought automobility to the masses also closed off the economic opportunities that were responsible for the original association between movement and social advancement. The large-scale, capital-intensive production pioneered by the auto industry produced a trend of economic concentration which crushed the small businesses on the industrial frontier which had once provided workers with opportunities for escape from the large firms. So although more Americans owned autos, they had fewer economic opportunities to drive to, and most of these employed the same rationalized methods of mass production and bureaucratic organization.

The automobile continued to be seen as a democratizing force in America, but increased emphasis was placed on the liberty and equality it brought in consumption, not production. Increasingly the automobile was seen as a leisure machine that improved the life of the masses by offering a temporary escape in off-work hours from oppressive working conditions. As auto ownership spread from bourgeoisie to workers, so too did the therapeutic ethos, which stressed the recreational benefits of automobility and other forms of commodity-laden leisure. Mass automobility made this recreational mobility available to all and was thus thought to further class equalization.

Many philanthropists and reformers of the era, like Cornelius Vanderbilt Jr, looked to the automobile "to solve the labor and social problems" by providing workers with an escape from the urban congestion that was said to breed class discontent. One commentator wrote that workingmen "who, in the late afternoon, glide away in their own comfortable vehicles to their little farms or homes in the country . . . will be healthier, happier, more intelligent and self-respecting citizens because of the chance to live among the meadows and flowers of the country instead of in crowded city streets." Although during the 1920s growing auto ownership did not facilitate actual suburbanization of workers, it did bring them temporary respite from industrial ills through recreational use. The Lynds' study of Muncie found that the automobile was increasingly the focus of working-class leisure activities like the Sunday drive in the country. And extended automotive escapes from the monotony of the job also spread to workers, as they made up an increasing proportion of autocampers and tourists.[28]

Many social reformers and commentators of the day believed that the congenial mixing of the classes in automotive leisure would overcome class segmentation and further democracy. Others hoped the automobile would equalize the classes by making workers property owners and giving them a stake in America's capitalist system. Ideologically conflating consumer goods with capital, a 1924 Chevrolet ad argued that car ownership made the "once poor laborer and mechanic . . . a capitalist – the owner of a taxable asset. . . . How can Bolshevism flourish in a motorized country having a standard of living, and thinking too high to permit the existence of an ignorant, narrow, peasant majority?"[29]

For an increasing proportion of American workers, automobile ownership was a symbol of their growing status and equality in the realm of consumption. The Fordist production process had largely stripped them of power and status at work, but with their higher wages workers bought back a semblance of freedom and control in their leisure time. If they could never be the equals of their bosses and educated technicians at work, at least they could live the same at leisure, consuming similar products and pastimes. The automobile symbolized this trade-off, for, as the Lynds wrote, it gave the worker "the status which his job increasingly denies, and, more than any other possession or facility to which he has access, it symbolizes living, having a good time, the thing that keeps you working."[30]

These cultural meanings attached to the automobile were part of a larger ideology of technological progress emerging in America. The growing abundance of mass-produced consumer goods encouraged Americans to measure their lives in technological terms. A better life was defined no longer as greater job responsibilities, development of talents, or closer social relations, but as more and better material goods. And the way to achieve this material abundance was not changing society but changing technology. Progress increasingly meant the consensual improvement of the technical apparatuses of society, not the conflictual reordering of its social relations.

The fear of mass production as dehumanization

Mingled with the praises sung to the democracy of mass consumption could be heard discordant voices expressing apprehensions about the dehumanization of mass production. The automobile was also an important symbol in this critical image of the emerging mechanical age. Complementing working-class resistance to Fordist production were intellectual lamentations that the machine age was destroying the human spirit. Paul Frankl, an American designer, wrote that: "Twentieth-century Man is in the toils of a new mistress . . . the Machine. . . . Roughshod she trampled over all traditional values; she crushed out the lives of men, women, and children; she destroyed the old beauty and replaced it with a 'new ugliness'. . . ."[31]

Many intellectuals attributed this "ugliness" of the age to mass production. This standardized production process undermined the bourgeois ideal of individuality by reducing people to interchangeable units and dooming "countless thousands to standardized virtues and machine-made existences," lamented Frankl. Mass production was also said to contradict democracy by reducing the common person to a mere bystander, "a simpleton who 'joy-walks' into the center of a swiftly moving traffic of ideas." And many, like American designer Walter

Dorwin Teague, worried that machine production undermined equality: "we have allowed it to generate social conflict, magnify inequalities and injustices, create appalling conditions of living which are as deleterious to human welfare as war itself. . . ."[32]

Because mass-produced products bore the visual marks of this dehumanizing production process, they became associated in the popular culture with the ugly side of the machine age. This association had been pioneered in nineteenth-century England by John Ruskin, William Morris, and others, who founded the Arts and Crafts movement on the idea that industrial products were ugly precisely because they reflected the violence done to humans in industrial production. They argued this production system destroyed the craftworkers' unity of design and execution, with devastating aesthetic as well as human results. Fordist mass production exacerbated this fragmentation, erecting an insuperable class barrier between these previously unified functions. As American designer Raymond Loewy argued, the machine age replaced the craftworker with the engineer, who gave priority in design to the technique of production over aesthetics. As a result, wrote Walter Dorwin Teague, "the machines let loose on the world a flood of imperfect and hence ugly wares as shocking as the black devastation that spread over so many fair countrysides and growing towns."[33]

The early mass-produced commodities that bore the visible marks of mass production were said to offend the senses. The stark, standardized, form required by machine production "generally signified the often harsh necessities of work," writes one design historian, "and as such was tolerated in its place, but art, in the form of decoration and ornament, represented for many people a deep aspiration for a better life." When transported to the domestic sphere of consumption, these mass-produced goods were constant reminders of the inhumanities suffered in all rationalized work processes and violated the emerging requirement that "the [domestic] environment should kill all associations with work."[34]

More so than other products, low-priced automobiles acquired this stigma of Fordist mass production, for they visibly testified to the unpleasant aspects of rationalized work. Their severe, rectilinear lines were clearly reminiscent of the unyielding machines that dominated production, and the fragmented look testified to a labor process filled with detail workers who produced separate parts with no vision of the whole. The obtrusive gaps and seams between parts were further testimony to a disjointed production process. And the rigid uniformity of these vehicles visibly indexed a production process that eliminated the variety and discretion of work.

These aesthetic associations with the bad side of mass production caused these cheap cars to be widely regarded as ugly. The Model T, the epitome of mass production, was singled out for aesthetic abuse. Earnest Elmo Calkins, an advertising agent and pioneer of mass consumption, admitted that the T was a good, economical car but complained that "it did violence to the three senses, sight, hearing, and smell" and constituted an "intrusion of more ugliness into a world that was losing peace and silence and the beauty that inheres in old things." In popular lore the car was lovingly revered as a dependable, hard-working companion but just as commonly regarded as ugly, noisy, and cheaply made. Model T jokes sprang up to good-naturedly ridicule its undesirable aesthetic qualities. Ridiculing its social stigma, one asked why a Model T was like a mistress. The answer: because you hate to be seen on the streets with one. Another joke poked fun at the T's loosely joined construction, with an owner stating he knew his speed without a speedometer: "When my Ford is running five miles an hour, the fender rattles; twelve miles an hour, my teeth rattle; and fifteen miles an hour, the transmission drops out."[35]

Because these early mass-produced cars bore the visual marks of mass production, they also testified to their owners' class position in that process. Visual comparison to the large, powerful luxury cars clearly revealed that autos like the Model T were produced by a different labor process and owned mainly by those dominated by that labor process. The qualities of luxury makes testified to their production by an un-hurried handicraft process, unified by skilled craftworkers executing their tasks without the domineering presence of the stopwatch or mechanical line. To own and drive one of these cars symbolized a particular position not merely in the distribution of wealth but also in the distribution of power in the economy that generated this wealth. Owner-ship of a Packard, Cadillac, or Lincoln said that the individual led an unhurried, discretionary life, unsullied by necessity or routine. These cars announced that their possessors were themselves unpossessed, free from the hurrying commands of human and mechanical masters, just like the craftworkers that produced them. Their unified, organic aesthetics testified to whole lives, undivided by the contradictory demands of degraded work and compensatory leisure. In sum, the luxury makes symbolized a life of control, command, discretion – over oneself and others.

By contrast, the cheap, mass-produced cars said that their owners were subject to the demands of mechanical and bureaucratic necessity, dominated by rationalized work in the factory or office. They testified to a life fragmented by the hurrying commands of others, subject to the cost-cutting concerns of supervisors and assembly lines. These individuals, their vehicles announced, were unable to rise above necessity, lacked the discretion and control to consciously unify their fragmented existence. They were the objects of alien necessities, both mechanical and human, that rendered their lives standardized, angular, fragmented.[36]

The popular culture and commentary of the day recognized that these contrasting automotive styles testified to the contrasting class positions of their owners. As Earnest Elmo Calkins wrote in 1927: "We had large gorgeously appareled cars at high prices, and small ugly useful cars at low prices. The car with the long wheel base and the stream line became the symbol of wealth. The stubby car which continued to retain the graceless lines with which it was born was the symbol of homely worth and modest circumstance." Novelists of the period used the hierarchy of auto makes to symbolize the class positions of their characters. In F. Scott Fitzgerald, the reader senses that the family that trades in a Ford for a Franklin is on the way up, but has not socially arrived because it cannot afford a Pierce–Arrow. In Sinclair Lewis's *Babbit* the protagonist's decision to buy a new car touches off a family debate about the proper symbol of their social class, leading the novelist to conclude: "In the city of Zenith, in the barbarous twentieth century, a family's motor indicated its social rank as precisely as the grades of the peerage determined the rank of an English family. . . ."[37]

These class connotations of automobiles were further reinforced by the manufacturers themselves, who used them to promote their vehicles. Snob appeal appeared as a new theme in the automotive ads of this period, with automakers appealing to buyers' aspirations for distinction by associating their cars with class privilege and the craft labor process that symbolized it. The luxury makes pictured their cars in the quiet, genteel settings associated with privilege: estates, country houses, resorts. Duesenberg ran a famous series of ads that pictured owners in positions of privilege and power, simply stating "He (or She) drives a Duesenberg." In one, a tall, slender woman is bathed in sunlight as she stands on a portico overlooking an expansive lawn being manicured by a crew of faceless gardeners. She is speaking to one of them, who stands in the shadows, hat in hand, on a step below the woman. The elegant script that states she drives a Duesenberg quietly associates the car with a command over the labor of others that is the essence of class privilege.[38]

Other advertisements for luxury makes appealed to class exclusivity and individuality to emphasize their differences from mass-produced autos. Some stressed their low volume of production. Others emphasized their cars were custom-built, as an ad for the Kissel Custom-Built

Six which stated that "the most painstaking care is taken, not only to make each car complete, but of the custom-built quality and exclusiveness demanded by, and expected of, Kissel tradition." An advertisement for the Roamer similarly played to the desire for class distinction. "The average automobile possesses about as much distinction as a black Derby," it stated, and then went on to claim for its car "a distinct individuality. The Roamer is custom-made – it is produced particularly for *you*, not just for a *market*."[39]

American popular culture of this period evidenced a deep-seated ambivalence toward the grand luxury makes driven by the wealthy. They were commonly revered as symbols of the good life aspired to by all, and turned up in Cole Porter songs, Fitzgerald novels, and Hollywood movies. But because many resented the fact that they did not and probably never would own one, these luxury cars also symbolized envied wealth and became the focus of a great deal of class resentment and antagonism. As one commentator stated, great cars like the Duesenberg seemed to be designed "to make luxury motoring both a gratifying pleasure for those riding in cars and a deliberate taunt to the less fortunate passed by." The lower classes did not take these automotive insults supinely, for they responded with symbolic aggressions of their own. Sometimes these were expressed directly, as in a letter to a magazine protesting that Model T owners were "held in contempt by the chauffeur of a big 'six' doubtless because a Ford has passed him on the hill; treated with brusqueness by many a garage man. . . . But what angers me most is when we are classed as a God-forsaken, poverty-stricken lot. . . . Many a Fordist could buy up a majority of these revilers; many a Fordist is their intellectual superior. . . ."[40]

Other symbolic expressions of class resentment of the luxury cars were contained in popular jokes and songs. Many Model T jokes resentfully asserted the car's superiority to the expensive makes. One cartoon showed a T passing a big limousine mired in the mud, and was captioned: "The big car fumes and throws a fit, but the little Ford don't mind a bit." An entire genre of songs argued the romantic superiority of the mass-produced cars and their owners. One, entitled "Ray and his little Chevrolet," asserted: "He laughs at Packards, Coles 'n Roamers, /Gets more girls than Ruth gets homers."[41]

The mass-produced cars that were the centerpiece of the emerging realm of mass consumption could not provide the compensation for and escape from Fordist production as long as they served as symbols of class, people's position at work. One attempt during this period to eradicate the class connotations of mass-produced products proceeded in the realm of ideas alone. In various schools of modernism – purism, futurism, constructivism – architects and artists defined the forms of mass-production as beautiful, and produced works that aped the fragmented, mechanical appearance of mass-produced goods. As purist architect Le Corbusier wrote: "The creations of mechanical technique are organisms tending to a pure functioning, and obey the same evolutionary laws as those objects in nature which excite our admiration." Part of the larger Progressive movement, these bourgeois architects and urban planners realized that the social conflicts unleashed by Fordist capitalism could be contained only by reconstructing workers' physical environment of leisure with consumer goods. But this physical reconstruction could succeed only if workers would accept in their homes the mass-produced goods turned out in factories. Machine aesthetics, which glorified the appearance of such goods, provided the intellectual justification for this program of bourgeois reform to restructure the working-class home and leisure.[42]

In the United States, this reform program sought to wean workers from the historic styles compatible with craft production and promoted the simple, austere furnishings produced by machines. But working-class Americans were not easily persuaded that the stark, severe forms of the machine were beautiful and should be welcomed in their homes. Unlike architects and reformers, workers had intimate contact with the workings of mechanized factories and were well aware of the human degradation and ugliness perpetuated by them. In their minds, as in the minds of most middle- and upper-class Americans, mass-produced products that bore the aesthetic marks of this labor process were ugly and inappropriate for the home, where they sought escape and compensation.[43]

So workers joined other Americans in seeking an aesthetic in consumer goods that concealed rather than revealed the marks of the production process, allowing them to temporarily forget the demands of work. They wanted consumer goods that had the look of nature, not the factory. The soft, rounded forms of the natural world provided relief from the harsh, angular world of capitalist mass production by referring to a realm of peace and harmony beyond or before the domination of things and people by the ruthless logic of profit. These organic forms were also reminiscent of craft production, an earlier, more natural form of labor in which people consciously controlled their own activities. Goods with this organic look were said to have "style," and were in high demand among all classes.

THE STYLE IMPERATIVE: THE DEMAND FOR OBSCURING AESTHETICS

This demand for style that hid the fragmentation of the factory began to influence the American auto industry in the early 1920s due to a complex combination of cultural and economic factors. Culturally, consumers became less and less fascinated with the technology and utility of the car. When the automobile was a novel machine, people were enthralled with its technology and wanted to see the latest technical developments that improved its utility. But by the mid-1920s, technical innovation had slowed down and nearly all automobiles possessed a uniformly high standard of performance. Consumers took for granted the car's technical functions and placed more emphasis on its social use as a symbol of status and progress.[44]

By this time, however, mass production had brought the auto within the economic reach of many Americans, diluting the social distinction of mere ownership. From this point on, writes one automotive historian, "the use of the automobile as a status symbol would be restricted to the type of car one owned rather than to automobile ownership per se." Because standardized, mass-produced vehicles connoted a lower-class position, buyers began to demand that their ugliness be eliminated, or at least obscured. They sought cars that borrowed the organic aesthetic of the craft-produced luxury vehicles, thus obscuring undesirable social connotations.[45]

Economic factors forced producers to rapidly supply cars with the style that consumers demanded. By the mid-1920s many feared that the American market for automobiles was nearing saturation. Sales to first-time buyers declined, as the proportion of American families owning an auto reached 55 percent in 1927. But bringing automobility to the poorer half of the American population was difficult, as both wage growth and auto price declines stagnated. Competition in this slowly growing market became intense, forcing automakers to distinguish their products from the horde of homogeneous vehicles flooding off assembly lines. But concentration in the auto industry – the Big Three now accounted for 72 percent of total output – prevented this competition from taking the form of price cuts or technological innovations. The small number of competitors reduced the pressure for price-cutting. And oligopolization also reduced the pace of technical innovations. Only the large corporations could afford the escalating costs of such innovations, but they were under little competitive pressure to do so. And they were loath to undertake changes that required replacing expensive production technology before it was fully depreciated.[46]

In this era of increased competition between a few oligopolistic giants, improvements in style emerged as the preferred method of distinguishing a company's products. It was cheaper and easier for mass-producers to alter the finish and style of the body than to pioneer mechanical changes in the parts underneath. And beautification of the ugly, cheap cars seemed to be what consumers wanted anyway, as they focused on the social symbolism of the car. So a combination of changing cultural meanings and oligopolistic economic structure produced the escalating emphasis on style.

The emergence of this style imperative was registered in the commentary and advertisements of the early 1920s. An auto reporter for *Scientific American* wrote in 1922 that since all cars exhibited a high level of technical performance, the annual shows of new models were reduced to body exhibits. "The buyer and the seller alike take it for granted that the car will take its owner where he wants to go at the speed that pleases him and with a minimum of attention from him and they concentrate their critical eyes upon the shape of the body. . . ." By 1925 *Automotive Industries* was editorializing that "great sales appeal is attached to an attractive automobile body." Even though slightly higher costs would be entailed in changing dies and tools to improve appearance, "a really good body design is well worth seeking and production considerations should not be allowed to becloud this fact."[47]

Advertisements for mass-produced cars reflected this growing concern for beauty and style. Technical features faded away, and appearance was prominently featured. Even the homely Model T promoted itself in a 1915 ad as "a car of style – beautiful in design – rich in detail of appointments." Advertisers often resorted to deception to appeal to style, changing the proportions of cars in their illustrations to make them look longer, lower, and rounder. Whether through illusory or real changes, automakers sought to give their inexpensive cars style by making them look like the expensive luxury classics of the day. As Thomas Hibbard, a pioneering auto designer, wrote: "large manufacturers in the mid-1920s began to realize . . . that sales could be stimulated by making high-production cars as attractive as the custom bodied cars on well proportioned chassis." These luxury cars were universally recognized as beautiful because they testified to a more human and integrated process of production. Although only the wealthy could afford these truly integrated, organic products, working people could and did demand autos that resembled them in appearance, possessed a facade of beauty that obscured the ugliness of the factory and their degraded position within it.[48]

So mass-producers began to alter the appearance of their cars to resemble the luxury makes, thus closing the aesthetic gap in consumption that testified to the class gap in production. Alfred Sloan, president of GM, summarized the new approach to design as "unifying the various parts of the car from the standpoint of appearance, of rounding off sharp corners, and of lowering the silhouette. We wanted a production automobile that was as beautiful as the custom cars of the period." Mass-production cars were lowered by chopping roofs, using smaller wheels and balloon tires, and mounting springs under the axle. They were also lengthened, if not in reality at least in appearance by adding aesthetic features like belt moldings that accentuated the horizontal dimension. And improvements in press technology made it possible to round off the corners of roofs, fenders, and radiator shells.[49]

Mass-producers of autos also sought to obscure the telltale marks of their fragmented production process by adopting the integrated appearance of craft-produced classics. They hid the fragmented conglomeration of loosely joined, dissilimar parts beneath a body whose pieces were smoothly blended into an aesthetic unity. The hood was raised, widened, and blended smoothly with the main body of the car by a flush cowl, a gently curved piece of sheet metal which replaced the awkward, steeply angled ogee cowl. Transitions between other body parts were handled with a similar eye to eliminating abrupt joints. Pains were taken to hide all signs of assemblage like rivets, nails, and screws. And this smooth, seamless body was extended to conceal the mechanical parts, as manufacturers became aware that people no longer wanted to see these. As Charles Kettering, head of General Motors Research Corporation, stated in 1927: "At first when cars were novelties, people were interested in what made them go. Now they wanted to be unconscious of the mechanism." So the crudely finished and assembled functional parts were tucked away under body extensions like side panels, which concealed the top frame rails, and sheet-metal aprons, which hid the engine bottom.[50]

Finally, automotive mass-producers superficially imitated the lustrous, hand-finished paint jobs of the luxury makes with the introduction of quick-drying Duco, or nitrocellulose lacquer. Lacquer dried quicker than varnish paints, and the new base could carry more pigment than previous types. In 1923 these colorful lacquers began to replace the drab black enamel finishes on inexpensive cars. And while Duco finishes did not achieve the brillance of varnish paints, they did produce a wide range of cheap color finishes on mass-produced cars, reducing their chromatic differences from the laboriously finished luxury cars.[51]

These and other aesthetic features pirated from the prestigous makes were promoted in the ads of mass-produced cars to lure buyers. An ad for a $695 Maxwell boasted a list of seventeen "high priced car features," including "Pure stream line body," "Concealed door hinges," and "Crown fenders with all rivets concealed." And just in case the copy failed to establish an affinity between these mass-produced cars and their high-class cousins, they were pictured in settings of privileged leisure like polo grounds, where the Maxwell was shown parked. The ads seemed to say that these cars that bore no stigmatizing signs of the factory allowed even humble workers to mix undetected with the leisure set in a classless utopia of consumption.[52]

This aesthetic piracy became prominent in the early 1920s, when GM, Dodge, and Chrysler began to meet the demand for style. The 1923 Chevrolet Superior was definitely "stylish" in the idiom established by the luxury classics, with its longer wheelbase, lower roof, higher hood, and less angular styling overall. The Dodge brothers, who had a reputation for producing rugged but plain-looking cars, caught the styling trend in the next year, offering a base model with a higher hood and flush cowl, and a higher-priced Special featuring a chrome-plated radiator shell, a deluxe interior, and other decorative refinements. And when Walter Chrysler introduced the first car bearing his name in 1924, it was widely recognized as a style leader for its smooth, rounded appearance, as well as its luxury-car features like side-mounted spare tires.[53]

Compared to these stylish cars, Ford's Model T appeared dowdy and antiquated. Owners stigmatized by its high, angular, mechanical look began on their own to "modernize" its aesthetics, giving rise to a burgeoning business in parts and accessories. Although some accessories addressed mechanical deficiencies, many were clearly aimed at disguising the T's mass-produced origins by making it superficially resemble the luxury classics. One kit contained a "streamline" hood and radiator shell which, an ad claimed, "makes the Ford look like a high-priced car." To replace the flat fenders of early Ts, some suppliers offered crowned fenders, "having the graceful, flowing, stylish lines and the rounding arch that you generally see only in high-priced cars." But the ultimate kits for disguising the Model T's factory origins offered entire "streamline" bodies to replace the rectilinear, fragmented production body.

Not wholly oblivious to the emerging demand for style, Ford began to introduce changes in the Model T's appearance that followed the trend toward the organic aesthetic of the luxury cars. The 1917 model appeared with curved and crowned fenders, a higher and larger hood,

Figure 6 1923 Chevrolet Superior four-door sedan, signaling the beginnings of style in mass-produced cars. The smooth, stylish body imitated the look of the luxury classics and obscured the mass-produced fragmentation underneath. (Courtesy National Automotive History Collection, Detroit Public Library)

and a rounded radiator shell. But further changes were not introduced until 1923, and by then the T was well behind the style leaders. In this year the T's body was lowered, the hood raised, and an apron added to the radiator shell to conceal the frame and crank mechanism. But Ford's inflexible mass-production technology caused these changes to be made slowly and incrementally, causing an aesthetic lag that ultimately resulted in declining sales.[54]

The emerging style imperative in mass-produced cars forced organizational changes in automaking corporations. Automakers first found it necessary to establish closer ties to their body suppliers in order to coordinate activities and achieve the unity of design that integrated the chassis and body into an aesthetic whole. In 1919 GM acquired 60 percent of its major supplier, the Fisher Body Corporation, and bought the remaining interest in 1926. Although Ford did not buy its major body suppliers, it did establish closer ties to the Murray Corporation by luring it to Detroit. To achieve the organic look, mass-production firms also began to shift design responsibilities away from body engineers, who gave priority to production, toward specialists whose sole concern was aesthetics. In the mid-1920s volume bodybuilders and automakers alike began to hire designers who developed initial working drafts on tracing cloth with india ink and ruling pens. Some companies bought out entire coachbuilding firms to obtain such design expertise. In the span of a few years in the 1920s, Fisher acquired Fleetwood, Briggs bought out Le Baron, and Murray purchased Dietrich Incorporated. Firms which could not afford these expenses often retained independent coachbuilders as consultants for the design of their mass-produced bodies.[55]

In the early days of the style imperative, the position of these new merchants of style within the American automobile industry was tenuous. Automakers were groping their way in a rapidly changing market with ad hoc changes in policy and organizational structure. During this transition period there was a great deal of conflict over this newly opened frontier of style. Within firms, established occupations and divisions fought the upstart stylists for control. And there was also considerable conflict between firms over the role that style would play in the automotive market. It would require two decades of struggle before style-driven mass consumption became the institutionalized complement to Fordist mass production.

Chapter 4

The struggle for styling I
The 1920s and the birth of automobile styling

One day in the early 1930s Harlow Curtice, the new general manager of General Motors' Buick Division, ventured to the third floor of the corporation's headquarters in Detroit, where the Art and Color Section was located. This was the corporate "beauty parlor," as some of Detroit's hard-boiled, no-nonsense automotive men referred to it, where the "pretty-picture boys" dressed up the automobiles that came off the engineers' drawing boards. The section was headed by a California transplant named Harley Earl, a style-conscious man given to wearing white-linen suits and purple shirts. But he was also a huge, powerful man who could curse, drink, and womanize with the best of the industry's engineers and production men. And he was determined to wrest the power to design cars away from them.

Curtice eyed the decorations that Earl and his staff had hung on his forthcoming Buicks and did not like what he saw. He quickly got into a heated argument with Earl, who told him that he did not know a "damn thing" about style. After a few more expletives were exchanged, Earl suddenly fell silent and strode toward his office, motioning for Curtice to follow. He picked up the receiver of the phone on his desk and pushed the button that opened a direct line to the office of GM president Alfred Sloan.

"Hello, Alfred, how are you?" Earl asked calmly.

"How's Carol, Alfred? And how are the kids? All right? That's good." Now the tone of Earl's voice grew notably harsher.

"Alfred, I'm here in the Buick studio with that son of a bitch Curtice, and he seems to be a little confused. He can't tell who's in charge of Buick and who's in charge of Art and Color. I thought maybe you could straighten out his ass for me."

Earl handed the phone to Curtice, to whom Sloan calmly stated: "Let him build anything he wants."[1]

Harley Earl created the first design division in a major automaker, which by the early 1940s had almost absolute authority over the look and shape of all GM cars. But in his first years at GM, he had to struggle against the entrenched power of production-oriented executives to realize his vision of automotive style. He was a charismatic leader, carrying out a revolution against the bureaucratic authority of engineers, division heads, and sales executives, and depending on the sheer force of his personality. His unlikely ally in this struggle for styling was Alfred Sloan, whose personal patronage and friendship Earl wielded as a weapon in his early battles.

Earl and Sloan were one of the industry's oddest couples. Sloan was the original organization man, a dispassionate champion of corporate bureaucracy and the bottom line. A frail, pale New Yorker who dressed conservatively, Sloan seldom got excited about anything, much less automobiles. By contrast, Harley Earl was a flashy, brash, athletic, perpetually tanned Californian who was easily excited, especially by cars. He absolutely loved them and wanted to transmit his love and excitement through style to the buyers of GM products. The two men could not have been more different. But they needed each other, and they knew it.

In the mid-1920s, Sloan was struggling to break the stranglehold that Ford's Model T had on half of the automotive market. He decided that instead of confronting Ford directly in a price war, he would cater to the emerging demand for style. So Sloan hired Earl to give his mass-produced products the appearance of variety and innovation. But could excitement and change be rationalized, turned into an impersonal cog in Sloan's corporate bureaucracy? This question would only be answered by a monumental struggle at all levels of American society.

AMERICA, 1925–1930: CONSUMER SOCIETY AND THE RISE OF INDUSTRIAL DESIGN

GM's marketplace struggle for stylish cars and Earl's organizational struggle for stylists were part of a larger societal struggle for style that emerged in the latter 1920s. As mass production and economic rationalization undermined the meaning and identity that people found in productive activity, they struggled to define themselves increasingly in terms of the things they consumed. But to bear this cultural burden, the products of mass production required more than mere utility. They had to have style – the individuality, wholeness, and progress that jobs in Fordist factories and bureaucracies lacked.

A rising material standard of living during this period allowed most Americans to express themselves through consumer style. While workers' wages rose more slowly than the income of the bourgeoisie, this growing class gap was obscured by improvements in the material well-being of American workers. Growth in industrial productivity and installment buying brought workers a broader array of technological conveniences like automobiles, radios, telephones, and washing machines. The privileged fraction of industrial workers was beginning to participate in the emerging consumer society.[2]

In the mid-1920s Robert and Helen Lynd found that the entry of workers into consumer society had effected cultural as well as material changes in their lives. They found in Muncie that commodities were increasingly the focus of workers' social status and personal identity. As one informant told the Lynds, people were socially placed "in terms of where they live, how they live, the kind of car they drive, and similar externals." Inspired by advertising, radio, and movies, workers joined the "business class" in seeking an ever-escalating material standard of living, and were thus "running for dear life in this business of making the money they earn keep pace with the ever more rapid growth of their subjective wants. . . . The working class is mystified by the whole fateful business."[3]

But not just any material possessions could mystify American workers into accepting the growing gap of power and wealth between the classes. The working-class recruits into the consumer army demanded products that had the elusive look of "style." The Lynds ascribed this demand for ever-changing style in commodities to the manipulative devices of business elites, who sought "to ram home a higher standard of living" by making the consumer "emotionally uneasy, bludgeoning him with the fact that decent people don't live the way he does." Many leaders in the emerging professions of consumer style agreed that their main mission was to stimulate demand through instilling dissatisfaction and new needs. But as others argued, the style professions did not manufacture needs out of whole cloth but appealed to a preexisting consumer demand. As one recent analyst of consumer culture writes: "Americans were not passive creatures subject to direct manipulation by wiley agents of capital. They became consumers through their own active adjustment to both the material and spiritual conditions of life in advanced capitalist society." And the most important conditions to which most Americans adjusted were those of rationalized work. Since the monotonous, fragmented, and degrading work of mass-production factories and offices provided few genuine satisfactions, working people looked hungrily to the consumer marketplace

for products that provided compensation for and relief from these conditions. They sought commodities with unity to compensate for their
fragmented activities in mass production. They demanded goods with
individuality to provide the distinction that their homogeneous jobs
could not. And in their things people sought a semblance of the progress
and improvement that they could not achieve in the leveled and segmented occupational hierarchies.[4]

But the structure of Fordism that denied these needs in production also
blocked their realization in consumption. The division of labor that
rendered workers skilless also prevented products from achieving unity.
The standardization of models that eliminated human discretion also undermined product individuality. The high cost of specialized machinery
limited the product changes that signaled progress. And all of these factors
distinguished mass-produced products from the craft-produced goods of
the upper classes. The problem facing mass-producers in the latter half of
the 1920s was meeting the escalating demand for stylish goods without
undermining the economies of mass production.

The solution to Fordism's dilemma was found by the new profession
of industrial design. In the mid-1920s, when saturated markets elevated
the priority of sales over production, these merchants of artifice
emerged to give mass-produced goods the superficial appearance of
individuality, unity, progress, and class without changing the foundation
of Fordism. In the United States the first industrial designers were artists
and illustrators with close ties to advertisers, wholesalers, and retailers.
Many of the profession's pioneers began as ad illustrators for agencies
like that of Earnest Elmo Calkins, who used fine art to create a "class
atmosphere" for products. By the mid-1920s large department stores
were also hiring commercial artists to sell standardized goods by placing
them in unique, stylish packages and dramatic, eye-catching displays.
Gradually these store stylists began to consult directly with manufacturers, shifting responsibility for the design of mass-produced goods
from company engineers to outside artistic consultants.[5]

These first halting domestic steps toward industrial design at mid-
decade were accelerated by important European influences imported in the
1925 Exposition Internationale des Arts Décoratifs et Industriels Modernes
of Paris. Here for the first time were ordinary objects that self-consciously
celebrated style and beauty. The Expo's underlying message – that style
was compatible with mass production – was more influential on American
designers than the angular, machine aesthetics of the objects. By the late
1920s design pioneers like Raymond Loewy, Norman Bel Geddes, Henry
Dreyfuss, and Walter Dorwin Teague were developing a distinctively

American design idiom based on obscuring the mass-production mechanism from which goods issued.[6]

American designers realized that to provide people with the domestic palliatives for economic ills, consumer products had to hide all their disturbing associations with Fordist production. In the words of designer Paul Frankl, the task of design was "the domestication of the Machine," the elimination of the fear people normally felt for machinery and its products so they will "no longer be restricted to the factory . . . [but] can now be admitted to Man's castle, his home." Raymond Loewy argued that the complexity and fragmentation of unadorned products were "extremely confusing," "a nightmare of confused engineering" for most people, since factory specialization deprived them of the knowledge needed to comprehend their functional unity. To eliminate this sense of confusion and impotence, designers obscured the complex mechanism with the superficial appearance of simplicity and order. Frankl recommended that industrial designers use simple lines because they "tend to cover up the complexity of the machine age. If they do not do this, they at least divert our attention and allow us to feel ourselves master of the machine."[7]

To achieve the reassuring appearance of unity, designers often hid all the functional parts under a sleek, sheet-metal shroud which gave the product an "organic look" – "the look of inevitability, of perfect adaptation to a designated end, to be found in living things," as Walter Dorwin Teague described it. Helping consumers forget the oppressive workplace required that designers also obscure the disturbing standardization of mass-produced goods, which reminded them of their own interchangeability on the job. As two advocates of industrial design wrote, "we are sick and tired of standardization. The demand for something individual and the desire not to be like everyone else is a permanent human desire." Designers gave mass-produced goods the appearance of individuality by attaching surfaces differentiated by color and ornament to obscure the standardized reality underneath.[8]

American designers realized that consumers also wanted in their products a sense of progress and improvement denied in their dead-end working lives. To give mass-produced goods this look of newness without disturbing product standardization, designers introduced incremental changes in style, or planned obsolescence. These continuous but slow changes in product appearance gave consumers the reassuring sense of rational progress that their lives otherwise lacked. And finally the emerging profession of industrial design stimulated the flow of factory goods to domestic refuges by giving them the look of democracy. To help consumers forget the class divisions of production, designers provided mass-produced products with the superficial signs of classy goods, thus facilitating a democracy of things that obscured the class structure.[9]

Industrial designers' attempts to recast mass-produced products to give consumers compensating style were not initially greeted with approval in industry. Although often advocated by executives in sales and marketing, beautifying designers met with outright hostility from engineers and production managers, who traditionally designed products with a focus on manufacturing efficiency. They resented designers dictating changes on the ephemeral basis of appearance and prevented the new profession from initially gaining much power in corporate hierarchies. However, the deepening stagnation of the late 1920s, culminating in the stock market crash of 1929, gradually impressed on corporate leaders the importance of stimulating sales through style.[10]

STRUGGLE OF THE AUTOMOTIVE GIANTS: GM STYLE VERSUS FORD UTILITY

The most important terrain for the struggle for styling in the second half of the 1920s was the automobile industry. This pioneer in Fordist mass production was the first to feel its principal contradiction of underconsumption. By the mid-1920s the market for new cars was dangerously soft, but Fordism's general weakening of labor prevented wages from rising enough to bring automobility to poorer workers. The auto industry faced the dilemma of stimulating the consumption of its product without raising the costs of its production.

During this period there emerged two strategies for overcoming this contradiction, each identified with its corporate champion. Ford extended its strategy of cost-cutting utility – offering a widely useful vehicle at a low and decreasing price – on which it had risen to industry dominance. When faced with slowing car sales in the mid-1920s, Ford's prescription was more of the same price-cutting medicine. But even drastic cuts in Model T prices did not stimulate sales, and Ford's market share slipped from 50 percent in 1923 to 15 percent in 1927. This strategy of cost-cutting utility failed because, first, finding new production economies to offset lower prices was increasingly difficult and expensive. Further, the demand for low-priced, basic transportation was increasingly filled by used cars, whose supply exploded as first-time buyers traded in their old cars for a new one. Finally, auto buyers were increasingly demanding comfort, convenience, and style, all of which were woefully lacking in Henry's humble vehicle. Sensing this, Ford made half-hearted efforts in the mid-1920s to stylistically update the Model T, but these were too little too late. Ford was forced to discontinue T production in 1927 to make way for the more stylish Model A.[11]

The second and ultimately triumphant strategy of stimulating consumption was pursued by GM, Ford's second-place competitor in the automotive race. Billy Durant founded the corporation in 1908 as a holding company to monopolize automobile production, but by 1920 his financial manipulations had left GM a sprawling, disorganized empire in the control of Pierre Du Pont. Du Pont appointed as his executive vice-president Alfred Sloan, a brilliant young executive who turned this loose conglomeration of competing companies into a corporate behemoth that dominated the industry for a half century. Upon assuming the reins of the corporation, Sloan began to devise a strategy to crack Ford's market domination. He ruled out head-on price competition in the low-priced field as "suicidal," arguing: "No conceivable amount of capital short of the United States Treasury could have sustained the losses required to take volume away from him at his own game."[12]

The astute Sloan suggested another strategy – fielding a graded hierarchy of autos blanketing all markets. Each of GM's car divisions would specialize in one price market and position its product in the upper range of that market, offering a better quality auto for a bit more money than the competition. Sloan's innovative product policy recognized that rising incomes and installment buying were replacing the mass market for basic transportation at a low cost with a "mass-class market," "the mass market served by better and better cars . . . with increasing diversity." He recommended that GM meet this demand for escalating quality with a hierarchy of better cars covering all classes, which would capture consumers' dollars as they moved up the consumption ladder. And GM would induce consumers to trade in their old cars by offering annually a new car in every class that was bigger and better.[13]

But Sloan's innovative product policy, authored in 1921, left unexplained important details, like how to produce a variety of constantly improving cars without undermining the standardization and high volume necessary for mass production. These details, especially what constituted "better quality," were thrashed out in an internal struggle that eventually shifted the power structure of Sloan's emerging bureaucracy. The engineering and technical people at GM, led by Charles Kettering, defined "better quality" as improved performance and economy. Kettering thought both could be achieved by his innovative air-cooled engine, which GM planned to incorporate in the 1923 Chevrolet in order to compete with Ford. But development of the "coppercooled" engine ran into technical problems that delayed production and interfered with Sloan's plan, which boldly stated that GM's purpose "was to make money, not just to make motor cars." He concluded that the pursuit of this "engineering dream" was undermining the "commercial-mindedness of our original strategic plan."[14]

Sloan ordered that the air-cooled engine program be side-tracked, and introduced in 1923 a Chevrolet with 9-year-old technology but a body of the newest style, with a lower roof, higher hood, and more rounded lines. Brisk sales of this newly frocked car convinced him that relatively inexpensive and predictable changes in automotive appearance were more conducive to profit-making than expensive and risky technological innovations. Sloan concluded that his plan "was valid if our cars were at least equal in [technical] design to the best of our competitors in a grade, so that it was not necessary to lead in design or run the risk of untried experiments." Thus it became the policy of GM not to be innovative in engineering.[15]

Upon his appointment as president of GM in 1923, Sloan began in earnest to implement his strategy of offering "better quality" cars by producing better-*looking* cars. In 1925 Chevrolet introduced another restyled version of the same old car, whose major features were, in Sloan's words, a "longer body, increased legroom, a Duco finish, a one-piece windshield with automatic wipers on all closed cars, a dome light in the coach and sedan, a Klaxon horn. . . ." This newly clothed Chevy boosted division sales to a new peak, convincing Sloan that his concept of better cars could practically mean improved appearance and more accessories. In 1926, the year in which Chevy sales nearly doubled and Ford sales dropped 25 percent, he wrote to Buick's general manager: "I am sure we all realize . . . how much appearance has to do with sales; with all cars fairly good mechanically it is a dominating proposition and in a product such as ours where the individual appeal is so great, it means a tremendous influence on our future prosperity."[16]

With automotive improvements thus defined in terms of appearance, Sloan's policy of offering continuous improvements came to mean regular changes in automotive appearance, that is, annual model changes. Automakers traditionally incorporated product changes on an annual basis due to the highly seasonal nature of production. But in the early industry, most of the yearly changes were mechanical improvements that enhanced the car's utility. As use of autos became less seasonal, innovations were often introduced at midyear, and many new models remained unchanged for several years. But Sloan's policy of offering cars continuously improved in appearance quickly led to annual style changes that spread throughout the industry.

In July of 1925, GM's General Sales Committee undertook a discussion of "Annual Models Versus Constant Improvement." Some sales executives argued against yearly models, stating that improvements should be quietly introduced whenever available. Arguing for annual models, Sloan replied: "That might be best in connection with some changes, but in the case of a different body it presents serious difficulties." He was already focused on appearance changes, designed to publicly proclaim that GM cars were pioneering automotive progress. Sloan's arguments carried the day, and GM instituted the annual model change, which created the illusion of technological progress to stimulate sales while leaving the mechanical realities largely unchanged to meet the demands of mass production.[17]

But Sloan wanted not just one but a whole hierarchy of "better quality, constantly improving cars," reasoning that the best way to increase volume was not to dominate one market segment but to increase sales in every segment. To do so he proposed central co-ordination of the previously independent divisions to make each specialize in one segment, for he believed that this "teamwork could thus attain increased volume at reduced cost." But increased volume would reduce costs only if the different divisions standardized and shared components, thus allowing their mass production. In 1923 Sloan established the General Technical Committee to implement cross-divisional sharing. The first fruit of this program was the 1926 Pontiac, a new car which demonstrated, in Sloan's words, "that mass production of automobiles could be reconciled with variety in product." Planned to fill the price gap between the low-priced Chevrolet and the middle-priced Oldsmobile, the Pontiac program reduced production and development costs by sharing a chassis, body, and other parts with Chevrolet. The Chevy body had to be slightly modified to fit the Pontiac, but there was so much parts interchangeability between the two that the cars bore a disturbing resemblance to one another. One GM executive wrote that when the Pontiac and Chevy were placed side by side, "you would have sworn it was the same body."[18]

The new program of corporate interchangeability thus raised the serious problem of differentiating structurally similar cars. The solution was once again styling. If the car lines were differentiated by appearance, then perhaps consumers would pay more for the same technology in a more attractive dress. GM could thus give consumers the distinction they desired without violating the standardization of mass production. As Sloan wrote: "People like different things. . . . It is perfectly possible, from the engineering and manufacturing standpoints, to make two cars at not a great difference in price and weight, but considerably different in appearance and, to some extent, different in technical features, both, in degree, built with the same fundamental tool equipment." As Sloan struggled to put flesh on the bones of his 1921 product plan, it became clear to him that the styling of automobiles was the key to the future success of the corporation.[19]

1927 AND THE TRIUMPH OF STYLE

The year 1927 was a turning point in the history of the American automobile industry, for it marked the triumph of Sloan's superficial styling over Ford's standardized utility. Despite attempts to aesthetically update the Model T, Ford's share of the market had dropped to a disastrous 15 percent by 1927. No longer able to ignore the handwriting on the wall, Henry Ford announced on May 25, 1927 that the company would immediately cease production of the Model T and concentrate on the design and tooling of an entirely new car, the Model A. Because Ford's facilities were so rigidly specialized, the changeover was costly, requiring six frantic months and $18 million. And the Model A revealed that Ford had yet to learn the lesson of the Model T's decline, for it was merely an updated expression of Ford's philosophy of one standardized, unchanging mass-produced motorcar for everyone.[20]

But at least Ford's new car was stylish, giving grudging recognition to the style imperative. Like many automotive men of his generation, Henry himself had no use for beauty on a machine and questioned the masculinity of those who insisted on putting it there. But he was forced by the success of the stylish Chevrolet to recognize that most buyers did not share his opinion. So he let his artistically inclined son, Edsel, work with body engineer Joe Galamb to design the body and outward appearance of the Model A. Edsel, who was president of Ford's Lincoln Division, followed the trend of bringing the look of craft-built luxury to the mass-produced car, borrowing many of the Lincoln's style features like rounded corners, a sweeping hood line, and fuller fenders. In comparison to the Model T, which bore aesthetic testimony to the incivilities of the mass-production factory, Henry's new Model A looked more civilized and acceptable in the world of leisure. One popular songwriter was inspired to declare that "Henry's made a lady out of Lizzie," associating the new car with the gender which supervised the civilized consumption retreat from the barbarous male preserve of production.[21]

Figure 7 1928 Ford Model A Tudor sedan, Henry's attempt to "civilize" the Model T. The car adopted the superficial aesthetics of the luxury Lincoln but nonetheless lagged behind the style leaders at General Motors. (Courtesy Henry Ford Museum and Greenfield Village)

But the real styling sensation of 1927 was not Ford's Model A but GM's La Salle, a new car from the Cadillac Division. This stylish but lower-priced cousin of the Cadillac luxury car was the first mass-produced car to have its appearance completely planned from bumper to bumper by one man, Harley Earl. Like Edsel's Model A, Earl's La Salle brought the look of the handcrafted luxury classics to the factory-produced vehicle. But unlike Edsel, who had to fight his art-abhoring father to bring style to Ford, Earl had the complete support of a corporate president who realized that the firm's future hinged on the appearance of its products.

The La Salle began as another of Sloan's efforts to plug the holes in his automotive hierarchy – this time at the high end, between Buick and Cadillac. The objective was to build a smaller, lighter luxury car that sold for just over $2,000, considerably under the $3,000 price of the cheapest Cadillac. To hold down costs, the La Salle, unlike the other Cadillacs, was mass-produced on specialized machinery and production lines. But Sloan and Cadillac head Larry Fisher knew it could not *look* like a mass-produced car if they wanted to charge a Cadillac price. As Sloan stated: "We wanted a production automobile that was as beautiful as the custom cars of the period." The task of camouflaging the mass-produced Cadillac was entrusted to the man who was to become the father of American automobile styling, Harley Earl.[22]

Earl had gained renown in Hollywood for building custom auto bodies for the stars. His father's Earl Automotive Works had a close connection to Don Lee, the Cadillac distributor on the West Coast, for whom it provided custom bodywork and accident repairs. In 1921 Earl's innovative work came to the attention of Cadillac president Richard Collins, who commissioned him to build six Cadillac sports sedans. Earl's work also interested the man who succeeded Collins as head of Cadillac in 1925, the brash and style-conscious Larry Fisher. When the two met at a Hollywood party, Earl bragged: "I can make a car for you, like your Chevrolet, to look like a Cadillac." To this tantalizing taunt Fisher replied: "If you can, you've got yourself a job."[23]

Two facets of Earl's work impressed Fisher. First, unlike other bodybuilders who developed their designs in wood and metal models, Earl used full-scale clay models. This pliable material resulted in designs that were less fragmented and mechanical and more unified and organic. Second, unlike many coachbuilders Earl designed not just the body but all the visible parts of the car, blending them together into a coherent, integrated form. This was exactly the "unified appearance" of the handcrafted cars that Sloan and Fisher wanted for their production

Figure 8 1927 La Salle convertible coupe, with designer Harley Earl at the wheel and Cadillac head Larry Fisher standing. The first production car designed as an integral whole by one man, it demonstrated definitively that obscuring style could be mass-produced. (Courtesy General Motors Corporation)

Cadillac. So early in 1926, Larry Fisher brought Earl to Detroit on contract to lend his unique style to the mass-produced La Salle. Using the dimensions given him, Earl developed five full-sized clay models, which so impressed top GM executives that they were immediately accepted and rushed into production.[24]

Introduced in March of 1927, the sporty little production Cadillac was an instant and unqualified success, evoking unheard of superlatives from journalists. The La Salle was touted as one of the most beautiful cars ever built and widely compared to the Hispano–Suiza, a luxury sports car from Europe. The comparison was not gratuitous, for Earl later admitted that "I stole a lot of stuff . . . [from the] Hispano." But such design larceny did not bother Sloan or Fisher a bit, for it was just this unified look of luxury that they wanted in their mass-produced Cadillac. For a mere $2,500, nearly one-sixth the price of a Hispano–Suiza, the buyer got many of the same custom-car features, like dual side mounts, wire wheels, folding windshield, a cross-brace between headlights, and original color combinations. It was not merely the accessories, however, but also the overall proportions of the La Salle that evoked the elegance and speed of the luxury classics. Earl's design was longer and lower than other production cars, and, like the hand-crafted classics, rounded off all sharp corners, thus replacing the mechanical look of rectiliner lines with the organic appearance of curvilinearity. And the whole car was blended into one harmonious whole that contrasted sharply with the fragmented, assembled look of most production cars.[25]

The overwhelming success of the La Salle and the final demise of the Model T proved the soundness of Sloan's product policy, which emphasized appearance. These events also convinced Sloan that he had found the individual to implement his policy. On June 23, 1927, the Executive Committee of GM approved Sloan's recommendations to create a new staff department "to study the question of art and color combinations in General Motors products," and to hire Harley Earl as its head. Flushed with the La Salle success, Earl returned to Detroit to inaugurate the Art and Color Section, the first styling department of an American automobile manufacturer.[26]

THE INSTITUTIONALIZATION OF STYLE: HARLEY EARL AND THE RISE OF ART AND COLOR

The crucial question facing Sloan and the rest of the industry in the late 1920s was whether the one-time styling success of the La Salle could be regularly reproduced within a bureaucracy geared to stable, predictable mass production. Could the aesthetic innovation and variety of Sloanist merchandising be reconciled with the uniformity and predictability of Fordist production? American consumers frustrated in their quest for individuality, empowerment, and progress in the mass-production process were demanding consumer products that provided at least sub-limated satisfaction of their desires. Ultimately, the question facing not only Detroit but the entire nation was whether consumer dreams could be mass-produced in sufficient volumes to placate restive Americans.

Sloan had reason to believe that Earl could reconcile style and Fordist production, could mass-produce consumer spectacles on wheels. Harley was born and raised in Hollywood, where his father had come from Michigan to apply his woodworking skills to making wagons and carriages. He had grown up with the movie industry, building vehicles both for its mass spectacles and its stars. Earl had thus learned at an early age to think of automobiles as entertainment for the masses, means of mental transport away from life's troubles, as much as mundane trans-portation from place to place. As he stated: "People like something new and exciting in an automobile as well as in a Broadway show – they like visual entertainment and that's what we stylists give them." Hollywood provided Earl not only with his philosophy of spectacular entertainment but also with a model for its mass production. The centralized studios harnessed the creative impulses of actors and directors into a routinized system that produced standardized movies at fantastic profits. They were particularly successful during the 1920s in creating wish-fulfilling spectacles that diverted a nation's attention from widening class in-equalities. By 1927 this son of a Michigan migrant was ready to take his celluloid lessons back to the Midwestern heartland of mass production and translate them into sheet metal.[27]

But when this carrier of the Hollywood entertainment ethos arrived in Detroit's auto establishment, he was not welcomed with open arms. The hard-nosed engineers and production men who had built and now controlled the auto industry thought of their product as a mundane vehicle of transportation, not an ethereal object of art and entertainment. For these men, beauty belonged in the parlor, not on an automobile. They had yet to grasp what Sloan and Earl already knew – the auto-mobile was part of the domestic refuge of consumption, and people wanted it to be as beautiful as anything in their parlors.

Alfred Sloan knew that Earl's attempts to beautify cars would chal-lenge the authority of body engineers, who had hitherto single-mindedly molded the metal to conform to production imperatives. Yet he was reluctant to force Earl's authority on his divisions. Sloan was in the midst of constructing a path-breaking divisionalized corporate structure, which centralized general policy decisions in the hands of top corporate executives but left to the operating divisions the details of implementation. Forcing detailed designs on the divisions would have undermined this structure, so he assigned Earl's new Art and Color Section an ambiguous position. It was made part of the corporation's general staff organization, but given the power to merely advise Fisher Body and the divisions on car appearance. As Sloan recalled: "I said to him, 'Harley, I think you had better work just for me for a while till I see how they take you.' With the support of Mr Fisher and myself, the new section, I hoped, would be accepted by the car divisions."[28]

Placing Earl's section in the central office staff directly responsible to the President lent it the prestige of Sloan's personal support. But by denying Art and Color line authority over the divisions, Sloan avoided challenging the power of divisional executives. This dependent position also gave Sloan greater control over the new styling function. In the 1920s he was trying to unify Durant's decentralized empire by monitoring the divisions through standardized accounting practices. But the uncertain and unquantifiable tasks of Art and Color were impossible to control through such bureaucratic rules. How could Sloan harness beauty for the business of building automobiles? As Max Weber recognized, the only alternative to bureaucratic control of organizations is personalistic control, power based on ties of kin and loyalty. If subordinates cannot be controlled by detailed instructions, they can often be made to act in the interest of superiors through personal loyalty, created in face-to-face interaction rituals. Sloan cultivated such a personal relation with Harley Earl, which allowed him to influence the highly variant tasks of automobile styling.[29]

The two were widely different in social background. Alfred Sloan came from a well-to-do New York family and an elite education, both of which trained him in the reserve and cultivated indifference of the upper bourgeoisie. Earl came from a working-class background, and although he attended Stanford University, he never outgrew the earthy language and manners he learned in his father's carriagebuilding shop. His speech was reportedly crude and ungrammatical – when he was not shouting expletives he could usually be caught mispronouncing words, most notoriously, aluminum. And Earl was given to temper tantrums and emotional outbursts. But he and the reserved Easterner Sloan came to be famous friends. They saw one another socially in Detroit, and each summer Earl spent a month with Sloan on board his yacht cruising and fishing off the coast of Florida. So when Earl needed some corporate firepower in a battle with an engineer or division head, he could call on his personal friend and patron Alfred. But conversely, Sloan could be sure that in his activities Earl would place the good of the corporation foremost, if for no other reason than his personal loyalty to its head.[30]

But Sloan's personal patronage did not totally overcome the resistance Earl encountered to his styling efforts, for, as one early Art and Color stylist recalled, "the higher-ups . . . didn't always understand these things or were too busy with other things." While some forward-thinking divisional executives like Larry Fisher and Bill Knudsen eagerly sought Earl's advice, most resented a California pretty boy telling them how to build automobiles. The conflicts with engineers were particularly vicious. While Earl's job was to constantly change cars, the production-oriented engineers were reluctant to alter their mass-production machinery once it had been set up. In his first years at GM, Earl constantly clashed with the engineers at GM's Fisher Body Division, who incessantly told him that his designs could not be mass-produced. The conflicts with the Fisher brothers were classic confrontations of cultural style as well as business philosophy. As Bill Mitchell, an early employee of Art and Color, recalled: "The Fisher brothers were small, . . . they wore homburgs, and what a contrast to this 6'4" man [Earl] who had a bronze complexion. He'd wear bronze suits, suede shoes – flamboyant was the word and outspoken, a tough man, and he'd cuss those Fisher brothers out. We called them the seven dwarfs. He'd say, 'Goddamn, you don't know what you're talking about.' He didn't have any respect because he was hired by Sloan."[31]

Engineers like the Fisher brothers thought of the stylists as a bunch of worthless "fairies" and "pantywaists" whose interference in design was unjustified. So even when a divisional executive accepted one of Earl's designs, body and production engineers often altered it as they saw fit. Such unauthorized alterations were the cause of an early Art and Color disaster, the 1929 "pregnant Buick." Earl designed a body with a slight bulge below the belt line around the entire car, but Fisher Body engineers altered it, pulling in the side panels at the bottom and adding five inches in height. The changes accentuated the side bulge, producing an unpleasant fullness that some said resembled an expectant woman. Earl was furious – "I roared like a Ventura sea lion" – but the car went into production nonetheless and was a sales disaster. This pregnant Buick embarrassment reinforced Earl's conviction to win unilateral control over the design of GM cars.[32]

In this Earl was opposed not only by engineers but also by divisional sales managers, who believed that their closeness to the market gave them privileged knowledge of consumer desires. They were often as conservative as engineers – if a model was selling well, they resisted changing it. Divisional salesmen were also worried that a central design division controlled by one man could not sufficiently distinguish the different GM lines. Sloan assured them that Earl was keenly aware of "the importance of having things different," but also agreed that it might be necessary to establish a duplicate styling organization in each division.[33]

Clearly, Earl's fledgling Art and Color Section had only a tenuous toehold in GM's emerging bureaucracy. With little official power and only the unreliable patronage of a few higher-ups, Earl was thrown back on his own personal resources to win influence for styling. And these, from all accounts, were considerable. Earl was undoubtedly talented, but not as an original designer. Most who worked closely with him agreed that he could not draw and rarely sketched his own designs. Nor could he clearly articulate his ideas. Earl stuttered and stammered in his attempts to communicate visual ideas to his designers, and often resorted to expletives and sexual metaphors because he lacked the technical vocabulary of design. Earl's verbal weakness developed into a taboo against design discussion in his organization, a norm enforced with the frequent rebuke, "I can see but I can't hear."[34]

Earl's real talent was his critical eye for design, which he focused firmly on the bottom line. Earl was an uncanny commercial critic, with an extraordinary ability to anticipate the sales success of a design. As he once wrote: "The only yardstick for measuring the success of styling is its success in the marketplace." Earl kept his finger on the pulse of the American marketplace to pick up trends and fashions. He was always bringing in fashionable goods of all sorts and vaguely commanding his employees: "Do something like this." Earl also had a keen understanding of consumer motivation. He knew that consumers wanted to be entertained, wanted to escape the mundane monotony of their daily lives into a dream where their denied needs could be at least superficially fulfilled. As he once candidly told a conference of GM executives: "The dream of the potential buyer must be discovered and satisfied and the buyer must be awakened with his dreams turned into cars that he can and will buy." Earl's true talent was this ability to probe the psyches of consumers and turn their repressed desires into salable visual styles.[35]

But Earl's commercial vision would have been ineffective without the sheer persuasive power of his personality. He used his eye for style to sell not only automobiles but himself, presenting a powerful, impressive figure wherever he went. Standing 6'4", weighing 235 pounds, and possessing a perennial sun tan, his physical presence always dominated the scene. And he called attention to himself with flamboyant clothes, wearing polychromatic linen suits with brightly colored shirts and ties. Earl coupled this imposing physical appearance with a tyrannical demeanor that cowered nearly everyone around him. His booming voice filled the largest of rooms with intimidating expletives, and his frequent rages sent all but the bravest of souls scampering for cover. One of Earl's earliest employees, Frank Hershey, recalled: "They were . . . physically scared of him 'cause he was 6'6" [sic], and he could look down on you with a fierce look that would just melt even some of the hardest executives."[36]

In other words, Harley Earl had charisma, which was exactly what the pioneers of automobile styling needed. They were revolutionaries, seeking to seize power away from the engineers and production experts who had entrenched themselves in the industry. As Max Weber recognized, those who would overturn an established order of traditional or legal-rational rule must have extraordinary personal powers. One Chrysler designer stated of the early design leaders: "They weren't exactly professional designers as much as strong, dominant actors. They had strong magnetism and very definite ideas." Charisma is above all an act, and Earl was a consummate actor. Indeed, GM stylist Frank Hershey stated that his persona was a "calculated image." "Earl had to become very macho to survive, because in those days the people in Detroit were pretty crude. Big, tough, hard-drinking, hard-talking blacksmiths." Beneath the tough, confident image he cultivated, Earl was often insecure, perhaps, Hershey speculated, because of his "ordinary background" and inability to express himself verbally. But when the towering, meticulously dressed hulk of a man stepped before an audience of divisional and corporate executives, he seemed to have absolute confidence in himself and his designs.[37]

Harley Earl was insightful enough, however, to know that charisma is ephemeral. So in his struggle to institutionalize the power of styling, he also sought to construct networks of personal friendship and loyalty to solidify what Weber called patrimonial rule. Earl quickly penetrated the automotive social circles of Detroit, cultivating friends at the country clubs and cocktail parties. He fit in well with the physically oriented, working-class culture of engineers and production men, for he too had come up from the shop floor. And Earl also used the resources of his section to do personal favors for influential executives like Larry Fisher, for whose yacht Art and Color craftworkers built a cabin.[38]

In the first years of his Art and Color Section, Harley Earl occupied himself not merely with external political struggles but also with internal technical organization. Before he could sell his designs to corporate executives, he had to organize a team to produce them. Earl had to find artists, engineers, and tradesmen who could design automobiles that were not only stylish but also functional and feasible to produce. He turned first to the existing bodybuilding shops, both mass-production and custom, and recruited draftsmen like Frank Hershey from Murphy Body and Gordon Buehrig from Dietrich Body. But Earl feared that the traditions of coachbuilders might inhibit their production of the constantly new and different styles necessary to disguise the standardized sameness of mass-production cars. So he expanded recruitment to include "anyone who was interested in design and showed some promise," recalled one of his early employees. He hired trained architects and interior decorators, as well as ad illustrators. Many of them knew little or nothing about the technical requirements of automobile construction. As Earl stated: "We combed the art schools, and then I had to train the ones we hired from the ground up. They were forever making something look good but you couldn't get into it." But for Earl the main qualifications for early recruits were a passion for cars and an ability to convey it to others visually. In Bill Mitchell's metaphor, they had to have "gasoline in their blood." Another requirement of recruits seems to have been a decidedly masculine gender. Earl was concerned that any hint of femininity would handicap his struggle in the rough-and-tumble, masculine world of the auto industry. By the beginning of 1928 Earl had recruited fifty people for the Art and Color Section – ten were designers, and all shared a macho love of the automobile.[39]

Harley Earl then had to mold this mix of diverse talent into a disciplined, centralized organization to convey a unified vision of automobile style. Several production and marketing imperatives made this centralization mandatory. First, to facilitate corporate interchangeability all divisional designs had to conform to the basic dimensional packages. Second, although the divisional cars had to look distinctive, corporate executives also wanted all GM products to have a recognizable similarity. This "corporate identity" helped to advertise the corporation and keep those trading up buying GM autos. Achieving both corporate identity and dimensional uniformity required a centralized aesthetic authority in the Art and Color Section.

The execution of annual model changes also required a centralization of corporate styling decisions. As Earl recognized, the purpose of such changes was to "dramatize progress." But to give consumers this sense of progress, annual style innovations had to be slow, gradual developments of the same visual themes, not drastic or random newness. There was also an important economic reason for such incremental changes. New-car sales depended upon relatively high trade-in prices, and drastic changes in style tended to depreciate these. Gradual style changes created the dissatisfaction with old models necessary to stimulate sales while allowing them to retain sufficient trade-in value to ease the economic burden of a new-car purchase. Such annual changes required a single authority with the power to impose a unified aesthetic vision on the corporation's cars.[40]

Understanding the necessity of aesthetic unity, Harley Earl went about constructing a rigidly centralized, personalistic organization of authority with himself at the center. The variable tasks of his artists, engineers, and tradesmen could not be controlled by impersonal, standardized rules but solely by the personal command and surveillance of an individual. Earl used the same resources to establish personal dominance over his inferiors that he used with corporate peers and superiors: charisma, intimidation, favors. "Mistearl," as his employees called him, was a ubiquitous, domineering presence in Art and Color, exercising direct control over every step of the design process. Displaying his flair for the dramatic learned from his Hollywood idol Cecil B. DeMille, Earl often strode into a studio wearing jodhpurs and riding boots, seated himself in a director's chair in front of a full-sized clay model, and began barking orders. Pointing to a line with his toe, he would demand that it be altered. As Bill Mitchell recalled, "he would sit there and everyone would run around like a bunch of monkeys." He brooked absolutely no departure from his personal vision of auto aesthetics. "Either go his way or get the hell out!" was the way Mitchell put it.[41]

Earl enforced his unilateral design decisions through personally dispensing both harsh punishments and endearing favors. He cowed and intimidated his employees by arbitrarily firing anyone he did not like or felt was not working hard enough. When Bill Mitchell once complained to Earl that he had one designer so scared he could not work, he replied: "Goddamn it. You tell that son of a bitch to get off his ass, or throw him out, throw him out into the street!" But there was also an endearing and generous side of Earl that could inspire great loyalty. He dispensed little favors, threw big parties, and engaged in small talk and banter with his employees. One designer recalled: "He'd come in, and we would all huddle up around him – he was like a big Smokey the Bear – and he'd always have something engaging to say." Earl also controlled his employees by inducing cut-throat competition between them, like, for example, telling one group of designers that compared to others their work "wasn't worth a damn." He also staged formal contests between different studios for a particular design. This dog-eat-dog, competitive ethos Earl cultivated undermined the cooperation and communication among designers necessary to form lateral coalitions to challenge his personal authority.[42]

But Earl's dictatorial control over the Art and Color Section did not initially give him much power to affect the overall aesthetics of GM automobiles. His organization merely applied color and trim features to bodies already built by GM's Fisher Body Division. Gradually, however, Earl succeeded in expanding the scope of his responsibilities to include the lines and form of the body. And as a result of the pregnant Buick episode, Sloan issued an order in 1930 that no changes be made in designs accepted from the Art and Color Section. Although the divisions were not obliged to accept Earl's suggestions, more did so voluntarily as his reputation and sales successes grew. But during this period Art and Color designs were still substantially constrained by the predetermined layout of the chassis.[43]

The work of the Art and Color Section typically began when a division seeking its assistance turned over the dimensions of the chassis it planned to produce. Earl then set his designers to work sketching ideas in small scale on paper, assigning one designer the radiator shell, another the grille, etc. From these sketches Earl would select a few for further development, synthesizing the various elements into an overall design. When he was satisfied with the basic themes, he ordered the sketches transformed into full-scale orthographic drawings, precise, two-dimensional renderings of the outlines of the car from the front, side, and rear views. Earl learned the importance of these full-scale outline drawings from his coachbuilding days, and spent a great deal of time on them. Once the basic lines were established, designers added color and shading to these drawings to give them a better feel for the form. These orthographics were then used to construct wooden templates for the full-scale clay models built next.[44]

These clay models allowed designers to blend the separate dimensional drawings into a unified, organic whole whose dimensions could be quickly altered. First, tradesmen built a wooden armature complete with wheels, then turned it over to the design team for clay application. Most of the sculpting was done by clay modelers, blue-collar tradesmen below the drawing designers in organizational rank. They heated up modeling clay then applied it over the armature, using the wooden templates to guide them. But sculpting the three-dimensional model required details of form unspecified by the two-dimensional drawings, so Earl and top designers often worked closely with the modelers. Earl liked to present his design ideas to executives at the clay model stage.

JUNE 25 1937

Figure 9 A full-scale orthographic drawing, in the General Motors Art and Color Section. These renderings defined the precise dimensions of the car, and were then used to construct full-scale clay models. (Courtesy General Motors Corporation)

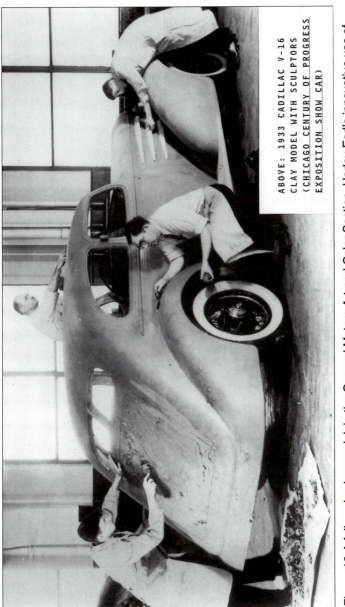

ABOVE: 1933 CADILLAC V-16
CLAY MODEL WITH SCULPTORS
(CHICAGO CENTURY OF PROGRESS
EXPOSITION SHOW CAR)

Figure 10 A full-scale clay model, in the General Motors Art and Color Section. Harley Earl's innovative use of clay models resulted in designs that were more unified and organic than those modeled in wood or metal. (Courtesy General Motors Corporation)

The size and fullness of a 9- to 12-foot sculpture could be quite impressive. And over the years Earl developed techniques that made the clay models look amazingly like real automobiles constructed of painted metal, glass, and chrome. Once the model was approved for production, Art and Color craftworkers constructed a replica out of wood or metal, from which dies for sheet-metal presses were produced.[45]

THE SLOW DIFFUSION OF STYLE

In response to consumer demand, then, Harley Earl began in the late 1920s to institute style as a regularized part of automobile production. The signs of a changing marketplace were not lost on other auto mass-producers, which also began to place more emphasis on the appearance of their products. As one trade journalist wrote in 1927: "Throughout the whole industry has grown a fuller conception of the commercial power of beauty. . . . And as this recognition has grown, so has grown also the number of actual attempts to bring skilled artists into the work of automotive producing organizations. . . ." In no other automaking company, however, did style have such a perspicacious patron as Alfred Sloan or such a persuasive practitioner as Harley Earl. Stylists in other companies labored under the stultifying dominance of old-fashioned engineers and hard-nosed production supervisors, for whom beauty was an unwelcome feminine intruder in their masculine preserve.[46]

The Ford Motor Company was the slowest to learn the lessons of style. The company was still dominated by the elder Henry, who clung to his philosophy of a standardized universal car for all and was reluctant to recognize the growing demand for diversity and progress. So as the novelty of the Model A wore off, sales began to decline. A few cosmetic changes in the car were introduced in 1930, but they were no match for the Earl-styled Chevrolets, which whittled away at Ford's market lead. By 1931 Ford sales were one third of their 1929 level, forcing Henry to shut most of his assembly plants and plan the terms of his surrender to the policies pioneered by GM.[47]

The remaining member of what would become the automotive Big Three, Chrysler, was much quicker than Ford to learn the lessons of style. Walter Chrysler was keenly aware of the changing market for automobiles, and his firm's first car, introduced in 1924, was an acknowledged style leader. But Chrysler relied mainly on the designers at its major body supplier, Briggs, for its styling until about 1928. By this year the corporation was following GM's policy of marketing a graded hierarchy of cars, and producing these economically through corporate interchangeability. For example, Plymouth, introduced by Chrysler in 1928 to compete in the low-priced market, was fundamentally the bargain-basement Chrysler 52 with minor changes.[48]

To superficially differentiate these mechanically similar cars, Chrysler set up its own Art and Color Department in July of 1928, obviously imitating Earl's GM group. Headed by Herbert V. Henderson, an industrial designer with experience mainly in interior architecture, the small department consisted of four other stylists. Unlike its namesake at GM, however, Chrysler's Art and Color Department was organizationally subordinated to the engineers, who reigned supreme in the corporation. Henderson reported directly to Oliver H. Clark, Chrysler's chief body engineer, who shared with others of his profession a view of "'styling' not as overall vehicle design but as something that involved ornamentation – the look of hubcaps, radiator shells, instrument panels, lamp housings and the like." So the responsibility of this early Chrysler styling group was severely limited, which was probably why in the late 1920s there was little aesthetic distinction between the corporation's Plymouth, DeSoto, and Chrysler lines. Clark designed all the bodies with an engineer's eye for cost-cutting production.[49]

During the late 1920s some of the smaller mass-producers like Hudson also set up styling departments in recognition of the increasing influence of appearance on sales. But the expense of retaining a staff of stylists forced most small firms to rely on outside consultants or independent bodybuilders for style expertise. They sometimes commissioned famous industrial designers on a one-time basis to lend their expertise and prestige to a model. But more frequently small firms relied on the body suppliers to design and decorate their cars' appearance. In the mid- and late 1920s, the big, mass-production body suppliers like Murray, Briggs, and Budd began to hire stylists away from coachbuilders to meet their clients' demands for better-looking bodies. These large firms with many clients could better afford a staff of designers than could a small automaker.[50]

Ultimately, however, the industry's growing obsession with style spelled the doom of both small automakers and their independent body suppliers. Annual style changes were hugely expensive, for they entailed producing new dies and resetting presses. In the early 1940s Sloan estimated that GM spent $35 million annually for model changes. The small, low-volume automakers could not shoulder such exorbitant costs. And increasingly neither could their body suppliers. The large variety of their products kept production runs low and costs relatively high. Frequent changes in bodies drove costs higher still. Some suppliers tried to control costs by inducing clients to share bodies, but this undermined their products' distinction. Gradually the large auto-makers began to build their own bodies or absorbed their suppliers to control escalating costs, spelling the end of the independent body-builders. The emergence of style as a competitive factor thus hastened the growth of automotive oligopoly.[51]

THE DIRECTION OF STYLE IN THE LATE 1920s

The automobile stylists who gained influence in America's automobile companies pushed the appearance of cars toward the general trends of America's emerging consumer society. They, like other industrial designers, were keenly aware of the attempts of average Americans to escape their increasingly monotonous, homogeneous, work lives in the realm of consumption. As one auto designer stated of this early period: "Escape – that was what a car was. A man's getting away from what and where you are. Get out, and if you don't like your environment or your little life, you get in a car and you can get away from it." As Earl put it, a car had to be designed "so that every time you get in it, it's a relief – you have a little vacation for a while."[52]

No one understood the car as an instrument of escape from industrial monotony better than Ned Jordan, head of the Jordan Motor Car Com-pany. Jordan made a name in the industry not with his cars but with the advertisements he wrote for them. He published four-color ads in popular magazines which, he admitted, appealed to the "suppressed desires" of buyers. Escape from monotony was the prominent theme, as in his most famous ad for the Jordan Playboy, entitled "Somewhere West of Laramie." Evoking the image of a carefree cowgirl in the wild West, the ad invited readers to: "Step into the Playboy when the hour grows dull with things gone dead and stale. Then start for the land of real living with the spirit of the lass who rides, lean and rangy, into the red horizon of a Wyoming twilight." Other Jordan ads, with titles like "A Million Miles from Dull Care," and "It's Vacation Time in Arcady," similarly used the theme of escaping the workaday world to freedom, romance, excitement.[53]

Automobile stylists gave their mass-produced cars the look of free-dom primarily by erasing the stigmatizing signs of the mass-production factory, the source of the dull, dehumanizing routines consumers were trying to escape. To give a car style meant covering up these telltale marks of fragmentation and homogenization by appending the appear-ance of craft-built luxury cars. These grand autos, produced by careful, unhurried craft labor, symbolized a life of leisurely autonomy far removed from the niggardly economies and repressive heteronomy of mass-production lines. One of their prominent features was the long-and-low look, which suggested these expensive cars were meant for sport and pleasure, not utilitarian transportation. The long hoods symbolized the powerful, sporting engines beneath, and the cramped accomodations eschewed mundane hauling in favor of romantically close comfort. The low-slung chassis also flaunted the fact that these cars were built more for speed than for practical transportation over rough and rutted roads.[54]

Harley Earl and others pirated this long-and-low look of luxury for their mass-produced vacation machines. As Earl once stated in retrospect: "My primary purpose for twenty-eight years has been to lengthen and lower the American automobile, at times in reality and always at least in appearance." Cars were lowered during this period by the introduction of the double-drop frame, which brought the body closer to the ground, and small, 18-inch wheels. Cars were also lengthened, in appearance and reality. The wheelbase of the low-priced Chevrolet grew from 103 inches in 1923 to 109 inches in 1931. And stylists made cars look longer than they actually were by stylistically emphasizing the horizontal elements. They did this by integrating the belt line of the body, which ran just beneath the windows, into one long, unbroken horizontal line that began at the radiator and flowed back to the rear. This "through-line," as it was called, caught the light and increased the appearance of length relative to height. Harley Earl was particularly obsessed with this feature. "He was very much for checking a highlight straight through – a long, straight through-line," recalled Bill Mitchell. Earl insisted that all clay modelers use a highlight gauge – a protractor device with a leveling bubble – to check the angle of light reflection from the belt line.[55]

In addition to the longer and lower proportions, the "unified appearance" of the luxury classics also distanced them from the realm of rationalized production consumers wanted to escape. This look of unity reflected a slow process of production unified by the knowledge and skills of craftworkers, and contrasted sharply with the disjointed appearance of cars mass-produced by detail labor. Earl and other stylists sought to give mass-produced cars merely superficial unity by stylistically integrating the surface to obscure the reality of fragmented mass production underneath. On the 1927 La Salle, for example, Earl's careful attention to every detail of style gave the car what Sloan called "the unified appearance" he was looking for. As one trade journalist wrote in

1927: "The outstanding feature of automotive design today probably is this trend toward harmony between all parts of the vehicle, both mechanically and artistically. . . ." By 1929 even the inexpensive Chevrolet was exhibiting the signs of the unified look. The hood was higher and wider, integrating it into the main body; the horizontal through-line flowed across and unified the hood, body, and doors; and the disc wheels were painted to match the bright body colors.[56]

Automobiles that had this look of custom-built unity gave their buyers at least the feeling that they were getting a quality product with which to forget their disqualification at work. As one long-time designer at Chrysler stated, seeing the mechanical complexity of a car "is a turn-off. But when it does look neat and trim, there is a perceived – and perceived is the operative word – a perceived better product. . . . They [designers] work on it very hard to try to get the customer perception to be at the highest level, even though it may not be the best car."[57]

Auto stylists and salesmen were also aware that people were seeking newness and progress in their consumer products to compensate for their monotonous, dead-end jobs in Fordist factories and bureaucracies. Earl's incessant admonition to his stylists was "Give me something new," for he understood that changing auto styles provided people with the appearance of progress denied them elsewhere. As one Ford designer stated: "Maybe it [style change] also says that things are getting better. If they aren't changing you know they aren't getting better. Maybe it's symbolic of the hope that they're always getting better."[58]

Annual style changes provided consumers with this superficial evidence of progress in their things. The trends toward longer and lower cars and more unified appearance were implemented in incremental, annual changes. GM products began to show signs of a styling cycle during the late 1920s. Every two or three years, the body and other appearance factors underwent a major redesign requiring new dies, which wore out in about three years anyway. Between these major style changes, stylists gave the model what they called a "face-lift," changing only minor features like grilles, taillights, fenders, and trim. Beneath the dazzling kaleidoscope of sheet-metal, however, the major mechanical components remained unchanged, sometimes for decades, allowing manufacturers to achieve large volumes demanded by mass production. And just in case consumers did not notice the sometimes slight changes made in annual models, GM and other automakers reinforced the illusion of progress with sophomoric model labels. So, for example, the 1927 Chevrolet carried the label Capital Series, which was changed in successive years to National, International, and Universal. Having reached the heady geographic expanse of the universe, the progress peddlers were forced to begin anew. While the superficial appellations soared to intergalactic heights, the actual technology remained tightly tethered to the terrestrial requirements of mass production. The "Stovebolt Six" engine that Chevrolet introduced in 1929 remained in production with only minor changes through 1954, over a quarter-century.[59]

While providing consumers with the illusion of progress, annual style changes also stimulated the sales of new cars by creating dissatisfaction with the old. Earl once admitted that: "Our big job is to hasten obsolescence. In 1934 the average car ownership span was 5 years; now [1955] it is 2 years. When it is 1 year, we will have a perfect score." But he preferred to call what he created "dynamic obsolescence," and stressed the economic benefits of the program to the entire economy. Earl and others said the process of trading in serviceable used cars for new ones not only provided cheap cars to the lower classes but also kept the capitalist economy of America growing, generating more jobs and profits. Planned obsolescence was, they claimed, good for consumers, the country, and, of course, the bottom line.[60]

Finally, automobile stylists knew that consumers also wanted products with individuality and distinction, qualities callously crushed by the homogeneous tasks of Fordist mass production. As one industrial designer told the Society of Automotive Engineers in 1928: "The objective of designing automobiles is distinction. They must be characterized by distinction, unless they have that, there is very little else they can have besides an engine." Bill Mitchell stated it more bluntly: "I know *I* like to have a car so that when I park it somebody says, 'Who the hell's car is that? . . . My God! I would not want to buy a suit like another guy." Stylists struggled to lend mass-produced cars distinction by stylistically differentiating mechanically similar models. Different bodies could make cars which shared numerous components look distinctively different. And by merely attaching different superficial details like moldings, taillights, grilles, and trim, even cars that shared the same basic body could be made to appear individual. Although the first hints of superficially differentiating style emerged in the late 1920s, the major efforts in this area awaited the 1930s and the Depression, which forced automakers into greater cost-cutting interchangeability.[61]

In the late 1920s stylists and others in the industry often attributed the growth in the importance of style to the specific demands of women. It was a commonplace among advertisers and designers of the day that women were wielding a larger influence on the household budget, so products had to be pitched to them. Ned Jordan echoed this opinion, stating "while men buy cars, women choose them." And what women were said to want in a car was comfort, beauty, and style. One writer reporting on the 1929 New York Automobile Show wrote that more than half of those present were women, and the automobiles reflected their predominance. "The feminine demand for line and color has overborne the mere masculine insistence on practicality, durability, power, and such dull and commonplace things. . . . In response to the silent but irrestible influence of woman, one-time squat, drab and formless cars have taken on such attributes of beauty as would have made Raphael stop dead in the streets of Rome or have caused Da Vinci to turn away from the last touches on 'Mona Lisa.'"[62]

Women were undoubtedly exercising greater influence on purchases of consumer goods. As Fordism separated and insulated consumption from production, it also gender-typed these realms with a rigid division of labor. Utilitarian production was the preserve of males, while women managed the domestic realm of consumption and were custodians of the nonutilitarian traits of beauty, comfort, and style. To perform their role women had increasing need of the automobile. But it is doubtful that "the woman's touch" was the main impetus behind the increasing emphasis upon automotive style. It merely provided the ideological guise for the appeal to the repressed needs of men and women alike. Both men and women were increasingly turning to the domestic sphere of consumption for compensation for needs denied in the rationalized workplace. To provide these substitute satisfactions, consumer goods had to hide their connections to the ugliness of mass production behind an obscuring veneer of beauty. But because the sexist ideology of separate spheres defined beauty as feminine, men could not admit that products appealed to them on this basis. Hence, manufacturers appealing to these repressed needs pitched their products to women, whose supposed influence on purchases men could use as an excuse to buy the obscuring and amnestic beauty that they also demanded. If manufacturers were really catering to women's specific demands, they would have hired women to design cars. But during this period auto designers were exclusively men. As one GM designer stated: "In those days, women were nothing, absolutely nothing. I don't think there are many women there now, and there never were any women at Ford. Never! Never! This is a man's world."[63]

But the emerging consumer society, in which both men and women looked to stylish, distinctive products as compensation for workplace indignities, required a stable, institutionalized guarantee of working-class consumption that was lacking in the 1920s. Workers could be cajoled to settle for the substitute satisfactions of consumerism only if they had enough cash to buy them. But unregulated Fordism prevented wages from rising as rapidly as industrial output, since it weakened craft unions and decreased employment per unit output. Consequently, during the latter 1920s production and profits soared as wages stagnated. The result was a massive overproduction crisis which nipped consumerism in the bud and opened up the festering wound of class inequalities that it had sought to conceal.

Chapter 5

The struggle for styling II
The Depression and the decade of streamlining

In 1933 two aesthetic visions of America's machine civilization were unveiled in the industrial heartland, reflecting the contested solutions to the nation's economic problems. At the Chicago World's Fair, whose theme was "A Century of Progress," corporate exhibitors offered a bright vision of a technological utopia, a not-too-distant future in which the scientific application of machinery would bring order and abundance to all. Reflecting this theme, automakers exhibited the first "dream cars," design prototypes giving the public a "glimpse into the future" of automotive evolution. The most innovative offered futuristic diversions by adopting the design idiom of streamlining pioneered by the technologically advanced aeronautics industry. Ford, for example, displayed the Briggs Dreamcar, a teardrop-shaped, rear-engined car with a periscope and unitized body construction. Even more spectacularly aeronautical was the Silver Arrow prototype produced by Pierce–Arrow, whose body resembled an airplane fuselage. These streamlined cars were part of an aesthetic vision that covered over the deprivations of America's Fordist system with the promise of a future of material abundance, achieved through the scientific invention of technological wonders like the airplane.[1]

But a competing aesthetic vision emerged during the Depression that revealed rather than concealed the social contradictions of America's machine civilization. This aesthetic of revelation was beautifully exemplified by the murals Diego Rivera painted on the walls of the Detroit Institute of Arts in 1933. Their focus was also the automobile, but Rivera stripped this American icon of the romance of its consumption to reveal the horror of its production. In the main panels the Mexican muralist penetrated the obscuring walls of the Fordist factory to reveal a productive machinery gone awry to enslave its human creators. But in separate panels Rivera juxtaposed to this oppressive application of modern technology its liberating potential, revealing the social basis of Fordism's problems.[2]

The revelatory aesthetic of Rivera and other American artists like Charlie Chaplin and Woodie Gutherie expressed an alternative path to progress – not inevitable technical evolution, but contingent social revolution, or at least radical reform. The Depressionary period in the United States was marked by overt conflict between the classes that stood behind each vision.

AMERICA, 1931–1945: CONFLICT, COMPETITION, CONCEALMENT, POSTPONEMENT

The economic depression that settled over America in the early 1930s strengthened the two stimuli that had given rise to industrial design in the 1920s: business competition in saturated markets and class conflict in repressive factories. Underconsumption reached epidemic proportions after 1930, increasing competition and sending business executives in search of some advantage over their competitors. And class conflict in Fordist production made it even more necessary for manufacturers to conceal its marks to sell their wares to consumers seeking escape. Consequently, this period saw industrial design become a crucial part of the corporate strategy to overcome depression by "streamlining America."

This slogan symbolized an elite program to restructure American economic institutions. The Depression dealt a death blow to the laissez-faire creed of the 1920s and raised a national outcry for rational economic planning. America's corporate leaders sought to steer this demand into a narrow program of "consumer engineering," a planned application of science and technology to stimulate consumption while leaving the basic structures of Fordist production untouched. Industrial design became an integral part of consumer engineering, for businessmen believed that consumer resistance to buying could be overcome by making mass-produced products more appealing and humanized. Industrial designers were increasingly called upon to give products new and beautiful surfaces that stimulated buying by overcoming consumer antagonisms to mechanically produced objects.[3]

Corporate leaders sought to mobilize the popular imagination for their program of consumer engineering with the polysemous notion of "streamlining." In the narrow sense, streamlining meant designing airplanes, trains, and ships to reduce their resistance to movement through air or water. But during the Depression this practice took on a broader cultural meaning. The sleek designs of transport machines became associated in the public mind with technological progress as such and the program to engineer recovery by the rational application of science and technology to industry. Business leaders proclaimed that the production of technologically advanced products, scientifically "streamlined" to better serve human needs, would stimulate consumption and lead the country to future prosperity.[4]

Industrial designers during the Depression applied sleek, streamlined surfaces to a myriad of products to offer consumers the illusion of progress, behind which hid the reality of technical and social stagnation. An old product wrapped in a smooth, modern shell stimulated consumer appetites for the new and reassured them that business was indeed engineering the country out of depression. In addition, streamlined forms also connoted order and stability. During these tumultuous times, many people longed for progress that was controlled and orderly, not fragmented and conflictual. The smooth, integrated shells of consumer products offered them the illusion of unity, a "spirit of order," as two advocates wrote, that obscured the underlying mechanical chaos that was a reminder of social chaos. By blotting out the fragmentation and the conflict of the factory, streamlined products also carried to consumers the desired connotations of cleanliness and hygiene. The look of factory work popularly signified dirtiness, for it was a reminder of the degradation of Fordized labor and the class distinctions that it bred. So industrial designers "cleanlined" many domestic machines like washing machines and refrigerators, that is, applied streamlined casings that concealed the dirty mechanism that symbolized the social insult of Fordist production.[5]

Although the streamlining movement portrayed itself as an expression of rational, scientific progress, it was actually part of a larger ideology of irrationalism that sought to substitute immediate sensory experience for mediated, rational thought. As design critic Donald Bush has recognized, streamlining was part of an "aesthetic of continuums" which included the stream-of-consciousness literature of Joyce and Faulkner, the pragmatism of Dewey and James, and the vitalism of Bergson. All privileged the uninterrupted, unreflective flow of immediate sensations over the interrupted, mediated reflection on experience. Rational thought necessarily entails disjuncture, an interruption of the stream of experience to isolate and place a fragment of it into a larger social and historical framework that gives it meaning. Aesthetic expressions like streamlining that emphasized continuity discouraged such rational analysis by depriving the mind of a critical pause and keeping it racing along to keep pace with the seamless rush of new experience. Streamlined consumer goods were meant "to keep the eye moving," to prevent vision from dwelling upon the fragments, which might reveal their origins in a fragmentary, dehumanizing production process. The spectacular unity, continuity, and cleanliness of streamlined forms kept consumers thoughtlessly dazzled and diverted from the Depression's historical realities of economic stagnation and class conflict.[6]

Under this corporate strategy of streamlining, the infant profession of industrial design flourished, producing sleek surfaces to give products the illusion of progress, unity, and hygiene. At first this shrouding frenzy focused on transportation machines like trains and autos, which received the futuristic look of aeronautics by the simple addition of a sheet-metal shell. Although arguably functional on such fast-moving machines, streamlining revealed its symbolic impetus when these smooth shells were attached to stationary objects like pencil sharpeners and washing machines. All consumer goods with this streamlined look of progress and unity quickly became objects of veneration among an American public eager for some deliverance from the stagnation and fragmentation of the Depression. And equally venerated were the designers who created these commodified illusions. Raymond Loewy, Norman Bel Geddes, Henry Dreyfuss, and Walter Dorwin Teague were celebrated as popular heroes, laboring in the public interest to pull the nation out of the Depression and into the technological future. The firms of these high priests of industrial design quickly grew from one-person operations to rationalized dream factories employing dozens of staff members and receiving regular retainers and special commissions from some of the biggest corporations in America.[7]

But during the Depression, the social divisions and disorder created by the machinery of Fordist production were not so easily obscured by streamlined consumerism. At first many Americans clung tenaciously to the palliative of domestic consumption, especially its central symbol of the automobile. The Lynds reported of Depression-era Muncie that even under severe economic strain "people give up everything in the world but their car." But as the Depression deepened, the refuge of domestic consumption was violated by economic hardships like lower wages, unemployment, and evictions. Woody Gutherie's sad refrain, "I ain't got no home in this world anymore," captured the sense of betrayal felt by those who had just begun to buy into the bourgeois dream of domestic abundance and stability. With the evaporation of domestic diversions, the rising tide of popular resentment was increasingly directed against its source in the system of production. Under the new auspices of the Congress of Industrial Organizations (CIO), the labor movement was revived at the grass roots with a focus not so much on wages and benefits but upon workers' control of the technology and organization of the Fordist factory that many were beginning to identify as the key culprit in the economic catastrophe. Other social movements also arose to challenge some of the basic tenets of the system of capitalist mass-production.[8]

Out of these popular protests and struggles of the Depression period emerged slowly an alternative vision of the future of America to contest the corporate program of streamlined consumerism. Although composed of disparate strands of unionists, populists, reformists, socialists, and communists, many of the movements were united by a conviction that a prosperous, just America for all could be ensured only by collective, not corporate, control of the economic machinery of the nation. The flood of popular demands for economic regulation and planning breached the dam of consumer engineering erected by corporate leaders and inundated the state at the local and national levels.

During this period the class forces behind these opposing visions of America's future – the corporate program of consumer engineering and the popular program of collective economic control – battled for power. The outcome of the clash was a compromise program of collectivized consumption which was gradually engineered by state managers. The state began to intervene on the demand side of the market to socially ensure a level of consumption adequate to absorb the production controlled privately by corporate giants. The first seeds of this compromise – most importantly, the Wagner Act and the Social Security Act – were sown during the Depression, but they did not germinate into a viable solution to the contradictions of Fordism until after the Second World War.[9]

The international hostilities postponed resolution of the domestic struggles over the economy. Stepped-up wartime production not only put America back to work but also froze the contending parties and policies in their tracks, awaiting the political thaw that only peace would bring. The production boom revitalized consumerist dreams among American workers, who were promised by wartime leaders that the mass-produced technology of destruction would provide the basis for a postwar technology of consumption hitherto undreamed of. But the state-coordinated program of war production also kept alive the radical alternative among unionists and leftists, who saw in it the beginnings of a collectively planned economy.

AUTOMOBILE STYLING'S DEPRESSIONARY RISE TO POWER

Just as automakers were pioneers in product styling during the exuberant 1920s, they also led the corporate campaign of streamlined consumerism during the sobering 1930s. The Depression dealt the auto industry a devastating blow, with production dropping from 5.6 million cars and trucks in 1929 to 1.4 million in 1932. Competition in this small, impoverished market became intense, motivating manufacturers to offer consumers more car for less money.

Under these conditions the grand luxury makes fared poorly, with their sales declining even among the securely privileged bourgeois. These American aristocrats felt their class privileges threatened during the Depression, and began to consider the ostentatious display of automotive wealth to be not only in poor taste but downright dangerous. One automotive historian wrote that class resentment of the rich was often directed against their luxury automobiles in the form of bricks and mob attacks. "Whether it was guilt or just plain safety, such experiences were reinforced by the overwhelmingly serious and austere mood of the times. By restricting lavish expenditures and indulgences to less ostentatious areas of their lives, the moneyed found they could achieve a sort of anonymous security, and this explains why the coachbuilt luxury car was one early deletion from the Good Life."[10]

Sales of luxury autos fell from 150,000 in 1929 to 10,000 by 1937, and their manufacturers struggled to survive. At first they fought among themselves for the diminished market with the horsepower weapon, offering bigger and more powerful V–12 and V–16 engines. But as sales continued to decline, many of the grand makes like Packard, Cadillac, and Lincoln stooped to compete in the middle- and low-priced markets for mass-produced autos. Those who did not so condescend – Pierce–Arrow, Marmon, Stutz, Auburn–Duesenberg – bit the Depressionary dust. The decline of these craftbuilt cars also spelled doom for the coachbuilding shops which supplied them with custom-built bodies – only a handful survived by 1945. As the grand luxury makes either died or downgraded, the aesthetic gap between them and the mass-produced cars closed, helping to obscure the widening class gap.[11]

The Depression also cut deeply into the market for middle-priced cars and expanded demand for low-priced cars, whose proportion of all sales grew from 52 percent in 1926 to 73 percent in 1933. In response, mass-producers also downgraded their line-ups, leaving them heavily weighted to the low end. General Motors slashed the prices of Pontiac, Buick, and Olds to crowd them into the sub-$,1000 market. Chrysler Corporation also squeezed the Chrysler, DeSoto, and Dodge lines down closer to the low-priced Plymouth. Ford made fewer changes, since it was not playing with a full line-up.[12]

To accomplish this price-cutting, mass-producers cut costs and economized. At GM some top managers suggested reducing the company's car lines from five to three in order to save money. But Sloan was reluctant to reverse his policy of model diversification and maintained all makes, arguing that even though their prices were similar their nominal differentiation was crucial for supplying the consumer demand for individuality. The Depression actually increased this demand, since Americans found little to distinguish their impoverished lives beyond consumer purchases. So auto manufacturers competing for a shrinking market could ill afford to ignore this need by offering homogenized products.[13]

The only way to maintain a diverse line-up of cars and simultaneously cut costs was to increase the sharing of parts between makes, thus intensifying the interchangeability programs that had emerged in the 1920s. Chrysler initiated an extensive interchangeability program in 1930, when Plymouths, Dodges, and DeSotos began to share common engines, chassis, and bodies. At GM parts-sharing was also stepped up. Divisions shared some mechanical components like suspensions and brakes, but engines retained their divisional uniqueness. The main focus of GM's interchangeability program was the body, the dies for which were enormously expensive. Despite some earlier attempts at interchangeability, as late as 1934 GM produced different bodies for each of the corporation's five divisions. With the costs of body production about to increase substantially with the introduction of all-steel construction and solid steel tops, and with no sign of relief from Depressionary cost constraints, GM began to search for solutions.[14]

In the early 1930s a solution was found by a key member of Harley Earl's Art and Color Section, Vincent Kaptur, the chief of body layout. Working with the engineering drafts of all the divisional bodies, Kaptur discovered that most of their dimensions were very close, within a quarter of an inch. He went to Earl and suggested: "Get the engineers together and commonize these bodies. Make them all use one, or get a compromise to have as few bodies as possible." By 1933 a common body, later known as the B–body, had been worked out for most models of Buick, Olds, and La Salle. In 1935 GM introduced the smaller A–body for Chevrolet and Pontiac and the larger C–body for Cadillac and the big Olds and Buick models. So in this year GM effectively reduced the number of basic bodies to three, saving the corporation millions of dollars in tooling and production costs.[15]

This decade's cost-cutting pressures thus exacerbated the dilemma that automakers had begun to face in the 1920s – reconciling the economies of mass production with the sales-stimulating effects of product diversity and innovation. Their solution was intensification of the trend toward superficial styling. Although capital shortages prevented companies from offering cars that were technologically different and innovative, relatively inexpensive differences in appearance gave Depression-deprived consumers the illusion of innovation and individuality.

This Depression-induced focus on style considerably strengthened the fledgling stylists in their organizational struggle with engineers and others for design supremacy. The styling staffs of the Big Three grew larger and more powerful during this period, although none came so far so fast as Harley Earl's Art and Color Section at GM. Earl astutely parlayed the perilous economic conditions into power for himself and his organization, pioneering a path to the top of the corporate power structure that would be followed by other stylists only after the war. His successful efforts were symbolized by his appointment as a vice-president of the corporation on September 3, 1940, making Earl the first in his profession to achieve this corporate rank.[16]

Harley Earl's struggle for styling supremacy

Earl and his Art and Color Section entered the Depression in a precarious position, with a long, uphill battle before them for a secure place at the top of GM's corporate bureaucracy. Divisional executives were not obligated to use Art and Color's services, so stylists had to struggle to win their confidence and displace the influence of engineers and sales managers. The engineers were particularly formidable foes, although the war was turning in Earl's favor. In 1934, for example, he won an important dispute over pontoon fenders for the La Salle, which were too deep to stamp out in one piece. Over their objections, Earl forced production engineers to stamp three separate pieces and hand-weld them together. In the late 1930s Earl found himself locked in another battle with engineers over the wide, rounded bumpers he wanted to introduce. When production engineers told him these could not be stamped, Earl worked with engineers in several steel companies to develop a thinner gauge of stamping steel. These and other technical battles convinced Earl that Art and Color needed its own engineers to provide technical expertise in the struggle against divisional engineers. So he assembled a group of "far-out, creative engineers," as one stylist called them, to assist stylists in technically achieving their objectives.[17]

But even as Earl undermined engineers' monopoly on technical knowledge, he still had a battle on his hands with the sales executives. Armed with the new tool of consumer surveys, they also advanced "scientific" pretensions to determine design. By 1932 the sales department of GM was surveying a million motorists a year for opinions on auto design and engineering. Most of these surveys revealed rational and practical consumers, who preferred dependability, economy, and safety in their autos over appearance and speed. Armed with such "scientific facts," the sales managers at GM hounded Earl to produce designs that catered to these rational demands and not the irrational desires he preferred to tap.

In the late 1930s they convinced top corporate executives to pressure Art and Color to build cars in accordance with one survey that revealed that consumers wanted less chrome, more headroom, greater visibility, and easier access. Peeved at the constant exhortations, Earl relented, spitefully remarking to one stylist: "By God, we'll design exactly what they want!" Earl's resentful efforts yielded the 1939 "box cars," B–bodied Buicks, Olds, and Pontiacs with high, square roofs, big windows, and little chrome decoration. Alongside the streamlined designs of other makes, these "survey cars" looked antiquated, forcing executives to give in and let Earl introduce all-new "torpedo" bodies in 1940 and 1941. This episode proved an important victory for stylists' intuitions over salesmen's rational surveys.[18]

Stylists knew intuitively that the surveys were wrong – automobile purchases were not determined by consumers' mundane calculations of convenience and economy but by their fantastic flights of fancy. As one long-time Chrysler designer stated: "An automobile is an emotional purchase. You're stupid to go out every year and buy a brand new car. . . . But the emotion says, 'Wow, isn't that nice.'" When confronted with sober survey questions, people responded with sober preferences for safety, convenience, economy. As a GM designer stated, "there is something inherent in this form that requires that people respond in a sane and rational way." But when confronted with a three-dimensional icon appealing to displaced desires, the response was nonrational, emotional. One designer characterized consumers as Pavlovian dogs, irrationally salivating at the stimuli created by stylists. "Give the dogs more dog food. . . . Keep feeding it to them in the right dose, and right amount, the right color and trim, and they're gonna come back and buy it. Why? Because it's an emotional buy."[19]

To avoid the obtrusively rational context of survey questionnaires, corporate sales executives began to solicit consumer responses to actual models or drawings of cars in tests called "clinics." But stylists argued that annual style changes rendered present consumer preferences worthless in assessing future models. Consumers judged the prospective models against aesthetic standards which stylists would have gradually changed by the time the car reached production. They could not currently tell designers what they wanted in the future, for the future was largely the artificial, arbitrary changes created by designers themselves to give consumers the illusion of progress.[20]

Harley Earl thus used the uncertainty and irrationality of consumer desires to defeat the design ambitions of fact-grubbing marketing departments. He knew if he could satisfy American consumers' displaced needs for individuality and progress and still meet the cost-cutting demands of the Depression, his Art and Color Section would become increasingly powerful. But to do so he first had to reorganize his design personnel and procedures. Until 1931 his small group of auto designers had worked together in one big room, with only ad hoc divisions of responsibility. But Earl became dissatisfied with these arrangements for, according to Strother MacMinn, an early Art and Color employee, the borrowing of ideas between designers resulted in a homogeneity of appearance between divisions. To achieve greater divisional distinction, Earl separated designers into studios devoted exclusively to one division and physically divided by large blackboards. Each studio consisted of a chief, three or four stylists, six clay modelers, and a blackboard man or draftsman. MacMinn recalled: "The idea of isolating the creativity that way was a stroke toward the individuality of each division's design or ideas." The new organization yielded results by 1933, when GM makes began to show distinct styling themes.[21]

These early attempts at greater individuality were quickly intensified in mid-decade, when GM launched its program of body interchangeability. Earl then confronted the conundrum of making the same body appear different. He accomplished this seemingly impossible feat with a sleight-of-hand manuever that testified to his ingenuity not only as an illusionist but also as an organizational politician. In 1933 Earl created a separate Body Development Studio and staffed it with his best designers and engineers. These experts, also called the Design Committee, worked with Earl and divisional engineers to develop the body shells, the basic structures of the common bodies which included the floor pan, roof, doors, and rear quarter-panels. They selected sketches from the divisional studios and developed them into a general design theme. Then they created the body shells in plaster or clay models and turned them over to the studios of the divisions which were to share them. There, the designers added on the details that made the mass-produced, common bodies seem unique: the bumpers, grille, hood, fenders, trim, etc.[22]

To further disguise the commonality of shared bodies, Earl encouraged designers to create identification cues that made each division's cars easily recognizable. He believed that people chose their purchases by the way cars looked on the road, and that to grab the buyer's attention a car had to be easily identifiable from a quarter of a mile away. In 1933 Frank Hershey and his Pontiac studio designed a model with the type of brash identifying cues that Earl was looking for. Although he rejected the overall design of the radically streamlined model, one incidental feature caught Earl's eye – a group of thin chrome strips that started at the bottom of the grille and extended up and over the hood. Hershey copied this feature from a racing car with a cast-aluminum oil cooler whose fins protruded through the hood. His chrome strips were non-functional, but this was just the sort of visual manifestation of speed and excitement that Earl wanted to distinguish the divisional makes. The "Silver Streak" strips appeared on the 1935 Pontiacs and became an identifying feature of the make, so that "any child could name a Pontiac a block away, which was exactly what Harley Earl intended," as one GM stylist recalled. By 1937 other GM makes acquired similar identification cues, which outwardly displayed their differences while disguising the inward homogeneity of interchangeable bodies.[23]

Most of these divisional identification cues were composed of chrome appliqué, for several properties of this brightwork made it ideal for camouflaging commonality. Chrome trim was cheaper to manufacture and change than features sunk into dies. And most importantly, Earl discovered that it could literally dazzle consumer spectators. As one GM stylist put it: "Mr. Earl . . . found that bright plating – in order to have its strongest effect – should reflect the bright sky directly into the customer's eye." This flash of light distracted consumers from the shared body panels and gave a "different proportional reading" of the common form. Earl and his stylists turned this chrome-plated deception into a science, studying angles of reflection to discover the most blinding forms.[24]

Earl found that this aesthetic differentiation of makes required, however, increased organizational distance between the divisional studios. In the early 1930s, these studios were separated only by blackboards, which were easily circumvented. After the introduction of shared body shells, Earl became concerned that the facile intercourse of designers might lead to the mongrelization of divisional distinctness. So in the fall of 1936 he ordered each studio surrounded by temporary walls and restricted access to its specific employees plus his Design Committee.[25]

The year 1937 brought physical and organizational changes for Earl's section that signaled its rise to the pinnacle of corporate power at GM. On January 3 Earl's staff, which had grown to around two hundred, acquired expanded quarters, moving from the General Motors Building to the top five floors of the new Research Annex Building B across the street. These new quarters provided all the space and facilities that Earl could ask for, including a lavish auditorium for presentations. To properly present autos as reified, ethereal objects and remove any terrestrial taint of alienated production, the auditorium walls were covered with majestic photomurals taken from a Colorado mountain peak. In conjuction with this move, the name of the section was changed from Art and Color to Styling at the insistence of Earl, who thought the former was a "sissy name." And on the same day Sloan appointed Earl to the powerful Engineering Policy Group, a high-level corporate committee responsible for initiating new product programs. "It will give you more authority when you talk to the presidents of these different divisions," Sloan told Earl of the position.[26]

Earl took the opportunity provided by new quarters to consolidate the organizational distance between divisional studios, separating them by locked doors to which only Earl and the Design Committee carried passkeys. The locked-studio system not only prevented homogenizing communication between studios, but also gave Earl absolute aesthetic control over the section. Since he alone possessed knowledge of all the aesthetic options available from the subordinate studios, only he had the power to select among them. Earl's centralized, patrimonial system divided and conquered his underlings, preventing the lateral communication necessary to organize opposition to his rule. And he further divided his subordinates by pitting them against one another in competition. This organizational control system resembled nothing more than a feudal kingdom, with King Earl at the center, surrounded by a group of close friends as ministers assisting him in subordinating the studio lords through isolation and competition.[27]

Earl used this centralized control system to create not only divisional differences but also corporate unity between GM cars. By carefully transferring both ideas and personnel between studios, he created a subtle family resemblance between GM makes, while retaining their distinction. As another automaker explained: "If a characteristic styling theme can be created for a broad line of products, the value of instant recognition is similar to the effect of a well-known trademark." And Earl's system also engineered the regularized style changes that connoted automotive progress, a characteristic all the more imperative in a stagnant economy. Since capital for costly mechanical improvements was short, the annual changes in body style begun in the late 1920s became increasingly important. As a technical assistant to GM's Sloan wrote, giving consumers evidence of progress need have "nothing whatsoever to do with engineering advantages or disadvantages" but could be achieved through styling. And even last year's body shell could be made to look new by changing enough superficial details. As Earl said: "The thing is to tool them into coming out with a car that has so many changes in little things, it looks entirely new."[28]

In the 1930s GM developed a styling cycle to regularize these annual model changes. The cycle began when the Body Development Studio produced an all-new body shell. For the next model year, the divisional studios made minor face-lifts of the shell, changing decorative details like grilles, bumpers, and lights. In the third year of the cycle, when the public got bored with the old shell, stylists made major changes to disguise it, including new fenders, hood, and deck. Then in the next year a new shell was introduced again because, as Earl stated: "After three years, even with lots of fresh accessories, you don't get a lift out of the car anymore." To hold down annual design and tooling costs, the corporation staggered the styling cycles of the shared shells. So, for example, in the model year that a new A–body was introduced, B–body cars got a minor face-lift, while cars built on the C–body received a major face-lift.[29]

In the late 1930s, Earl stabilized and consolidated these complex programs by initiating his own training program for auto stylists. Although the main motive was to supply his expanding section with trained personnel, Earl also used his training school to socialize designers into his aesthetic and organizational norms. Supervised by several of Earl's most experienced stylists, trainees followed a 1-year, highly competitive course focused on designing experimental vehicles. Students were evaluated every three months and either fired or promoted to the next segment. Upon graduation these new stylists were placed in the Advanced Design Studio, where they developed new design ideas until chosen by one of the studio chiefs to join a production team. Because these trainees were constantly competing for the attention of their instructors and potential bosses, by the time they arrived in the production studios they had thoroughly absorbed not only styling techniques but also Earl's competitive system that kept designers divided and firmly under his control. Many of the industry's early designers were trained in GM's design school. Although some eventually defected to Ford or Chrysler, they reproduced there the system Earl pioneered at GM. There was no escaping the growing influence of Earl, inside or outside of GM.[30]

The rise and fall of styling at Ford and Chrysler

The conditions of the Depression forced even the obstinate champion of automotive utility, Henry Ford, to recognize the increasing importance of appearance and style. By 1931 the declining sales of his Model A had convinced Ford of the need for a drastic change. So in 1932 he introduced the Ford V–8, a new automobile that signalled his capitulation to the policies pioneered by GM. The car was the first low-priced V–8 in the industry, but more importantly it came in fourteen different models, reproducing GM's policy of offering a variety of superficially differentiated models on a standardized, mass-produced chassis. And the bodies of the Ford V–8 were more stylish than ever, designed by Edsel Ford and Joe Galamb to capture the custom-built look of the Lincoln. But despite this new car, Ford sales in 1932 dropped to their lowest level since 1914, largely due to the decline in the entire market. The deepening depression convinced Ford that sales had to be stimulated by methods other than utilitarian engineering. Surrendering to GM's styling policy, Ford began in 1933 to update the appearance of his cars yearly. And to accomplish this the company formed its first styling department.[31]

To head the Ford styling department, Edsel Ford chose Eugene T. "Bob" Gregorie, a draftsman who had come to his Lincoln Motor Company after working briefly in Earl's Art and Color Section. Unlike Earl's separate division, which reported directly to the president, Gregorie's new styling department was placed under the authority of the Engineering Group. Ford stylists were thus subordinated to body engineers like Joe Galamb, who resented their role in design, and production men like Charlie Sorensen, who placed speed of production over beauty and style. But like Earl, Gregorie had a corporate patron who understood the growing importance of automotive appearance – Edsel Ford. A sophisticated patron of the arts, Edsel had an excellent eye for design and worked closely with Gregorie developing the appearance of Ford cars. He was determined to win control of styling for the new corporate section and assisted Gregorie in battles with Ford engineers and production supervisors. Although it remained nominally under the authority of the Engineering Group, Gregorie's styling department had won effective control of design by 1936. Unlike Earl, who had to cajole several layers of GM's bureaucracy, Gregorie, operating in the personalistic Ford empire, had only to sell his designs to Edsel. Together the two could push their preferences quickly past the most recalcitrant engineers and production supervisors.[32]

In the mid-1930s, the small Ford styling department had but one car line to design, not five like Earl's Styling Section. But as Ford began to imitate GM's graded hierarchy of cars, the styling staff was given responsibility for rendering this diversity compatible with mass-production. At first they merely differentiated the Ford V–8 body shell into two trim packages, Standard and Deluxe. Then in 1938, responding to the Depressionary demand for cut-rate diversity, stylists gave the Deluxe line a different hood, grille, and fenders.

In 1939 Edsel moved Ford even closer to GM policies by convincing the company to introduce the completely new middle-priced Mercury line. Taking a page from GM's lesson book, the upscale Mercury shared many parts with the downscale Ford, including the engine and body shell. Bob Gregorie recognized that this mechanically similar Mercury had to be stylistically differentiated from Ford "to give it prestige . . .," to appeal to people seeking "to step up socially." Although he convinced Edsel to nominally dissociate the Mercury by removing its Ford nameplate, Gregorie was less successful in aesthetically dissociating the two lines. The Mercury bore a striking resemblance to the 1939 Ford Deluxe, especially in the all-important front. Although Ford sought to imitate GM's policy of interchangeability between car lines, Gregorie's small, inexperienced styling staff was less adept than Earl's larger, complex organization at disguising this mass-produced monotony.[33]

Further growth and development of the modest styling group was held hostage to the internecine warfare at Ford. Although Edsel was nominally president, Henry was a powerful force and still fundamentally hostile to the his son's ideas on automobile style. While Edsel was alive, he held his father's disdain for beauty at bay and built a niche for Bob Gregorie's staff within the strife-torn company. But when he died in 1943, so too did Ford styling's hopes for greater influence. Gregorie quit shortly thereafter, and even though Henry Ford II rehired him in 1944, without Edsel there would be no strong role for styling until the postwar reorganization of Ford.[34]

As at Ford, styling at Chrysler during this period rose rapidly under the protection of a powerful patron, and just as rapidly declined upon the patron's death. The corporation's small Art and Color Department entered the 1930s subordinated to the dictates of Chrysler's powerful engineering staff. But the engineers' domination lessened during the decade as Walter Chrysler acquired a personal interest in design. The company introduced interchangeable bodies in 1930, and because they were designed by unimaginative body engineers, they looked interchangeable. Feeling the competitive pressure to achieve greater distinction, Walter Chrysler began to work personally with custom-body designer Raymond Dietrich, who was hired as a consultant in 1932 and became the unofficial head of the Art and Color Department. His leadership improved the overall style and differentiation of Chrysler cars, but styling's influence was still limited.

Then in 1934 Chrysler introduced a radically new car, the Airflow, which was developed by the company's engineers with no input from the stylists. The spectacular failure of the Airflow convinced Walter Chrysler that innovative engineering was not enough to sell cars and led to the rapid rise of styling's importance within the corporation. After the Airflow flop, Chrysler hired Dietrich as the official head of Art and Color and elevated the power and reponsibility of the department. Walter Chrysler developed a close relationship with Dietrich, and under his patronage the styling chief built a strong department. Despite continued fights with the engineers, Dietrich brought the corporation back from the Airflow disaster with more conventional styling, careful differentiation of shared bodies, and a program of incremental annual changes.

But Chrysler styling's rise to prominence was short-lived, undermined by the departure of its patron before it could institutionalize power. When Walter Chrysler's failing health forced him to abandon his active company role in 1938, Dietrich resigned and Chrysler engineers quickly retook the ground they had lost to styling. Although the new Chrysler president, K.T. Keller, was a sophisticated art collector and patron, he viewed the automobile as a utilitarian machine, not an aesthetic object. His sole design considerations were cost and service, so under his reign the engineers and their views prevailed. While other automakers produced sleek, streamlined cars, Chrysler products remained boxy and stodgy. Keller personally dictated product packages with high, square dimensions, boasting that people could get into a Chrysler without knocking their hats off. Consequently, Chrysler styling limped along in the late 1930s with a small, demoralized staff.[35]

THE BATTLE FOR THE IDEOLOGY OF STREAMLINING

As the stylists grew in number and influence during the 1930s, they advocated an aesthetic that captured popular hopes and frustrations and diverted them into channels that bolstered the faltering capitalist system. This aesthetic was streamlining, the movement that fetishized the sleek, rounded forms of the latest transportation technology. What were originally functionally engineered forms on fast-moving machines became, in the distorting reflection of social struggles of the period, an ideological fetish for the technological progress that corporate capitalists promised would take America to a consumer utopia. When applied to the bodies of mass-produced automobiles, these sleek, organic forms made the old mechanical parts beneath look modern and disguised their origins in the increasingly discredited machine process of Fordist production. The streamlined machines of the decade thus helped divert popular efforts from struggles to change America's system of production to the frictionless achievement of a dream world of consumption.

The idea and effort to streamline automobiles was by no means new to Depression-era America. Since the invention of the motor vehicle, engineers, scientists, and tinkerers had tried to improve its performance by reducing wind resistance. European engineers pioneered the application of the emerging science of aerodynamics to cars. High gasoline prices and heavy horsepower taxes forced them to maximize engine efficiency, and the reduction of wind resistance was a relatively simple way of doing so. In the early 1920s engineers like Germany's Edmund Rumpler and Wunibald Kamm and Hungary's Paul Jaray experimented with teardrop-shaped cars in wind tunnels. Some of these shapes made their way onto racing cars and even production vehicles by Maybach, Audi, and Mercedes–Benz.

By the late 1920s the United States also had its advocates of automotive streamlining, like Alexander Klemin of New York University and W.E. Lay of the University of Michigan. Their wind-tunnel experiments in auto aerodynamics were motivated by the obsession to find the technically perfect form, which would allow the automobile to function in the most efficient way. Many believed this form to be the teardrop, a rounded, elongated, air-foil shape. These aerodynamic tests attracted the attention of American automotive engineers, who saw in them an emerging body of knowledge that might help them to build practical, efficient cars. And, perhaps, they also saw this science as a weapon against an organizational enemy that was beginning to threaten their power – the stylists. Not only did aerodynamics make design a technical task once again, but it also gave engineers claims to aesthetic values, for truly streamlined forms were said to be beautiful as well as efficient. Thus, in 1931 the art director at GM's Campbell, Ewald ad agency told a group of automotive engineers that "a car designed along aerodynamic lines to more properly function at high speeds will automatically become more beautiful than the conventional, modernized buggies of today. . . ." If the subjective pursuit of beauty could thus be transformed into an objective science, the power of the stylists could be dealt a devastating blow.[36]

For these reasons aerodynamics excited automotive engineers in the early 1930s. Trade publications and professional meetings were filled with reports and debates about teardrop designs, rear-engined cars, wind-tunnel tests, and drag coefficients. And several American engineers began to construct experimental streamliners. In 1933 architect-engineer R. Buckminster Fuller built his Dymaxion car, which sported three wheels, front-wheel drive, rear-wheel steering, and a rear-mounted engine, all enclosed in a body that was a near-perfect teardrop. A year later an aviation engineer, William B. Stout, presented his streamlined vehicle, the Scarab. Because he believed teardrop shapes to be unstable in side winds, his rear-engined car was shaped like a turtle or a beetle.[37]

These functionally engineered experimental cars ideologically strengthened engineers in their organizational struggle against stylists, for they testified to the effectiveness of streamlining and legitimated the return of auto design to engineers. But these streamlined machines also helped to legitimate the interests of corporate capitalists in the larger societal struggle raging during the Depression. These technological wonders made palpable the corporate promise of a streamlined consumerism to be ushered in by science and technology, and diverted people from the struggle for real social progress.

So the functional streamlining of consumer goods by engineers was ideological enough. But the aesthetic streamlining of products by stylists would become even more so. What automotive engineers believed would be a weapon in their struggle to control design was seized by their organizational enemies and turned against them. Stylists used streamlining not merely to divert people from the lack of social progress but also to disguise the lack of real technological progress in automobiles. Industry stylists won the organizational struggle to control streamlining because of their superior understanding of the automobile as a ideological icon in American culture. Earl and his ilk understood well that the automobile was valued more for its symbolic than its functional power, as testimony to progress and success in the consumption world insulated from Fordist production. Efficiency, savings, productivity – these qualities were part of the miserly logic of production, from which people sought to escape in leisure through surfeits of goods consumed in purposeless extravagance. Understanding this, stylists treated streamlining not as engineering efficiency but as aesthetic beautification which assisted in concealing and compensating for Fordist work.

From the beginning of the auto industry, streamlining was more an aesthetic than an engineering function. The word first emerged in the 1920s to describe the rounded, flowing lines of the luxury classics, which were judged aesthetically superior to the square, boxy forms of mass-produced cars. These rounded, organic "streamlines," which required careful, slow craftwork, connoted a life of leisure removed from the cost-cutting concerns of engineering efficiency. They also concealed more of the car's mechanical parts, which could remind consumers of the rationalized labor process they were seeking to escape. Finally, streamlined luxury cars appeared more beautiful because they were visually associated with the excitement of the emerging aviation industry. As early as 1909 these cars tried to borrow the image and prestige of aviation. But this airplane obsession drastically intensified in the late 1920s, when Lindbergh's trans-Atlantic flight cemented in the public mind the association of aviation with progress, excitement, and adventure. Manufacturers of luxury autos tapped these meanings visually by giving the smooth, integrated look of flight to the surface of cars.[38]

So the American automobile industry entered the Depression with two competing visions of streamlining. The engineers promoted a functional engineering of the automotive form to achieve economy, while the stylists pushed an aesthetic styling of the automobile's skin to cover the mechanicals and carry connotations of progress and romance. Both carried the ideological potential to divert public attention from the social misery of America, but the cultural and economic conditions of the era favored the stylists' vision of aesthetic streamlining. Consumers were already committed to the automobile as a cultural icon, symbolically removed from the mechanical concerns of efficiency and economy. And the economic straits in which the automakers found themselves discouraged the expensive technological innovations required for functional streamlining. It was safer and cheaper merely to alter the contours of the skin to give autos the look of newness, technical progress, and luxury that streamlining connoted.

As the luxury makes declined during the Depression, the battle over streamlining was fought almost entirely in the market for mass-produced cars. In 1931 stylists launched the first offensive with the Reo Royale Eight, the first mass-produced car to display the streamlined aesthetic. Designed by Amos Northrup, a stylist at Murray Body, this pathbreaking car did not alter traditional automotive proportions, as did the functional streamliners, but merely rounded, integrated, and extended the body surfaces. At the front, the V–type radiator was surrounded by a smoothly rounded, peaked shell, and the headlights were mounted in elongated pods. The heavily radiused fenders had rolled-under edges that extended close to the ground to conceal the frame side rails. The sides of the body also extended out and over the top of the frame, further obscuring this functional member. This aesthetic of concealment was carried through to the rear, where a double curvature panel swept out at the bottom in a "beavertail" that covered the fuel tank.[39]

Aware that consumers liked to pride themselves on being practical and economical, Reo promoted these streamlined style features as functional. The rounded fender edges were said to increase fender strength and reduce paint chipping. And Murray proudly proclaimed that the overall shape reduced wind resistance, producing wind-tunnel tests showing that at 80 miles per hour the new body reduced horsepower requirements by 12 percent over the previous year's body. But as one Murray designer admitted in the *Journal of the Society of Automotive Engineers*, "the results at 60 m.p.h. are not quite so interesting, and at 40 m.p.h. are not to be considered." He went on to justify this functional smokescreen for streamlined style, stating: "radical departures from the customary shape of a useful object like the automobile should be made with at least the excuse of some utilitarian purpose; that is, beauty disguised in usefulness is more attractive than beauty by itself." With the aesthetic appeal to people's repressed desires carefully disguised as functional, the streamlined Reo was an immediate public sensation.[40]

Confident that he had tapped into the Depression-era consumer psyche, Northrup made even bolder pronouncements in the idiom of streamlining in his 1932 design for another struggling automaker, Graham. For the Blue Streak he extended the aesthetic of concealment, rendering the auto an integrated, organic unit that might just as well have dropped from the skies as issued from the Fordist factory. The most radical innovations were up front, where for the first time a decorative chrome grille was placed in front of the radiator. This concealed the functional part and provided a vehicle for aesthetically blending the car's front with the rest of the body. The Blue Streak grille was gracefully tilted back to suggest speed and echo the slope of the fenders and windshield. At the bottom it blended gracefully into a splash pan or "modesty panel," which covered all the immodest reminders of mass production like spring horns and frame members. The fenders also received concealing "skirts" or "valences," which closed in around the wheels "hiding the unsightly and hard-to-clean undercarriage."[41]

Figure 11 1932 Graham Blue Streak convertible coupe, one of the first mass-produced cars to incorporate aesthetic streamlining. Designed by Amos Northrup, this car's major features – radiator grille, splash pan, fender skirts, and beavertail – concealed mass-produced parts and gave it the look of organic unity. (Courtesy National Automotive History Collection, Detroit Public Library)

The success of these aesthetically streamlined cars created a styling stampede among the larger mass-producers. By the 1933 model year, the influence of Northrup's cars was seen far and wide, as chrome grilles, V'd radiators, fender skirts, and beavertails became commonplace. Perhaps the most thorough changes were seen in General Motors' A–bodied Pontiacs and Chevrolets, about which President Sloan wrote that "the body was extended in all directions in an attempt to cover some of the ugly projections and exposed parts of the chassis which were still in evidence." *Business Week* was not fooled by automakers' public claims that aerodynamic efficiency motivated these changes. The primary purpose of the new models, it stated in 1933, was "to accelerate the senility of the old ones. . . . Streamlining is the principal device to hasten obsolescence."[42]

AIRFLOW: THE DISASTROUS DEFEAT OF FUNCTIONAL STREAMLINING

Automotive engineers did not surrender to the stylists' first offensive but answered with a bold counterattack for functional streamlining from Chrysler, the corporation known for its powerful and innovative engineers. Three of its best, Fred Zeder, Owen Skelton, and Carl Breer, developed the Airflow, a car radically innovative in engineering and aesthetics. Breer claimed the idea for the Airflow originated one day in 1927 when, having stopped his car to admire a flock of geese, he discovered the flying formation was actually a squadron of fighter planes. Inspired by the way aviation engineers imitated nature's aerodynamic forms, he wondered if similar forms might improve automobiles. Through wind-tunnel tests assisted by aviation pioneer Orville Wright and others, Breer discovered that the conventional sedan generated less air resistance going backward than forward, and he became dedicated to engineering a scientifically streamlined car.[43]

The initial prototypes for the Airflow had rear-mounted engines, but problems with the design forced Breer to change to a conventional front location. To attain the tapered aerodynamic tail, the engine was pushed up over the front axle, allowing the rear seat to be moved forward off its traditional perch on top of the rear axle. Chrysler engineers discovered that this radically new configuration was not only more streamlined but also created a smoother ride and more interior room. The car's body was conceived as functional packaging for this radical architecture, engineered to reduce air resistance and increase strength. Designed largely without the assistance of stylists, it was a masterpiece of functional engineering. The Airflow body pioneered unitary construction, in

Figure 12 1934 Chrysler Airflow four-door sedan, beside the streamlined train *City of Salina*. A marvel of functional streamlining, the Airflow was a commercial disaster because it radically transformed traditional automotive architecture and symbolism. (Courtesy Chrysler Historical Collection)

which the previously separate body and frame were constructed as an integral, weight-bearing structure. Body panels were welded to a bird-cage framework of steel girders, which was in turn bolted to a shallow frame, yielding a highly rigid but relatively light structure.[44]

The stylists were, however, allowed to add their touch to the Airflow's incidental body features, in order to appeal to women, according to one engineer. To visually dramatize the Airflow's streamlined engineering, the stylists chose Art Deco themes in much of the ornamentation, inside and out. The bumpers and the hood vents were arrayed in the three-tiered configuration popularized by this style. The interior was also starkly modernistic, with hygenic rubber mats instead of carpeting and seats cradled in a frame of chrome tubing. The stylists' greatest challenge, however, came in the car's front, where streamlining replaced the vertical prow with a bulbous, sloped hood that blended smoothly into the fenders. To relieve this bulky mass, stylists added a grille of fine vertical chrome bars extending far up the hood.[45]

In promotion of the Airflow, which premiered in 1934, Chrysler hit on all the ideological themes of streamlining. The car was depicted as an application of the most advanced principles of science and was pictured alongside streamlined dirigibles, airplanes, and trains. The results of wind-tunnel tests were widely publicized, revealing that the Airflow reduced the coefficient of drag 15.6 percent over a standard 1932 sedan, a rather modest achievement. And the strength of the body's unitary construction was dramatized by sending an Airflow over a 110-foot cliff, then driving the relatively undamaged car away under its own power. But Chrysler carefully avoided associating the car with the technology of Fordist mass production, which was increasingly discredited by the Depression. The Airflow was promoted not as a mechanical construction but as an organic creature, "designed . . . in accordance with this natural law [of streamlining]," as one ad stated. The car covered all mechanical connotations with a streamlined shell and then justified that shell by the laws of nature, providing a naturalized excuse for its social obfuscation of dehumanized production.[46]

Aware of the increasing importance of style in selling automobiles, Chrysler executives also promoted the Airflow as fashionable and beautiful. But they were careful to stress that the beauty of the Airflow came from its functional design, not tacked on ornamentation. Streamlining guru Norman Bel Geddes, who was hired to publicize the Airflow, stated in an ad that "when the line and contour of a motor car start with the problem of what a car is designed for . . . the result is a great motor car."[47]

But the consuming public did not agree that beauty necessarily followed from functional engineering. Although the Airflow was an engineering success, pioneering advances that were widely emulated by other automakers, it was a sales disaster, sending Chrylser into financial straits from which it almost did not emerge. Production delays caused by tooling difficulties dampened initial enthusiasm for the car and led to rumors that it was a lemon. Although the first production runs did have problems, the Airflow generally fulfilled the engineers' promises, performing admirably in speed and endurance tests. Nevertheless, it sold only about 18,000 units in the first year, and only the sale of its conventionally styled cars saved Chrysler from financial ruin.[48]

Poor sales indicated a problem more fundamental than engineering and performance, and most thought it was appearance. As designer Henry Dreyfuss stated, the functional design was "a case of going too far too fast." People during the Depression wanted evidence of progress in their things, but stylists understood that they wanted slow, reassuring progress. Thus, aesthetically streamlined cars like Northrup's Blue Streak merely rounded off the edges of conventional automotive architecture. But Chrysler engineers leaped radically ahead into functional streamlining, abandoning many of the visual elements of the traditional form and leaving many consumers feeling themselves victims of technological progress beyond their control. The most important of these elements was the distinctive prow or "face," formed by the vertical grille, free-standing headlights, and detached fenders. The Airflow melted these distinct elements into a round blandness. Further, moving the body forward left the hood short and stubby, robbing the auto of the long hood line that connoted power and speed. And the car's ubiquitous curves made it look heavy and bloated, "so bulbous, so obesely curved as to defy the natural preference of the eye for horizontal lines," wrote *Harper's* editor Frederick Lewis Allen.[49]

Part of the Airflow's problem was that it appeared not only too unfamiliar but too functional. The car's curvilinear lines gave it an organic look, but the Airflow's organicism was starkly functional, frugally purposeful with no excess of ornament. The car displayed immense expanses of barren sheet metal, bereft of the entertaining appliqué that Harley Earl so deftly designed. There was very little to look at beyond the streamlined silhouette economically designed to "cheat the wind." And Chrysler promoted the car mainly by appealing to utilitarian needs, "the things that people really need and want in a motor car. . . . Comfort, safety, performance, and economy. . . ." For most working Americans these rational qualities were alien impositions, forced upon them by the cost-cutting pressures of Fordist production. They did not want to be reminded of this enforced deprivation and denial in their leisure time but wanted products with luxurious distractions and entertainment. The starkly functional Airflow provided no such entertainment.[50]

Neither did consumers want to be reminded of the terrestrial hazards of driving when soaring in their celestial dream machines. Images of accidents and collisions brought consumers back to earth and the cold realities of automobility. So pictures of Airflows flying off cliffs to demonstrate their safety and strength were probably received with anxiety, not enthusiasm. The industry was just beginning to learn the lesson that "safety doesn't sell." As Harley Earl once said in opposition to overt safety appeals: "We are trying to make the slogan 'Driving for Fun' a reality. I think it can be too if we take the annoying things out. . . . We don't believe you should be conscious of accidents. If you were on a boat, you would not want life preservers all over the table; it suggests too much."[51]

After the Airflow's appearance problems became apparent, the corporation devised a strategy to divert disaster by giving greater influence to stylists. Raymond Dietrich was assigned the task of refashioning the offensive face of the Airflow, which he did by extending the hood and adding a conventional grille. Impressed with his efforts, Chrysler officials hired Dietrich to offically head the Chrysler Art and Color Department and gave him responsibility for styling a conventional companion model for the Airflow, the Airstream. In place of the radically functional streamlining of the Airflow, this car gave customers the comfortably progresssive cues of aesthetic streamlining, borrowed from Northrup's Graham and Reo models. These and other carefully styled cars sold well enough to pull Chrysler out of its financial tailspin.[52]

The entire industry concluded from this episode that even meticulous and innovative engineering could not sell an ugly car, and that beauty could not be calculated by engineers' equations but only intuited by stylists' probing of consumer emotions. The Airflow disaster thus helped stylists wrest the technical bludgeon of streamlining out of the engineers' hands and turn it against them in the transformed shape of an aesthetic scalpel that surgically probed consumer psyches for sales advantages.

THE TRIUMPH OF AESTHETIC STREAMLINING

Now more influential than ever, the stylists pushed their own aesthetic vision of aerodynamics. Streamlining increasingly became a look that had little to do with reduced wind resistance and increased performance. GM's president Alfred Sloan admitted as much in a 1935 letter to stockholders, writing that "the contribution of streamlining is definitely limited to the question of styling" and calling the belief that streamlining increased automotive efficiency a "popular mistake." Automotive experts corroborated this opinion, at least in so far as conventional streamlined styling was concerned. One test found that the coefficient of drag (CD) of a streamlined-style 1933 sedan was .0014, a difference from the .0018 CD of a typical 1922 sedan that yielded real economies only at high speeds. And many features of streamlined style were exposed as downright dysfunctional from the standpoint of safety. Henry Crane, Sloan's personal assistant for engineering matters, argued in a 1939 article that low, streamlined cars with rounded roofs, heavily sloped windshields, and sleek fastbacks reduced and distorted the driver's vision. Despite these severe problems, Crane stated that "streamlining has been the badge of up-to-dateness in all forms of industry, and we must continue with it and make the best of it."[53]

Automobile stylists moved toward superficial streamlining despite these dysfunctions because the style was embedded in consumers' psyches as a sign of modernity and progress, the type of reified improvement that they hoped would transport them away from the Depression into a consumer utopia. Aesthetic streamlining also assisted stylists in humanizing and individualizing the cold, homogeneous auto that was a reminder of alienated Fordist production. This was achieved through an essential element of this styling idiom – extending the body to cover previously exposed mechanical parts. Fender skirts covered the undercarriage, body sills concealed frame rails, beavertails hid gas tanks, splash aprons obscured spring horns and shock-absorber mounts. As one Chrysler designer stated: "More mechanical things showing makes a car look machine-like. . . . It takes away from the romance." Industrial designers like Raymond Loewy realized that mechanical complexity intimidated and confused consumers, so they covered it up with smooth, organic shells that had the look of nature, not the factory. Aesthetic streamlining thus reified – i.e., obscured by naturalizing – the alienated human relations of Fordist production so as to make its products more palatable to consumers seeking refuge from these relations.[54]

To convey the unified look of nature, the streamlined style also concealed the signs of assemblage, which conjured up images of fragmented assembly lines. Stylists sought to close up body gaps and seams, and hide hinges, fasteners, nails, and screws. And great efforts were made to match the contours of panels. The result of this visual suppression of assemblage was a sleek, almost seamless form that kept the eye moving and prevented the concentration of thought on signs that testified to the fragmented process of production. As one automotive historian wrote, "the most stimulating automotive designs are balanced to keep the eye from attending any one form separate from and more than the rest." The incessant flow of the streamlined aesthetic thus prevented the interruption of experience required for a rational, mediated analysis of mass-produced goods. The irrationalist eye flowed effortlessly over the obscuring shell, allowing these consumer objects to enter the insulated realm of consumption without stirring up any rational reminders of their social origins.[55]

Auto stylists in all of the major corporations rode the streamlining craze for all it was worth, appending the look of unity, organicism, individuality, and progress to fragmented, standardized, mass-produced automobiles that were starved for real mechanical improvements during this decade. Two years after the Airflow disaster, Ford cast its lot with the trend and introduced the highly influential Lincoln Zephyr, capitalizing on the fame of the streamlined train of the same name. Like the Airflow, it was originally engineered as a venture in functional streamlining, complete with a rear-mounted engine, and a teardrop-shaped, unitized body. But when Ford executives mandated that the car share mass-produced Ford components, Zephyr's innovative engineering was sacrificed to cost-cutting economies. The car that premiered in 1936 was a conventional front-engined car that was poorly engineered but beautiful to look at. John Tjaarda and the Briggs stylists captured the excitement and concealment of aesthetic streamlining without losing the familiar automotive features. The hood was long and flat, the grille was slanted but still vertical, the front fenders were rounded pontoons, and the rear fenders concealed the wheels. The wide body moved out over the frame rails, entirely concealing them and leaving only narrow strips as running boards. The overall effect of the Zephyr was lithe and graceful, and it was popularly recognized as the epitome of modern style.[56]

Automotive stylists were quick to publicize the lesson to be learned from the relative success of the Zephyr over the Airflow. As David Holls, a GM designer and auto historian, stated: "The Chrysler Airflow was an engineering masterpiece, without the help of a designer. The Lincoln Zephyr was a masterpiece of styling and design with an absolute total lack of engineering below the surface." While the Zephyr set trends and sales records, the Airflow was "a commercial disaster." Aesthetic streamlining thus emerged triumphant.[57]

This design idiom was further advanced by the appearance in the same year of the widely influential Cord 810. Designed by Gordon Buehrig,

Figure 13 1936 Lincoln Zephyr four-door sedan, beside the DC3 airplane. This conventionally engineered but aesthetically streamlined car was a commercial success, reinforcing the case for elevating superficial styling over engineering innovation. (Courtesy Henry Ford Museum and Greenfield Village)

another of Earl's early employees, the car was wrapped in a sleek, unified shell that carried the cohesion and concealment of the streamlined idiom to new heights. Masking the fragmented look of assemblage was an integrated body that flowed smoothly from nose to tail. The radiator and hood were no longer separate but integrated into one elegantly long and flowing nose, surrounded by a bank of louvers that concealed both radiator entry and cooling vents. In front of the hood was a long splash apron that extended down to the bumper and concealed the front-wheel drive mechanism and chassis components. Elongated pontoon fenders closed in around the wheels, and body sides came out to conceal the frame rails and eliminate the running boards. Parts previously appended to the form were now carefully incorporated – mechanically retractable headlights were concealed in front fenders, taillights were flushed into rear fenders, and the gas-filler cap and radio aerial were hidden beneath the sheet metal. There was no trace of a hinge or rivet on the body, which was also bereft of tacked on decorations. The interior was aesthetically integrated with the exterior by a similarly aeronautical motif that utilized aircraft-style gauges and throw levers.[58]

The Cord 810 was widely influential in the industry, especially at GM, where Buehrig originated the design while working in Earl's Styling Section. The wrap-around bars of the front began appearing on many GM cars, as did the pontoon fenders and the absent running boards. But one feature of both the Cord and Zephyr that Earl would not emulate was the clean, unadorned surfaces. He had an aversion to undecorated expanses of sheet metal, perhaps because they looked too stark and economical, like the Fordist factories from which he was trying to give consumers a vacation. Earl wanted not merely to take their eyes on a trip but also to give them something to look at along the way. As one auto historian stated: "He wanted the customer to be able to walk around a car and be entertained the entire trip. He really felt it was very important to keep finding exciting things." Earl knew that chrome appliqué could entertain consumers and, as two design critics stated, "detract attention from the basic faults" of the car, like gaps, seams, and surface flaws in the body. And he also believed that brightwork could conceal the signs of physical deterioration like dents, dirt, rust, and faded paint. By thus distracting consumers from the unpleasantries of automotive production and operation, chrome geegaws helped maintain the value of used cars, on which new sales depended. Finally, one GM designer claimed that Earl used brightwork to enhance the value of a car by literally giving it the look of money. "The whole things stems clear back to the day when bright coins meant something, had a value and, therefore, brightness was a desirable factor."[59]

Another feature of the influential Zephyr and Cord that Earl countered in his cars was their light and delicate look. Earl took his streamlined style in the direction of beefy bulkiness, using large-radius curves that made his cars appear not only bigger but more powerful. Driving these more "substantial" cars gave people a feeling of importance and respectability that was often denied them on the job. And because Earl knew that Americans equated size with value, these bigger-looking cars made it seem they were getting more for their money. As Ford stylist Bob Gregorie stated: "If a man went to look at a Cadillac, for the same money it looked like twice the car as the Zephyr. It was full. . . . It looked like a heavy car, and that is what people wanted. . . ."[60]

The rise of bigness, of quantity, as a standard of automotive value was part of the general degradation of quality effected by Fordism. In replacing skilled craft labor with unskilled, machine-minding work, Fordism degraded not only the quality of products but also the standards of judgment by which they were assessed. Disqualified workers no longer possessed the knowledge to judge the quality of consumer goods, so they substituted quantity as a standard, following the dictates of a market economy that reduces everything and everyone to a quantitative value. In autos, as in other commodities, bigger, or at least bigger-looking, became better.

Earl's brand of beefy, chromed-up streamlining was well exemplified by the innovative 1934 La Salle, a model he introduced to save the sinking little Cadillac. The basic forms of the car – slanted windshield, long, tall hood, "suitcase" fenders (pontoons with cropped ends), smooth integration of parts – were all borrowed from Buehrig's Cord 810 design. But unwilling to let these forms speak for themselves, Earl tacked on a grabbag of appliqué clichés to entertain consumers and disguise the interchangeable sheet metal shared with Olds. He borrowed from racing cars the tall, narrow grille and the round exhaust ports on the hood sides. From racing airplanes came the two-tiered "biplane" bumpers and the streamlined pods for headlights and taillights. And there was no lack of chrome appliqué, molded in Art Deco style. Here was the master of styling clichés at his best, taking the mundane economy of shared sheet metal and mass-produced running gear and turning it into the exciting entertainment of a seemingly powerful and streamlined racing machine. The design was a styling sensation, quadrupling La Salle sales by 1936 and setting style trends that would persist until the middle of the fateful 1950s.[61]

Figure 14 1937 Buick Y–Job experimental car, with Harley Earl at the wheel. The car epitomized Earl's brand of beefy, chromed-up streamlining, which gradually trickled down General Motors' line-up. (Courtesy General Motors Corporation)

In 1937, Earl's aesthetic streamlining was given a bold push forward by an experimental Buick designed for him by Olds studio head George Snyder. Known as the Y–Job, the two-passenger sports convertible dramatically extended Earl's longer-and-lower philosophy, measuring almost 20 feet in length and just 58 inches in height. The main forms were classic Earl – softly rounded, bulbous, and muscular. The rounded fuselage body lacked running boards and had suitcase fenders which were almost integral with the main body. The front fenders blended smoothly with the hood at the face, where the normally upright grille was replaced by a low, horizontal one. And there was lots of chrome trim to dazzle the eye. The only features that could pass for engineering innovations on the Y–Job were power appliances – the retractable headlights, windows, and convertible top – which expressed Earl's goal of removing from driving all the manual work that could spoil an automotive "vacation."[62]

The Buick Y–Job plotted Earl's styling course in the late 1930s and 1940s, as he rationed out in small doses the features of this futuristic prototype to GM production cars. The newest features were introduced in the corporation's top makes and then allowed to trickle down the automotive hierarchy. This policy was motivated by both marketing and cost concerns. The initially high cost of a new feature could be borne only by the high-priced cars. But as production experience and volume grew, unit costs fell, making it feasible to introduce the feature on lower-priced cars. However, trickle-down styling was probably motivated more by marketing than cost considerations. Cosmetic innovations were introduced in the higher-priced makes to differentiate them from the low-priced cars and establish their prestige. The lower-priced makes could then borrow this prestige simply by tacking on the style trinkets of their high-priced cousins. While the Chevies and Pontiacs puffed themselves up with last year's hand-me-down fashions from the Cadillacs and Buicks, these rich relations would maintain their distinction by adding new geegaws.[63]

The first production car to incorporate the features of the Y–Job was the 1938 Cadillac 60 Special, a smaller, personalized sports sedan designed by Bill Mitchell. The car was long and low, with a fuselage body and fulsome suitcase fenders. Although the car was a sedan, Earl and Mitchell gave it the sporty feel of a roadster by designing a light roof whose thin pillars and blind rear quarters made it look like a convertible top. Gradually the features of Earl's aesthetic streamlining trickled down the GM hierarchy of makes. By 1941 even the lowly Chevy was wide, long, and low, with a horizontal grille, no running boards, and headlights and taillights faired into fenders.

The entire industry followed the Earl idiom of streamlining by the early 1940s. As American involvement in the war loomed on the horizon and arms production began to drag the economy out of its Depressionary doldrums, long, low, earthbound airplanes seemed more than ever to be the wave of the future. The cars of Ford and, to a lesser extent, Chrysler adopted low, organic forms, blending all the previously projecting parts into one integral whole. And on these smoothly stream-lined forms grew more and more chrome appliqué, especially at Chrysler. Only the still separate fenders suggested that the auto was in actuality a mechanical assemblage of parts and not an organic creature of flight grounded by some evolutionary fate.[64]

STREAMLINING FOR WAR

America's war effort had ambivalent effects upon the struggle of competing visions of America's future. On the one hand, stepped-up wartime production, planned and regulated by the government, strengthened leftists and labor unions and kept alive their hopes for a popularly controlled and democratically planned economy. But in other ways the war strengthened the appeal of the streamlined consumerism advocated by corporate America. Increased employment and rising wages renewed consumers' faith in Fordist production. And Fordism's proficiency in producing spectacular weapons for the war became a source of national pride and patriotic fervor. These benefits of wartime Fordism began to overshadow the inhumanities of Depressionary Fordism in the popular mind.

In 1942 the American automobile industry ceased the production of streamlined dream machines and devoted its resources to the mass production of streamlined war machines. The industry's extensive involvement in aircraft production consolidated in the public's mind the association between automobiles and airplanes that stylists had initiated in the 1930s. But production of actual aircraft and other weapons resulted in the depletion and dispersion of these agents of aesthetic streamlining. Most stylists were shifted out of the automakers to other defense industries, and those who remained were assigned jobs designing weapons.

One popular wartime job for stylists was designing camouflage for military vehicles and weapons. In fact, Harley Earl tried to keep his entire Styling Section together by converting it exclusively to camou-flage work. Although Earl's scheme was unsuccessful, it is revealing that Earl viewed his stylists as experts in the art of camouflage, of superficial disguise. Through the clever manipulation of form and color, Earl and the profession he created assisted automakers in their market-place battles by obscuring from consumers' view the presence of a mass-produced machine. If Earl's dream makers could hide the ugliness of an entire factory for mass production, surely they could obscure the brutality of a few weapons of mass destruction in a war which was ultimately a struggle for mass-production markets.[65]

In their spare moments away from war work, however, Detroit's stylists continued to develop automotive dreams whose opiate effects on American consumers did not have to await actual production at war's end. In the diminished styling departments designers worked evenings and weekends developing streamlined designs that drew on the excite-ment and romance of the wartime aircraft they often worked on during regular hours. Many of their sketches and clay models imitated the monocoque shape of an aircraft fuselage, integrating the previously separate fenders into rounded bodies. On top of these fuselage bodies sat rounded tops with lots of curved glass, obviously imitating bubble-top airplane canopies.[66]

These aircraft-inspired designs were part of a larger cultural climate of consumer speculation that legitimated the American war effort. The American government emphasized that the country was at war to defend freedom and democracy, but most Americans had come to define these abstract principles in the concrete terms of consumerism. Freedom meant the ability to flee the heteronomy of Fordist production to the autonomy of domestic consumption. Democracy meant the ability to choose from a plethora of products within this insulated realm. Realizing these asso-ciations, American leaders also promoted the war as a battle for America's consumerist way of life. An ad for the 1945 Buick, for example, featured the brilliant car emerging from gloomy scenes of war, and stated that for many fighting men victory "will mean such pleasures as an open road, a glorious day – and a bright and lively Buick. . . . We aim to make those Buicks . . . [that] will fit the stirring pattern of the lively, exciting, forward-moving world so many millions have fought for." In the pages of popular magazines and in the speeches of politicians and industrialists, Americans were told that the end of hostilities would free the nation's mighty machinery of production for the manufacture of spectacular consumer goods based on wartime technology.[67]

The automobile was the keystone in this promised postwar utopia of consumer technology, and stylists were instrumental in putting these promises in palpable form. They speculated that postwar autos would incorporate all the advances of wartime aircraft, if not functionally at least aesthetically. Writing in the *New York Times*, Walter Dorwin Teague predicted that the application of aviation technology to autos would produce not only light, fuel-efficient cars but also hybrid auto-airplanes affordable by most Americans. *Collier's* magazine printed futuristic drawings from GM's Advanced Design Studio depicting airplane-like autos that were steered by radar and powered by atomic fuel. In a *Saturday Evening Post* article entitled "Your car after the war," Harley Earl predicted low, racy cars with the aerodynamic lines and curved windshields of airplanes.[68]

Despite these fantastic predictions about engineering advances, auto stylists characteristically borrowed the prestige and romance of wartime airplanes for peacetime cars by imitating their superficial forms. And one propitious event that would shape this aesthetic direction took place shortly before America entered the war. In 1941 Harley Earl and some of his stylists were allowed to view the Air Force's new P–38 Lightning pursuit plane. Although security restrictions prevented them from standing closer than 30 feet, this was close enough for them to fall in love with the look of the plane's twin tail booms, each with a vertical stabilizer. Bill Mitchell, head of the Cadillac studio at the time, recalled: "We all admired the P–38's streamlining and individuality in design, with its twin fuselage and twin tail fins." When the stylists got back to the studios, Earl put them to work adapting its features to automobiles, with one of the resulting designs incorporating the fins on the rear fenders. Thus, the air war of the 1940s inspired what would become the fin wars of the 1950s – the bizarre contest of stylists to outdo each other in the application of superficial aviation clichés to postwar dream machines.[69]

Chapter 6

1950s' fins and the triumph of fantastic styling

Sometime late in 1947, an agitated Harley Earl stormed into the Cadillac styling studio, where he confronted the object of his rage – the full-size clay model of the 1949 Cadillac. At the end of both rear fenders were little bumps of sheet metal that incorporated the taillights. Frank Hershey had put these tail fins on the 1948 Caddy at the behest of Earl, who had stolen this aeronautic cliché from the P–38 Lightning pursuit plane. But somehow these infatuating little symbols of aviation had been transformed in Earl's eyes into annoyances of the first order.

Earl screamed at Hershey, who was working on the 1949 model: "Take those damned fins off the back. Nobody likes them. They don't belong on a Cadillac." Cadillac executives had received several complaints from dealers that neither they nor their customers liked the fins. So Earl, ever sensitive to the slightest signals of the marketplace, quickly reversed himself, ordering the fins off the new model. Hershey, however, decided to let his boss cool off and think about this enraged decision. Some days later Earl came roaring back into the Cadillac studio, asking "Did you take the fins off?" When Hershey replied he had not, Earl was relieved. "Oh, thank God! The public loves them. Leave them alone. Don't touch them." Thanks to Earl's aesthetic about-face, the infant fin survived the tribulations of its first year and by 1959 had grown to fantastic heights and spread to all American automobiles.[1]

This incident illustrates the aesthetic uncertainty of American automobile styling at the dawn of the postwar era. The industry's preeminent pulse-reader, Harley Earl, knew where he wanted to take auto styling – toward long, low, cliché-ridden dream machines that spoke more of stratospheric travel than mundane transportation. But he seemed uncertain whether the consuming public would follow him. Would the return of peace and prosperity for the first time in seventeen years find most Americans rushing to realize the dreams of consumerism begun in the 1920s? Or would they seek to realize the vision of a collectively and democratically regulated economy that emerged in the Depression and grew in wartime cooperation? In 1947 the answers to these questions were still being forged by postwar struggles, but the battle was already shifting to the forces of consumerist containment.

AMERICA, 1946–1959: CONFLICT, CONSUMERISM, COLD WAR, ANXIETY

The end of the war brought a political thaw that resurrected the un-resolved Depression-era opposition between advocates of an unregu-lated, consumerist capitalism and a publicly planned and regulated economy.[2] Labor quickly let its voice be heard, launching the largest strike wave in the country's history. The nearly 5 million workers who struck in the first year of peace demanded not only wage increases but also continuation of the political and shop-floor controls they exercised over production during the war. Ultimately, however, militant workers were forced to drop progressive demands and settle for simple wage increases. The 1948 election of the stick-wielding Truman over the third-party challenge of New Dealer Henry Wallace, who was supported by labor's left wing, signaled the end of incipient government planning and a return to unfettered corporate capitalism.

The corporate containment of the threatening ambitions of labor was effected largely by the enticements of consumerism. Workers in America's large corporations surrendered any claims to controlling their own economic activity in exchange for a bigger piece of the corporate-controlled pie, institutionalized in contractual provisions for cost-of-living increases and wage hikes tied to economic growth. This consumerist diversion of workers' postwar desires required not only the state's coercive labor laws, like Taft–Hartley, but also its benevolent budgetary policies. Private con-sumption, especially of the all-important automobile and detached, single-family home, required an infrastructure of public goods and services. To facilitate home ownership, the federal government underwrote the mort-gage market with Federal Housing Administration mortgage insurance and Veteran's Administration mortgage guarantees. To further the auto-mobilization of America, it financed the construction of a vast network of interstate highways beginning in 1956, with the passage of the Interstate Highway Act. These public subsidies for private consumption were feebly justified as national defense measures, necessary to transport and disperse a population under threat of attack by America's emerging archenemy, Soviet communism.

However erroneous, this national-defense justification reveals the propensity of Americans during this period to conflate consumerism and Cold War ideology. They had long been conditioned to associate the strength of American capitalism with its technology, which they believed rendered the United States impervious to attack. The country had just triumphed in one war due largely to its ability to produce masses of destructive weapons. As the international belligerents quickly re-arranged themselves for the new Cold War against communism, Americans assured themselves of success due to their superiority over the enemy in not merely military but also consumerist technology. Because American rights and freedoms had now been successfully confined to consumerism, the ideology of communism was held to be hopelessly unappealing to Americans, who could hardly be expected to surrender the "freedom" to choose among a tantalizing diversity of competing commodities for the coercion of a planned economy and its communist queues to purchase drab, standardized goods.

This equation of consumer technology with national superiority was dramatized for the nation in the infamous "kitchen debate" between Cold Warrior Richard Nixon and communist chief Krushchev. In the summer of 1959, when the United States and the former Soviet Union exchanged exhibitions of goods, Vice-president Nixon delivered the opening speech at the American exhibition in Moscow, claiming that the American system was superior due to the number and variety of its consumer goods. Later in an impromtu debate in the kitchen exhibit, Nixon defended the variety of available washing machines against Krushchev's claim that one kind was enough. He asserted an equation close to the heart of most Americans – freedom was consumption, and the best defense against communism was an economic system that gave consumers the freedom to choose among a dizzying variety of super-ficially differentiated washing machines.[3]

Due to heavy public subsidies, a suburban utopia of privatized con-sumption became available to the privileged core of American workers after the war. Large-scale, mass-produced housing developments like Levittown, New Jersey sprouted on the outskirts of many American cities, attracting some 30 million new suburbanites between 1945 and 1960. Many of these were working-class refugees from urban congestion. And although suburbanized workers did not lose all notions of class distinction on the job, at home they began to define themselves as part of the middle majority of Americans, sharing in the superficial equality of America's homogenized market of consumer goods. Mass consumption in leisure blurred and ulti-mately obscured the class distinctions of work. And within the sprawling middle-American community of consumption, there was sufficient choice of superficially differentiated goods to convey a sense of individuality within the mainstream.[4]

But one did not have to dig far beneath the superficial appearance of consumer contentment to unearth an uneasiness that could not be consumed away. This was the age not only of limitless consumption but also of anxiety and guilt, and the two were causally linked. As Freud wrote in the early 1930s, guilt and anxiety are the inevitable concomitants of "civilization," that is, the society of Western capitalism. The basic desires of the human organism are diverted into other channels by society's restraints, but because they do not achieve true satisfaction, their relentless energy remains. Substitute satisfactions are repeated compulsively without dissipating the drive's impulse, which must find release in outward aggression against the source of denial or inward aggression against the ego, that is, guilt. So it was, it seems, with the desires that Americans displaced into suburban consumption. Blocked in their true realization, American desires for autonomy and community were channeled into privatized, reified commodity consumption. And because such substitutes were inherently unsatisfying, they were compulsively repeated in a frenzy of futile and limitless consumption. Some of the unexpended energy of displaced desires inevitably found its way into the seamy side of the psyche, in the forms of anxiety, guilt, and aggression.[5]

The age of anxiety was uncovered by both elite and mass culture during the 1950s. Despite their rise to respectability and relative affluence, the working-class wives interviewed by sociologist Lee Rainwater expressed a boredom with their daily lives and an anxiety and uncertainty about the future. They found escape in wishfulness and religion. Popular films and plays like those of Arthur Miller and Alfred Hitchcock revealed despair, decay, and violence just behind the privatized doors of suburban pseudocastles. Part of the anxiety of the period was precipitated by a fear of losing one's identity in faceless crowds of consumers. Concerns about overconformity and the rise of a mass society were expressed in best-selling books like David Riesman's *Lonely Crowd* and William H. Whyte's *Organization Man*. In reaction to the fear of conformity, popular movies and books of the decade often celebrated the deviants, rebels, and misfits, as in James Dean's *Rebel Without A Cause*.

By the end of the decade the hitherto nameless forces that threatened American individuality were popularly identified as the merchandisers of the consumer utopia themselves. Vance Packard's best-selling *Hidden Persuaders* of 1957 pointed the finger firmly at the sales departments and advertisers, who used psychology to penetrate consumers' souls and turn their deepest desires against them. These paranoid fears of manipulation and subordination were largely the product of psychological projection, by which Americans redirected their self-aggression for settling for superficial consumer indulgences to an external enemy. As long as the criticism of America was confined to the sphere of consumption and did not trace its roots back to the source of perverted consumerism in capitalist production, solutions for these anxieties of the age would be sought in rebellions of style and taste alone.[6]

The decade's ill-defined guilt and aggression were brought into focus in the fall of 1957 by events that raised national doubts about the nature of America's consumerism. First, the economic recession interrupted the postwar economic expansion, raising doubts about the dream of unlimited economic growth. Second, on October 4 the former Soviet Union launched its first Sputnik satellite, beating the United States into space and raising deep doubts about America's consumption-based society. The Sputnik was immediately interpreted as a threat to America's military superiority, for it was deployed by an intercontinental ballistic missile more powerful than any yet developed by the United States. But when it exposed the inferiority of America's machines of destruction, by inference Sputnik also cast doubt upon the nation's machinery of consumption, which had been ideologically associated with military technology since the war. Many commentators questioned the superficiality of America's consumer goods and the national priority on them. *Life* editors scolded Americans for being undisciplined and placing luxury before liberty. "We should each decide what we really want most in the world. . . . A Cadillac? A color television? Lower income taxes? – Or to live in freedom?" Already anxious about overindulgence, America's consumers now had a focus for their guilt – America's lagging defenses.[7]

Americans in the late 1950s began to channel their consumer guilt away from domestic targets and toward an external enemy, chastening themselves for a space race with the Soviets. Not only did this re-channeling of discontent protect the Fordist system, but it also offered Americans the social purpose which individualized consumption could not. The scope of this purpose was extremely limited, as was most Americans' participation in its achievement. But with it John Kennedy and others engineered an ideology to mobilize the internalized aggres-sion of America's consumer society toward an external enemy and consequently justify imperialist forays to maintain the stranglehold on the world's resources that Fordism demanded.[8]

THE POSTWAR AUTOMOBILE MARKET: STYLING, OLIGOPOLY, BEAN COUNTERS

During this decade the American automobile was at the center of this postwar system of consumerist containment and Cold War ideology. The explosion of suburbanized consumption that contained the larger ambitions of working Americans depended on expanded automobility, not only for physical transportion to suburbia but also for cultural insulation and gratification within it. During the decade, the automobile industry blazed a path of fantastic, escapist consumption that brought to fruition the trends in automobile styling set in motion back in the 1920s.

This heyday of automobile styling did not begin immediately after the war. In the first few years of peace the Big Three took advantage of an unprecedented seller's market to offer merely warmed-over versions of prewar models, leaving new model production to the desperate independents. But by 1949 the leisurely efforts of the automotive giants finally resulted in their first new postwar models. This flood of new cars satisfied the backlog of demand, and the seller's market turned into a highly competitive buyer's market by 1953. And the weapon automakers chose for the new competitive struggle was a familiar one – styling.[9]

Confronting a market in which unit demand was falling but discretionary income was rising, the industry's giants embarked on a two-pronged offensive to capture a larger share of the consumer's income. First, they decided that if they could not sell more cars, they would "sell more car per car," that is, load up each car with an array of accessories that raised the unit price. Second, the major manufacturers sought to accelerate market turnover, stimulating consumers to buy a new car more often. To accomplish both prongs of this assault the automakers turned to their shock troops in the styling departments. Instead of offering risky and expensive engineering innovations, the Big Three merely offered consumers bigger and more frequent doses of superficial style changes. In the mid-1950s, the usual 3-year interval between major body changes was shortened to two on many models, and off-year face-lifts became more drastic. And all models, even the low-priced ones, were loaded down with superficial luxuries and conveniences that were previously confined to the top-of-the-line luxury makes. The intent of most of these accessories, like automatic transmissions and power windows, was the insulation of the driver from the physical labor and sensations of automobile operation. After a day of drudgery in the Fordized factory or office, no one wanted to hop into his or her escape express to suburbia only to be forced to labor at another recalcitrant machine.[10]

This postwar market offensive resulted in unprecedented power and influence for the stylists of the major manufacturers. In the early 1950s the Big Three beefed up their war-depleted styling staffs with huge infusions of personnel and resources, and gave them more freedom of design than they had ever dreamed of. One consequence of this unilateral focus on styling in postwar automobile competition was the consolidation of automotive oligopoly. Style changes were enormously expensive – a major body change could cost $200 million, while an off-year face-lift could run up a $50-million bill. So when the Big Three accelerated the style cycle in the 1950s, the low-volume, low-profit independents could not compete and were consequently devastated. By 1955 iron-clad oligopoly had descended on automotive America, with the Big Three dominating 94 percent of the market. Style was both the cause and consequence of oligopoly in the industry. The costs of style changes proved prohibitive for any but the biggest producers, but the concentration of business by the giants also ensured that style would remain the preferred manner of winning market share. The lack of competition removed the pressure to lower prices, and attracting consumers through technological innovation was too expensive for the big producers with large investments in fixed capital.[11]

So in the increasingly concentrated auto industry of postwar America, consumers got the same old technology wrapped in dazzling and quickly changing packages which sold for ever-escalating prices, while the Big Three got soaring returns on their investments. The entire system of shared monopoly was regulated by the biggest of the big, General Motors, which enjoyed a 50 percent market share. When GM set its car prices, the other two-thirds of the Big Three dutifully fell in line. GM officials shamelessly admitted before Congress that they determined their industry-leading prices by first deciding how much money they wanted to make and then pricing cars accordingly. Consequently, the corporation's average annual return on net worth between 1946 and 1967 was 21 percent, far above the 9 percent return of the average American manufacturing company.[12]

The increasing importance of style as a sales stimulus and competitive tool in the postwar industry swept into power not only the stylists, who appended the deceptively pretty surfaces, but also the finance men, who calculated the dividends of deception. In this oligopoly, industry executives needed no longer to display leadership in production and product technology but merely an ability to control costs and calculate the prices of products from a desired profit and a projected volume. So increasingly it was the accountants or bean counters who ran the Big Three, men whose veins ran not hot with gasoline but cold with cash.

The trend toward control by finance men was initiated in the 1920s by GM's Alfred Sloan, who introduced financial controls to govern his sprawling automotive empire. But Sloan was also a trained engineer with extensive knowledge of manufacturing operations. As long as he was at the helm, the financial obsession was tempered with automotive understanding. But this compromise came unstuck when Sloan retired as chairman of the board in 1956 and left a string of accountants to succeed him. A similar trend toward financial control was evident at Ford and Chrysler. When Henry Ford II took over as head of his grandfather's disorganized empire in 1945, he hired as his executive vice-president a GM accountant, Ernie Breech. And to assist Breech in the financial regime, he also hired eight experts from the Air Force's Office of Statistical Control, known as the "Whiz Kids." Chrysler trailed the other big automakers in instituting bean-counter control, retaining through the 1950s engineers as top executives and thus a reputation for technological innovation. But by the late 1950s poor sales forced Chrysler to place greater emphasis on styling, which brought to power the accountants, beginning with Lynn Townsend in 1961.[13]

THE ORGANIZATIONAL TRIUMPH OF STYLING

As styling emerged in the postwar industry as the preeminent competitive tool, the Big Three scrambled to rapidly rebuild their styling departments, which had been depleted and dispersed by the war. The task was less formidable at GM, which had a large and powerful organization of stylists before the war. But building a styling organization was more difficult at Ford and Chrysler, which had entered the war with small staffs still subordinated to powerful engineers. For them, getting into the styling game required a reorganization just short of a revolution.

Ford's lesser copy of GM styling

As soon as Henry Ford II took over the scattered disarray of Ford Motor Company, he set his small, subordinated group of stylists to work on a car to save the company. In 1945 Bob Gregorie's team showed him and Ernie Breech their proposal for the all-new 1949 Ford, a model that continued the big, bulbous aesthetic they developed during the war. But Breech had his doubts about the car, so he asked his friend George Walker, an independent industrial designer, to view the model. When

Walker said that the company would go broke with the car and that he could do better, Breech and Ford decided to hire him as an outside consultant and pit his designers against Gregorie's in-house group. When both models were unveiled at a competitive showing late in 1946, Ford executives chose Walker's, and Gregorie quit in a huff.[14]

The reason for stimulating this styling rivalry went beyond getting the best car. Because the competition gave Ford managers a number of options from which to select, it also gave them power over the increasingly important stylists. This divide-and-conquer strategy proved so useful that Ford managers institutionalized it in 1947. Walker and his team were retained as outside consultants housed in Ford buildings, duplicating and competing with Ford's in-house styling staff, which was rebuilt with an infusion of personnel. Breech accomplished the latter by raiding the styling staff of his former employer, GM. These GM transplants brought with them Earl's pioneering organizational and aesthetic techniques, but not Earl's power. Breech kept the enlarged Ford Styling Office firmly subordinated to the Engineering Department and divided by competition. As one former Ford designer recalled, Ford managers "encouraged sort of a dog-eat-dog thing, pitting studio against studio, pitting designer against designer, to the point that even some designers would sabotage competitors' designs."[15]

By 1955, however, even the obstinate old-timers realized that the division and subordination of styling at Ford was hurting the company. Top Ford executives began to understand that to compete in the ever-accelerating race for novelty and beauty, stylists had to be given more independence and freedom. One particular incidence seems to have dramatized this requirement. After Walker's model for the 1955 Ford was approved by top executives, Ford engineers altered it, as was their custom, to shave costs and eliminate production difficulties. This time, however, the alterations were near disastrous, for in this era of novelty, the 1955 Ford appeared ominously similar to the previous year's models. Walker's strong objections were heeded by top managers, resulting in his appointment as vice-president in charge of styling on May 2, 1955. On this occasion, Henry Ford II told Walker: "George, I want you to run this styling like your own business. And don't you let anybody ever tell you what to do, even me!"[16]

Elevating Walker to the rank of vice-president increased both the economic and symbolic capital of stylists at Ford, sending a signal both to the auto-buying public and to Ford employees that the corporation was serious about style. The Ford Styling Office was given a new, $11.5 million styling center, in which Walker, obviously imitating GM, created four production studios and an advanced studio. The styling staff grew to 650 by 1957, and salaries were increased to attract and retain personnel. Recalling the effects of these drastic changes, one Ford stylist, John Najjar, stated: "Here were five separate studios, all geared up to go. The designer had come into his own. The morale was high."[17]

George Walker ruled his new styling domain in the same flamboyant, charismatic manner that characterized the early days of Earl's reign at GM. The son of an Erie Railroad conductor and a former professional football player, he came from a working-class background which imbued him with the same physical, masculine subculture shared by the automotive engineers. Although trained in art, Walker, like Earl, was a working-class kid at heart and knew how to relate to the tough men who dominated engineering. As he recalled: "I got inside of them [the engineers], but the other designers didn't, and talked their language and talked styling, talked football, talked baseball – everything."[18]

Like Earl, Walker ruled through personal friendships and charismatic encounters. He hired trusted friends and long-time employees, Elwood Engel and Joe Oros, to help manage the office. And to control others outside his inner circle, Walker staged attention-grabbing encounters in a flamboyant personal style. As he stated, "a stylist has got to show style in his cars, in his home, his clothes and his person." His ostentatious wardrobe of forty pairs of shoes and seventy suits was an important part of his self-presentation, as was his $50,000 office, replete with sumptuous leather couches, a jungle of tropical plants, and a black lambskin carpet.

Although devoid of Earl's outbursts of temper, Walker's charismatic rule at Ford was not without its ugly side. He reportedly used his personal power to sexually harass women employees, hiring and retaining only those who yielded to his sexual advances. Such sexual licentiousness seems to have been common among stylists, perhaps to publicly testify to the masculinity of their profession and head off suspicions of homosexuality. But Walker seems to have exercised a less coercive hand over the men. He schmoozed and ingratiated himself to his stylists in order to, as *Time* put it, "keep his temperamental underlings happy." And he gave his underlings more creative license than Earl, merely making suggestions and not dictating a unilateral aesthetic direction.[19]

Walker's styling organization also differed from Earl's in having less corporate authority. Earl entrenched the power of his department in the foundation of the young bureaucracy at GM, strategically situating it at the coordinating hub of all decisions about new models, annual changes, line-ups, and interchangeability. But by the time Ford stylists gained greater power in the mid-1950s, control of these important functions had been implanted in a separate staff department dominated by marketing experts, Product Planning. This office was responsible for the development of new product programs. And although they received data and advice from the styling, marketing, and engineering departments, product planners formulated these into a definitive "package," specifying the car's type, price, dimensions, and engineering. Walker's Styling Office merely designed the external appearance of the approved package. As one Ford stylist stated of his boss, George Walker "did not know interchangeability, he did not know production figures . . . all he was interested in is having a shape on the vehicle." Even the appearance of the car was subject to the approval of divisional managers and product planners, who often demanded radical changes in the full-scale models. Consequently, Ford stylists usually presented several partially developed models among which managers chose, in stark contrast to Earl's presentation of one fully developed model which managers were forced to take or leave. So although the Ford Styling Office of the mid-1950s was formally modeled on the GM Styling Staff, its power paled in comparison to the original.[20]

Chrysler styling trails the climb to power

The stylists at the Chrysler Corporation also experienced a rapid ascent in organizational independence and power during the 1950s, but one that left them short of the height reached not only by GM's stylists but also by Ford's. The Chrysler Art and Color Department entered the postwar era still under the domination of the corporation's powerful engineers, who remained wedded to the notion that automobiles were bought mainly for efficient, comfortable transportation. In a 1948 article, *Collier's* quoted Chrysler president K.T. Keller as stating: "The buyer is proud of his car's symphony of line. . . . But he bought the car to ride in, and his satisfaction in the product depends on whether or not it is pleasant to sit in while it is moving." Keller and his engineers unilaterally shaped Chrysler's postwar cars to their outmoded utilitarian ethos, offering consumers high, upright, square boxes that looked more like tanks than the streamlined torpedos that consumers wanted. Nevertheless, they sold well in the immediate postwar years due to the backlog of consumer demand, convincing executives that their approach was correct. So in the early 1950s Chrysler put its money into plant modernization and engineering innovation, not styling. But in 1952, when the market for cars turned more competitive, Chrysler's sales fell behind Ford's for the first time since 1935. Reading the handwriting on the wall, top executives surrendered their utilitarian philosophy and turned to the stylists for salvation.[21]

Late in 1952 Chrysler's new president, Tex Colbert, gave the job of designing the corporation's new 1955 car line-up to stylist Virgil Exner. On the strength of his work, Exner was appointed director of styling in 1953 and given more design discretion, although the Engineering Division still exercised ultimate control of design. Exner's modern-appearing "Forward Look" cars of 1955 were an immediate success, doubling the previous year's sales and winning even greater independence for Chrysler stylists. By 1957 Chrysler styling was not only in the style race but leading it, forcing even Harley Earl to play catch-up.[22]

Virgil Exner's success was not fortuitous, for he was an extremely talented, experienced designer who had trained with the best. He majored in art at Notre Dame and in the late 1920s joined Earl's Art and Color Department, where he rose rapidly to head the Pontiac studio from 1934 to 1938. He then joined Raymond Loewy's firm as a designer for its major client, Studebaker. But a rift with Loewy in 1949 sent him to Chrysler as head of its advanced styling studio. There Exner produced a series of show cars that were so favorably received at auto shows that when Chrysler decided to breathe new life into its moribund styling, he was the obvious choice. Like Walker at Ford, Exner used GM Styling as a model for his revived department, reproducing its centralized body development studio and the series of divisional studios. And the Chrysler organization was also held together by the dominant personality of its head. Virgil Exner was a flashy, flamboyant leader, whose spectacular presence led his underlings to dub him the "chrome-plated man." His silver-gray silk suits shone like the decorative metal, and, combined with his silver-white hair and deep tan, made a very impressive image indeed.[23]

Yet several characteristics set Exner apart from his counterparts at GM and Ford and may have prevented him from achieving their level of influence. First, unlike either Walker or Earl, Exner was a real designer, whose hands-on involvement in the daily details of design may have detracted from the organizational politicking necessary to secure more power for stylists. Second, by temperament the Chrysler styling chief was more remote and less personable, which may have impeded the creation of the personal loyalties necessary to unify his underlings and cajole his superiors. Third, and finally, he seemed more intellectual than the other styling chiefs. In a profession which eschewed theory, Exner was all too ready to offer abstract explanations for his designs, regularly publishing his ideas in industry journals. This tendency to theorize may have prevented him from gaining influence over the industry's thoroughly practical engineers.[24]

For these reasons, in addition to the entrenched power of Chrysler engineers, Exner gained less independence for stylists than did Earl or Walker. Although he was officially promoted to the rank of corporate vice-president in 1957, Exner still reported to the chief engineer, whose cooperation he needed to realize his pioneering designs. During the mid-1950s, when Chrysler styling rode a wave of success, the engineers seemed willing to go along. But when consumers began to sour on Exner's designs, this cooperation evaporated, and Chrysler engineering reverted to its dictatorial ways.[25]

GM styling's struggle for maturity

During the 1950s the GM Styling Staff blazed a path to new heights of corporate power, but not without some delays and detours. GM's styling group was being transformed from a personalistic organization dominated by a single, charismatic head into an impersonal, rule-governed bureaucracy. And as Max Weber recognized, the routinization of charisma is often a painful process. Immediately after the war, Harley Earl began to reassemble the talented styling team that had been dispersed and depleted. With aggressive recruiting and training policies, he amassed a force of some 1,200 people by 1956. This expanded staff was necessitated not only by the increasing scale of tasks but also by their enlarged scope, now encompassing the design of GM's nonautomotive products.

By the early 1950s the Styling Staff's old quarters in the Research Annex Building B were bursting at the seams, so Earl began to press Sloan for a new, expanded facility at a suburban site. According to Bill Mitchell, Earl's purpose was to achieve not merely more space but also more independence by putting greater distance between his stylists and the divisional managers at corporate headquarters. By 1956 Earl's dream was realized in the $125 million Technical Center in suburban Warren, Michigan, a facility that housed not only styling but GM's other technical staffs as well. The campuslike atmosphere of the facility, with its artificial lake and expansive lawns, was far removed from the cost-cutting exigencies of the corporation's financial and manufacturing centers, inspiring stylists in the creation of spectacular autos that obscured the real capitalist logic of rationalization and domination.[26]

The costly Tech Center was testimony to the importance of Earl's department in the 1950s. During this decade, as never before, styling was king at GM. Earl got whatever resources he wanted and built whatever he pleased. Used to working within the limitations of manu- facturing costs and engineering feasibility, GM stylists were giddy with their new-found freedom. As one described this period: "There were these huge cars, this freedom of space, and a wonderful, naive sense of doing anything you wanted."[27]

During the 1950s, the planning of GM products fell largely into the hands of Earl's Styling Staff. The statistical models of market researchers were pushed aside in favor of stylists' intuitive feel for the consumer's psyche. In consultation with divisional managers, stylists developed the packages and styling concepts for new cars. After Earl obtained the largely perfunctory approval of the Engineering Policy Group, the Styling Staff took over the project and required no further approval until presentation of the final model. During the 1950s, GM stylists often by-passed even this simple process, secretly preparing full- scale models without approval. Then Earl sprung the dramatic models on unsuspecting executives, who often found the three-dimensional dream machines more irresistible than paper programs. And if execu- tives failed to fall under their charms, the provocative models were often placed in automobile shows to whip up public support for production.[28]

Unlike those at Ford, the marketing and sales staffs at GM had little influence over design during this decade. And the once-powerful engineers also played a minimal role. During the 1950s Earl dominated the engineers as never before, demanding that they shape automotive technology to conform to the fantastic visions of the stylists' dream world. In a 1954 article even the chief engineer of the Cadillac Division admitted that: "Styling dictates, to some extent, what engineering must do." Engineers were limited largely to after-the-fact technical contortions to turn whatever the stylists had dreamed up into a functional automobile.[29]

Ironically, however, just as his Styling Staff achieved organizational supremacy at GM, Harley Earl's personal dominance as its aesthetic leader began to decline. By the mid-1950s, he had pushed his auto-as- entertainment aesthetic to its limits, and did not know where to go from there. The younger stylists, most of whom had received formal training, preferred clean forms over chrome encrustation, and light and subtle lines over Earl's rounded, heavy-looking cars. Earl's aesthetic was the product of an earlier era, when the stylist's task was to make the small, mass-produced cars emulate the size and substance of the craft-built classics. But in the 1950s, when even the cheapest cars were puffing themselves up with overbearing self-importance, this aesthetic was no longer distinctive. The younger stylists were learning to distinguish automobiles with subtler nuances of form, not obvious tricks of size and ornamentation.[30]

This generational revolt brewing inside GM broke out in the fall of 1956, precipitated by the introduction of Virgil Exner's 1957 Chrysler models. When someone rushed into the styling studios to report the news of Exner's revolutionary cars, a group of GM stylists drove to a nearby Chrysler assembly plant to sneek a peek. As David Holls, a Cadillac designer, recalls: "these cars had absolutely razor-thin roofs and wedge-shaped bodies, and it was just absolutely unbelievable! We all went back and said, 'My God, they blew us out of the tub.' And here [at GM] were these ugly, heavy, old-fashioned looking things." Without authorization from Earl, who was on vacation, the young rebels scrapped their current designs and started new ones. Realizing that he had lost his touch, Earl let the new designs go into production when he returned. After this he withdrew from his active role in design, ceding more influence to his second in command, Bill Mitchell. Earl's mandatory retirement at sixty-five on December 1, 1958 and the appointment of Mitchell to succeed him, at his suggestion, made official his relinquishment of aesthetic leadership to the younger generation.[31]

In selecting Bill Mitchell as his successor, Harley Earl chose a man cut from the same cloth as him. Having served under Earl for twenty-three years, Mitchell had thoroughly absorbed his principles of aesthetics and organization and was determined to preserve them. Like Earl, he wielded personalistic power cultivated through dramatic encounters and personal ties. But in his reign at the Styling Staff, Mitchell drew on a source of power initially unavailable to Earl – the rules and procedures of the corporate bureaucracy. The power of the GM Styling Staff no longer depended on the charisma and connections of its head but was now invested in rule-governed positions and policies. Thanks to Earl's struggles, the styling chief was a vice-president of the corporation, with an official position on some of its most powerful standing committees. And the power of stylists within the corporation was institutionalized in GM's written policies on new model development, car line-ups, and planned obsolescence. Mitchell's personal ties and dramatics were thus more of a supplement to than the foundation of his rule.

Earl also institutionalized control of the Styling Staff in a centralized bureaucracy governed by rules and procedures. At the top, monopolizing decision-making power, was the vice-president, who alone had access to all information. He and his Design Committee chose from the options developed by designers, who were organizationally and physically isolated in locked studios. To enforce his decisions, the styling chief relied increasingly on a routinized career hierarchy and less on personal favors and punishments. And the aesthetic standards upon which stylists were judged were also routinized. Earl translated his imprecise sense of style into rules that could be objectively taught and enforced, like those governing highlights, chrome reflection, and gradual yearly changes.

Earl's bureaucratic system regularized car design, rendering the individual visionary at the top largely but not wholly obsolete. The programs of planned obsolescence and model differentiation still required a head that could invent or inspire new, distinctive designs. It was this unroutinized, unstandardized creation of automotive difference that Earl could no longer deliver. So when a new aesthetic vision came from outside GM in the form of Exner's cars, Earl was pushed aside in favor of a new generation of leadership.

THE AESTHETICS OF THE POSTWAR DREAM MACHINES

In this postwar era, the organizational dominance of the stylists combined with the consumerist channeling of American desires to produce an unprecedented period of fantastic automotive excesses. Through the wildly contorted sheet metal of their automobiles consumers dreamed the fulfillment of their desires for freedom, power, and distinction as they rushed frantically between their suburban retreats of consumption and their urban centers of alienated production. And these dream machines often assumed horrific, nightmarish forms that were almost as terrifying as delightful, revealing that all was not well in the fantasy world of American consumers.

The realization of automotive reification

Before automobile stylists could paint these metal fantasies of power and autonomy, they first had to create a seamless sheet-metal canvas that completely obscured its social origins in fragmented, class-divided factories. Before the 1950s stylists had been only partially successful in achieving this long-held goal, for mass-produced cars still appeared as mechanical assemblages of separate parts. But the first new postwar cars eliminated the last traces of this assembled, mechanical appearance by incorporating all the fragments into one unified, organic shape. Resembling the monocoque shells of sleek wartime airplanes, they had rounded, curving forms that incorporated hood, fenders, body, and top into one smooth shape. These reified forms appeared first on the products of the independent automakers like Kaiser–Frazer and Hudson, both of which produced 1947 models with fenders flushed with the main body. Major producers like Packard and Mercury introduced cars with such "slab sides" in 1948 and 1949, respectively.[32]

Some critics, however, thought that these first round, bulging cars looked heavy, resembling inverted bathtubs more than airplanes and sending stylists in search of alternative solutions to integration. Raymond Loewy's firm designed a 1947 Studebaker that was more succesful in capturing the light, poised look of flight on an enclosed body. Styled by Virgil Exner, the Champion model was long and low, like the other postwar cars, but the front and rear ends were tapered, lightening its appearance. And the monotony of the slab sides was relieved by the slight separation of the rear fender. George Walker's 1949 Ford also attempted to lighten the envelope body. Although smooth and rounded, it had tighter, flatter lines that were more reminiscent of aircraft, as were the ornamental incidentals like the prop-spinner grille.

Not merely the appearance but also the mechanicals of the 1949 Ford offered drivers escape from the unpleasant reminders of Fordist labor. The new 3-speed transmission had short gearing that made top gear adequate for nearly all purposes, since Americans did not want to work at gear shifting in their leisure time. Neither did they want to be subjected to a mechanical jolting reminiscent of Fordist production. So Ford engineers gave their car the independent front suspension by coil springs already used by Chevrolet and Plymouth, which produced poor handling but also the marshmallow-soft ride that Americans were coming to expect from their escape machines. Postwar cars like the Ford were losing not only their mechanical look but also their mechanical feel, insulating their drivers' compensatory leisure lives from their degrading work lives.[33]

The 1949 Ford was a big success, selling over a million units and beating out Chevrolet in model-year production. But subsequent sales revealed two shortcomings of the car relative to emerging style trends. The first was its size, which was shorter and narrower than Ford's 1948 model. As America entered the exuberant postwar expansion of the 1950s, consumers demanded big, substantial cars, although not ones that looked tubby and heavy. The second weakness was the car's clean, unadorned lines, which were almost totally devoid of ornamentation. This plain-Jane car gave consumer spectators almost nothing to hold their visual interest, but confronted them with monotonous expanses of uninterrupted sheet metal. Their visual trip around the car was unbroken but unentertaining, like a flawless vacation to a destination where there is nothing to see or do. Harley Earl understood that the designer had to give consumers some entertainment to hold their interest and relieve the monotony of their daily lives. His philosophy of design as an entertaining vacation blossomed and grew to outrageous extremes during the 1950s.[34]

Bigness and power: the psycho-economy of size

Earl's aesthetic preference for longer, lower, and wider cars was also realized in the 1950s, which saw automobiles grow rapidly not only in external dimensions but also in internal horsepower. This growth occurred disproportionately among the cheaper cars, as buyers of bottom-of-the-line models demanded the size and power that had once been the exclusive prerogatives of the luxury class. And they wanted all the comforts and accessories generally found on the latter. So the automakers' strategy of selling more car per car found enthusiastic consumer endorsement.

Since their entrance into the consumer society, America's working people had demanded cars that aped the size, power, and look of those driven by their bosses. But the conditions of postwar America made this demand stronger than ever before. Expanding automation during this decade eroded further the skills by which people judged the quality of consumer products and brought easily discernable quantity to the fore as the central standard of judgment. Fordist mass production eroded not only the perception but also the existence of quality differences in automobiles. As the market for the craft-built luxury cars declined during the Depression and on into the postwar period, their manu-facturers moved downscale, adopting mass-production methods and components. The only remaining way for automakers to distinguish their lines was by quantity – more expanse, horsepower, and accessories.

Further, bigger, gadgety consumer goods like cars were about the only outlet left for American aspirations after the war. Alternative avenues to a better life like progressive politics and workplace control seemed closed off permanently, and the only road on which most Americans were advancing was income. So to convince themselves that they were in fact "richer" and "living better" than ever before, Americans went on a spending spree, and the commodity they demanded most as a symbol of success was the big automobile. As George Walker told *Popular Mechanics*: "The American public is aggressive, it's moving upward all the time . . . and that means bigness. When the American workingman gets a little money he wants a bigger house and he wants a bigger car."[35]

Some commentators interpreted the demand for big cars, particularly among the working class, as competitive emulation – people were trying to look better than others by adopting the qualities of higher-class autos. But such arguments miss a more subtle use of goods as symbols. While working Americans used cars as status symbols, the image they sought was one not of superiority but of participation in mainstream America. In his study of the consumption habits of working-class women in the mid-1950s, Lee Rainwater found that, unlike middle-class women, they valued goods not for their distinctive qualities but as testimony to their acceptance in the "large middle, 'core culture' of the country." This working-class quest for community through consumption became especially salient in the 1950s, as many workers moved out of urban neighborhoods with distinct class and ethnic identities into the amorphous suburbs. Isolated from their traditional reference groups and worried about fitting into these new communities, workers looked increasingly to consumer goods like large, luxurious automobiles to prove they were part of the increasingly prosperous American community.[36]

At the beginning of the postwar period, American automakers did not anticipate this growing consumer demand for bigger, more powerful and luxurious cars. Predicting a postwar recession, Ford and GM developed during the war programs to produce small, inexpensive cars. But both programs ran into trouble, as automakers discovered that small cars were almost as costly to build as big ones. And the unexpected postwar boom made Americans willing and able to pay premium prices for bigger cars symbolic of their social mobility and belongingness. So the small-car plans were scrapped, much to the delight of the stylists, who preferred the big cars over the little ones. As Bill Mitchell said: "It's hard to do a small car. It's like tailoring a suit for a dwarf." The huge barges gave stylists more sheet metal to sculpt and display their artistic prowess. And because the bigger cars were more profitable, corporate officials were willing to invest more money in decorations uniquely styled for them.[37]

During the decade of the 1950s, then, Detroit's automotive offerings quickly ballooned to enormous proportions. Typical was GM's best-selling Chevrolet. Between 1946 and 1959, the cheapest two-door Chevy sedan grew 13 inches in length and 7 inches in width, and was lowered 10 inches. These increased dimensions also added 400 pounds in weight. Ed Cole, the division's head, said he wanted to make the low-priced car "look as big as we possibly can" in order to move into the rapidly growing medium-priced market. He also introduced high-priced and heavily accessorized models to the top of the line, while eliminating the stripped-down Chevies at the bottom. By 1958 the top-of-the-line Impala model was as long, low, and chromed up as just about any Pontiac or Oldsmobile, putting it in solid competition with these makes.[38] This upward push also resulted in enormous increases in power. The decade of the 1950s saw the start of a horsepower race that would stretch through the 1960s and end only with the first oil price shock of the 1970s. The horsepower of the average automobile engine increased from 110 in 1946 to 180 in 1956, with the biggest engines approaching 400 horsepower by the decade's end. Low-priced cars like Chevrolet that offered only 6-cylinder engines at the beginning of the 1950s could hardly be bought with one at the end, when the overwhelming majority of American cars were equipped with high-compression V–8 engines that developed over 200 horsepower.[39]

Unable to admit their real motives, American consumers deceived themselves that there were rational advantages to the bigger, more powerful cars. And the automakers encouraged this self-deception. The heavier cars were said to be safer because they "held the road" and protected their passengers in collisions. And many claimed that powerful engines gave drivers a margin of safety when caught in a jam and also reduced engine wear. In actuality, just the opposite was true. The big, powerful monsters were more unsafe, for improvements in steering and braking lagged behind increases in power and size. Huge body overhangs, pillowy soft springs, tiny wheels and brake drums, and absurdly slow steering all made these huge dream machines a nightmare to control. These heavier, more powerful cars were also costlier to operate. They consumed more gasoline, oil, and tires, and even minor collisions were costly to repair due to the huge expanses of non-detachable sheet metal that had to be straightened and repainted. American motorists also had to pay out billions in increased taxes to redesign streets and highways to accomodate the wider, longer, heavier, and faster autos. Finally, the rush to bigger, more powerful cars increased the initial purchase price of American automobiles. The average wholesale price of a car increased from $1,270 in 1950 to $1,822 by 1960, twice the increase of all wholesale prices during the decade.[40]

Although in the 1950s all cars increased in size, power, and price, the largest proportional increases came in the cheaper lines. As the low-priced Chevies, Fords, and Plymouths crowded in close to the middle-priced Oldsmobiles, Mercuries, and Dodges, the high-priced makes did not maintain their relative distance from the upwardly striving hoi polloi. In fact, most of the luxury makes moved down to capture the upper reaches of the expanding middle-priced market. This resulted in the culmination of a trend that originated in the 1930s – the homogenization of the automotive market. During the decade of the Great Depression the gap between luxury cars and the mass-produced makes narrowed, as the wealthy settled for the inconspicuous commonality of the cheaper makes. But the culmination of this decline in true luxury cars awaited postwar America, in which the ostentatious display of great wealth seemed to violate the democratic rhetoric that originated in the "collective sacrifices" of the war and continued in the "classless" consumer society of the 1950s. So the surviving luxury marques downgraded even further – in price, pretension, and mechanics.

The path to luxury car survival was blazed by Cadillac, which resorted to mass production to lower prices and increase sales. But its success depended in large part on a shrewd marketing campaign that balanced exclusivity with down-to-earth democracy. The Cadillac was portrayed as everyman's luxury car, exclusive but within the reach of nearly everyone in an era of rising incomes. Tapping into the period's ethos of upward mobility, the car was marketed to "the man on his way up," he who had earned his success and wanted to enjoy it. Although still expensive, the car was priced at a level not far beyond middle-priced cars. While in 1930 a Cadillac sold for four times the average car price, by 1955 this differential had been reduced to 1.7. And in the hands of Harley Earl, the GM flagship was styled in a bold, brash aesthetic that appealed to the masses, unlike the 1930s statements of reserved and leisurely wealth.[41]

This combination of condescending luxury makes and social-climbing cheap cars produced a flatter automotive hierarchy for consumers to climb. By the end of the decade, the qualitative differences in engineering, construction, and aesthetics between the automotive classes had virtually disappeared, replaced by small quantitative differences in size, horsepower, chrome, and price. The higher-class cars were not different, but merely excessive, possessing more of the qualities that all cars shared. Consequently, the classes of autos no longer bore direct, symbolic testimony to the classes of American society. The luxury marques no longer testified to an appropriating position of power free from the hurry of assembly lines, nor did cheap cars display their owners' enslavement to the cost-cutting system of unbending discipline. What a car like the Cadillac displayed was not qualitatively superior power in production, but quantitatively greater income in the market, which allowed the owner to buy more of what everyone wanted. This homogenization of the automotive market ideologically obscured the real class hierarchy of production power behind a substitute hierarchy of consumption in which people were differentiated by income extracted from the supposedly equitable market. An America in which the working man's Chevrolet closely resembled the rich man's Cadillac was a society that could unabashedly call itself "classless."

Escape and entertainment: dream cars lead the way

The economic and cultural climate of postwar America brought to fruition not only Harley Earl's longstanding preference for longer, lower, and wider cars, but also his philosophy of automotive entertainment and escape. After the deprivations of the Depression and war, Americans were ready for some diversion from the debilitating struggle to make ends meet. They escaped the growing problems of the industrial city by moving to the suburbs, but found themselves isolated in a monotonous landscape devoid of geographic and social landmarks. Suburbanized Americans sought relief in the entertainment of commodities and their channels of circulation. Buying became a collective diversion, with the media that facilitated consumption – television, radio, popular magazines – providing the unifying images of the spectacle to the isolated suburbanites.[42]

The automobile was the central icon in this spectacle of consumption. Increasingly the rhythm of American life was set by the cycle of artificial obsolescence engineered in Detroit. However monotonous life was on the job or in the suburbs, Americans could always count on the fall introduction of new models to generate some excitement. As Harley Earl stated in 1958, "car styling is fast rivaling the popularity of baseball and the weather as a leading national topic of conversation among the people of all ages and both sexes." Sensing that the time was right, Earl pushed his philosophy of spectacular entertainment to its absurd limits during the decade. The epitome of this aesthetic were the show vehicles created and displayed by GM's Styling Staff during the 1950s. These wild, fantastic "dream cars" probed consumer psyches, engineered the illusion of progress, and led consumers as well as other automakers to Earl's aesthetic ideals.[43]

Although automakers had occasionally produced dream cars for fairs and shows since the 1930s, the practice became institutionalized only in the 1950s, with the initiation of GM's Motorama Shows. These annual automotive extravaganzas grew out of Alfred Sloan's luncheons for New York's financial elite held each January in the Waldorf–Astoria hotel during the National Automobile Show. In 1949 GM executives decided to turn this exclusive showing into a popular affair which emphasized entertainment and escape. From rather modest attempts to make technology more exciting, the Motoramas quickly blossomed into full-scale entertainment extravaganzas, with stage productions that included original songs and coreography, top-flight performers, and show girls. But the real stars of these spectacles were the dream cars produced by Harley Earl's Styling Staff, which included original design prototypes as well as modified versions of GM production cars. Earl's fantastically entertaining Motorama cars attracted so much popular attention that Ford and Chrysler were forced to produce their own dream cars.[44]

Harley Earl justified these dream cars as a way "to test public reactions" to various design features, the most popular of which were incorporated into production models. But this rationale is at best partial. While a few popular prototypes did affect production design, more frequently the influence moved in the opposite direction. By admission of stylists at all of the Big Three, most of the dream cars were designed after the production cars and purposely incorporated some of the latters' features. As one Chrysler designer stated: "they'll build a show car that takes some of the features of that [production car] and carry them to an extreme to heighten the excitement." This deception prepared buyers for the new production cars and left them with the impression that these were technically progressive due to their resemblance to the futuristic dream cars. So the dream cars were mainly vehicles of consumer manipulation whereby designers led the public by the nose down a path they had already charted.[45]

These advanced, futuristic vehicles also sought to create for the entire corporation the image of a scientific and technological pioneer. For this reason, one Ford designer called them "propaganda cars." "They sort of implanted the assumption that one of these companies has a better feel for advanced thinking and technology than the other company." But the ultimate purpose of these fantastically futuristic dream cars was to entertain and excite the audience with a grand spectacle that put them in the buying mood. With these cars stylists sought to tap the unfulfilled desires of American consumers and bring them into sheet-metal reality. As Harley Earl told a private conference of GM executives in 1955:

> This dream must be turned into cash, the dream of the potential buyer must be discovered and satisfied and the buyer must be awakened with his dreams turned into cars that he can, and will, buy.
> How? Like this!
> With a spectacle that will excite the mind to the limits of its imagination. With a Motorama. . . . Styling's elaborate exhibition, all

for the purpose of enhancing the product, kicks off a buyer's splurge wherever it appears.[46]

Dreams come to life, desires transformed from the lifeless phantoms of the ideal world into the fantastic metal of material reality – this was the essence of Earl's automotive credo, which he embodied in the Motorama spectacles. He had learned this trick of diversion from the Hollywood movie industry. But film was inferior to Earl's automobiles for this purpose. Like the religious utopias that diverted consciousness in early capitalism, film realized desires in a sublimated mental world that evaporated when spectators left the theater. But the automotive utopia was materialized in tangible commodities – it was the opium of religion come down to earth.

The dream cars of the decade drew heavily on the design idiom of the emerging space age to divert and entertain spectators. The visual cues of jet planes and rockets resonated with the psyche of consumers at a number of imbricated levels. As in the 1930s, airplanes were on the leading edge of technological progress, so consumers searching for some sign of improvement in their lives naturally gravitated toward gravity-defying transport. And planes and rocketry symbolized the military power of America, not only in the past world war but in the emerging Cold War. American leaders ensured people that superior missiles would guarantee the triumph of Americanism against communism, and visual crossbreeding of this technology with consumer goods ensured them that their private lives were similarly superior. Finally, space transport carried connotations of escape, promising to deliver Americans from earthly limitations to a new frontier of opportunities.

The way in which auto stylists mobilized the connotations of air travel in dream cars is typified by Earl's pioneering prototype, the Le Sabre. Named after the F–86 Le Sabre fighter jet, the 1951 dream car embodied numerous technical advances, but the most dramatic and influential innovations were in the car's styling. The lightweight body was dramatically low even by today's standards, measuring only 50 inches in height. The Le Sabre also introduced the wraparound windshield, inspired by the canopies of jet aircraft. Although the curved glass distorted the driver's vision, it captured the look of flight that Earl wanted. The front of the car converged on a round grille simulating a jet-intake, while the rear ended in a round jet-exhaust nozzle. And rising off each rear fender was a towering fin simulating the vertical stabilizers on jets. All these tacked-on airplane clichés had the same dizzying appeal of an amusement park ride.

The Le Sabre dream car also pioneered in the technology of insulation, introducing conveniences that removed the unpleasantries of driving that could quickly bring imaginary pilots back to earth. Built-in power jacks removed the labor from changing a flat tire, and the convertible top automatically closed when raindrops struck the central console. All this and more equipment was controlled from a dashboard that was a gadgeteer's delight, containing sixty-three separate switches, buttons, and indicators. Earl liked to use the Le Sabre as a testimony to the advanced thinking of the Styling Staff, bragging that its features inspired countless advances in production cars. But only the styling clichés appeared on production cars, where they served as superficial signs of technological progress.[47]

Other famous dream cars similarly utilized the fantastic imagery of futuristic aeronautics to entertain consumers and capture their displaced desires. The 1959 Cadillac Cyclone had sides resembling two missiles and terminating in exhaust nozzles and tail fins. Ford produced a futuristic mock-up of a nuclear-powered car, the Nucleon, to mobilize the public optimism for the new form of energy. And when dream cars were not entertaining consumers with promises of otherworldly transport, they drew on terrestrial symbols of escape by borrowing the names of exotic vacation spots like Monte Carlo, Biarritz, Florentine, and Caribe. In both sheet-metal and moniker, these dream machines promised to transport their passengers beyond the profane world of monotonous production and suburban isolation into an extraordinary realm of exotic experience. They were millenarian movements on wheels, religious utopias in steel.[48]

Escape and entertainment: production in the wake of the dream

The production cars designed by the increasingly powerful and unrestrained stylists were practical versions of the dream cars, only slightly constrained by the mundane considerations of production costs and utility. During this period, the automakers gave stylists more leeway to realize their fantastic vision of the automobile. And with all the major corporations now in the styling game, the style competition quickly drove stylists to outrageous heights. Gene Bordinat, a Ford stylist, recalled: "We got carried away . . . the designer who had always reached for the moon hoping just to get half way there, because of these [financial and manufacturing] contraints, was now reaching for the moon, and they were saying, 'Okay, go ahead and get the damn moon.'"[49]

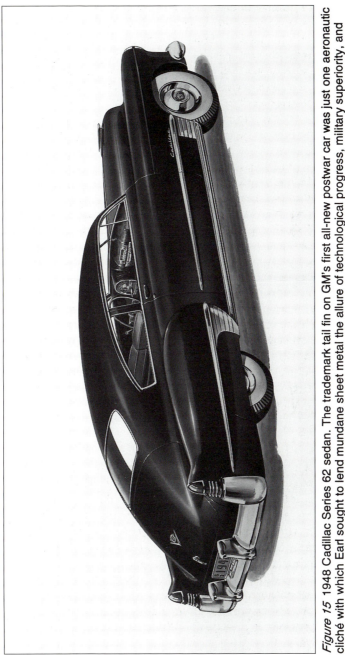

Figure 15 1948 Cadillac Series 62 sedan. The trademark tail fin on GM's first all-new postwar car was just one aeronautic cliché with which Earl sought to lend mundane sheet metal the allure of technological progress, military superiority, and escape. (Courtesy General Motors Corporation)

In 1948 Harley Earl fired the first volley in the postwar style war with the introduction of the fabulous new Cadillac, inspired by the P–38 Lightning aircraft. The nose of the car was rather pointed, like the plane, and accented by two protruding bullets on the bumper. And the dummy chromed scoops on the rear fenders simulated the functional air entries on the P–38. But the most distinctly aeronautical feature of the new luxury car was the little fin on each rear fender. The initially controversial tail fin was placed there not merely as a symbol of airborn escape but also of distinction. As Earl stated: "Cadillac owners realized that it gave them an extra receipt for their money in the form of a visible prestige marking for an expensive car." Earl's airplane allusions also resonated with the nationalist ideology of the postwar era, for they symbolized America's military superiority over past and present enemies.[50]

Earl pushed his aesthetic of aeronautical entertainment and escape further in 1949, when the remainder of GM makes got new bodies. Buicks and Pontiacs did not yet have fins, but their squared-off rear fenders suggested rudderlike formations. And a new aeronautic motif appeared on the Buick, the infamous portholes. Named Venti-Ports, the holes in the sides of the front fenders were reminiscent of the exhaust ports on fighter planes. Originally fitted with hoses to facilitate heat dissipation from the engine, the portholes were sealed off at mid-year, reportedly because a California high-school principal complained that some of his male students used those on his Buick to relieve themselves. Thereafter, the Venti-Ports served merely as another of Earl's differentiating styling cues. The 1949 Buick was also notable for its aggressive, twenty-five-tooth grille, which seemed to express America's sneeringly superior attitude to the rest of the world. War-impoverished Europeans called it the "Dollar Grin."[51]

On GM's 1949 line-up, Earl introduced two more airplane clichés of questionable value: the "hardtop convertible" and curved glass. Stylists used curved, two-piece windshields to get that jet-canopy look, despite knowledge that they distorted driver vision and increased flying fragments in collisions. In further pursuit of the airy look, stylists introduced a sedan top with no side pillars, named the hardtop convertible because it imitated the open look of a convertible with the top up. Supported only at the front and rear, these hardtops collapsed much more easily in rollovers than traditional sedan roofs. But they gave drivers the free, open feel of a convertible while sealing out noise and pollution. With the addition of conveniences like air conditioning and radios, commuters to the utopia of suburban consumption were insulated from reminders of urban blight and deluded themselves that they were going on a pleasant, free-wheeling drive in the countryside as they crawled home on dirty, congested freeways past the forgotten victims of Fordism.[52]

Between 1950 and 1956, Harley Earl and his GM Styling Staff extended and intensified these entertaining themes of aeronautics and escapism, setting the styling pace for the other automakers to follow. Tail fins and grilles grew larger, the glass area expanded, chrome brightwork proliferated, and the number and brilliancy of automotive colors grew. Earl's fantastic 1950s' cars were superficial exercises in attention-grabbing ornamentation that displayed little artistic unity. "They had one theme coming up one side, and another going down the other," recalled one GM stylist. Earl knew, however, that these were not works of art but dream machines, calculated outlets for desires repressed and perverted by Fordist production into bizzarely irrational forms of consumption.[53]

Stylists in the two other major American automakers slavishly followed Earl's fantastic path of design. Ford styling caught on quickly, replacing its smooth, clean, envelope body of 1949 with chromed-up collections of airplane clichés, replete with hardtops, curved windshields, bullet grilles, tail fins, and jet-exhaust taillights. After a slow start in the 1950s styling race, Chrysler stylists picked up their pace in 1955 and raced to the forefront in 1957. Virgil Exner's 1957 Forward Look line-up boldly pushed Earl's aeronautic aesthetic to its limits. The cars were dramatically longer, lower, and wider than any other production models, with razor-thin roof pillars and tail fins that seemed to soar into the upper atmosphere. While Earl's rounded, bulbous cars were aesthetically stuck in the early age of air travel, Exner's Chryslers captured the lean, angular lines of the jet age. These cars propelled Chrysler sales skyward and left GM stylists stunned and confused, bested at the game they invented. But they vowed to regain the lead, and their desparate efforts led to some of the most outrageous automotive extravagances in history.[54]

While GM dominated the styling game, Earl firmly enforced his rule of incremental change on the entire industry. He rationed out style changes on GM cars, and Ford and Chrysler trailed behind, faithfully imitating Earl's innovations. But by the mid-1950s the erstwhile followers had the resources to challenge the style leadership of GM. Anticipating the trends already established by Earl, Exner leapfrogged over the leader, usurping its incremental changes. Chrysler's 1957 advertising slogan – "Suddenly, it's 1960" – revealed Exner's strategy. He effected in one year the changes that Earl would have rationed out over three, making cars about as long, low, wide, glassy, and finny as they could be.

Figure 16 1957 Dodge Royal Lancer hardtop coupe, one of Virgil Exner's Forward Look cars for Chrysler. Their low, lean lines, soaring tail fins, and ethereal roofs dramatically usurped Earl's incremental changes, touching off a style war that escalated into absurdities. (Courtesy Chrysler Historical Collection)

As soon as the stabilizing dominance of GM was displaced, the search for novelty spiraled out of control. In their attempts to introduce ever newer models, automakers shortened the cycle for major body changes from three years to two. And the styling on these ephemeral models became haphazardly bold, introducing changes so wholly unanticipated and dissociated from previous years that they appeared merely different, not new. And the search for quantitative differentiation also careened out of control, with cars adding more chrome, more headlights, more taillights, more glass, longer bodies, and higher fins. When in 1959 tail fins could get no higher, they assumed the contorted shapes of batwings and eyebrows. By this year even Virgil Exner, the initiator of the fin wars, had to admit that "it was obvious that I'd given birth to a Frankenstein."[55]

There was, of course, no shortage of functional excuses for even the most monstrous of styling features. Exner claimed that wind-tunnel tests proved his tail fins stabilized cars in strong cross-winds, but these effects were achieved only at speeds of over 60 miles per hour. Harley Earl said his wraparound windshields "move[d] the corner pillars out of the way to provide really sweeping vision," but admitted that appearance was his main motive for this design feature. Bill Mitchell claimed that lower cars improved handling and lessened the dangers of rollover, but both claims were largely erroneous. These functional excuses were an ideological cover that stylists provided for themselves as well as consumers, who could not admit that their automotive dollars bought desublimated gratification of displaced desires, not safe transportation.[56]

Gadgetry, gender, and cold war: the ideology of insulation

Another automotive excess justified by a flimsy ideology was gadgetry. Cars of the 1950s were burdened with a barrage of technological superfluities like automatic transmissions, air conditioning, power steering, and power brakes, which enhanced not their utility or safety but merely the convenience and comfort of operation. The following are examples of another class of more frivolous innovations pioneered during the decade that may be described only as useless gadgetry: power seats, power windows, power locks, automatic headlight dimmers, automatic speed control, automatic air suspension, automatic signal-seeking radios, automatically opening windows, automatic antennae, and polarized sun visors. And this was also the age of push buttons, during which the operating control for almost every part of the car was converted to this form of activation that was considered the epitome of convenience.

As in an earlier era, women were most often blamed for the worst automotive excesses of the 1950s. The weaker sex, it was said, demanded these labor-saving conveniences to facilitate their operation of the family car. And even when they were not driving, they were said to demand all the comforts, conveniences, and beauty of the modern home in their automobiles. A 1957 article in the *General Motors Engineering Journal* claimed that women were the deciding influence in 70 percent of auto purchases, and went on to state that Harley Earl "credits women with inspiring increased beauty in car interiors, for the rapid growth of power accessories, and for today's tasteful and eye-appealing colors."[57]

As if to prove their devotion to female consumers, the major automakers began to hire women stylists during the 1950s. The Ford styling department hired two women in 1945, and by 1947 there were six on staff. Earl's GM Styling Staff hired its first female stylist in 1946, and by 1958 employed nine women in design. But these women were employed exclusively in the low-ranking interior studios, where they were expected to bring the "woman's touch" to the colors and fabrics of the passenger compartment to turn it into the family's "second living room." Women were discriminated against not only in job placement but also in wages. And they faced the degrading attitudes of male designers, who referred to them as "women designers" and claimed "they would not last."[58]

The miniscule number of women designers indicates that their real function was symbolic, as public testimony to the automakers' concern for women's needs. One woman in GM's Styling Staff stated that Earl "thought it would be good P. R." to have a few female designers, who were paraded before the public as part of a promotional campaign targeting women. Part of this GM campaign was the production of "Fem" show cars, designed by the women stylists and displayed at the 1959 Motorama. Painted up in gaudy colors and loaded down with outrageous accessories like seal-fur lap robes, perfume atomizers, and pink umbrellas, these fem cars were meant, in the words of GM designer Suzanne Vanderbilt, to "advertise the fact that they had women in design and show people what they did." But the women designers actually resented these cars as signs of their separate and inferior status at GM.[59]

In other propaganda aimed at women, automakers promoted the fashion and beauty of their cars by comparing them to the latest in women's fashions. And power features were also aimed at women, with one 1955 Chevrolet ad claiming these "make driving it as dreamy as dancing with your best beau." But a Willys advertisement gave away the secret of these appeals to beauty, style, and comfort – while ostensibly aimed at women, their real target was men. The ad pictured a stylish woman standing beside the car but was written in a male voice: "Here I'd been buying the same old kind of car, year after year, never asking the little woman what she wanted. . . . When I saw that car, and realized how beautiful it was. . . . I determined to buy an Aero Willys for my wife."[60]

The dirty little secret of automotive sales was that men made the major decisions. A majority of working-class women surveyed by Lee Rainwater in the mid-1950s stated that decisions about auto purchases were entirely their husband's. Then why did automakers pander to "women's tastes?" Because this provided male buyers with an excuse for purchasing a car with the qualities that they wanted but could not admit. Gene Bordinat, an important Ford stylist, claimed that the same automotive style appealed to both sexes, but: "Don't forget that husbands and wives tend to use each other for crutches. I remember . . . a man [who] showed up at the country club one day with a new car in lavender. The boy at the door complimented him. Said that sure was a good-looking car. He said 'Oh, yes, my wife liked the color.' Maybe she did, but so did he. He just couldn't admit it." Like the man in the Willys ad, he used the "little woman's" tastes as a cover for his own.[61]

Most designers recognized that both men and women demanded in their cars beauty, comfort, and convenience. Both sexes, particularly among the working class, wanted a beautiful, effortless automobile that insulated consumption from all the ugly reminders of drudgerous work, at home and the factory. But sexist ideology prevented men from consciously admitting it. Suburbanization made the separation and gender-typing of the spheres of labor and consumption more rigid than ever before. The masculine sphere was rationalized, cost-cutting production, while the feminine sphere was nonutilitarian consumption and reproduction that was insulated from and compensated for the indignities of production. Men as well as women placed increasing emphasis on consumption to fulfill their needs, but because this sphere was defined as feminine, males could not admit it. They had to consume the comfortable, nonutilitarian qualities of goods vicariously through their wives.

One connotation of gadgetry was more masculine, however, and could be consciously mobilized to appeal to men – technological superiority in the Cold War. If "improvements" in appearance, ride, power, and drivability were linked to the race for military superiority, then men felt more comfortable consuming them, since weaponry was preeminently masculine and provided a special sort of gender-typed insulation. Identification with the military superiority of the nation insulated men from and compensated them for their class inferiority in workplace. Automakers used these associations to sell dream machines loaded with gadgets and accessories. Buick launched a blatantly militaristic campaign in 1958, naming one model the Airborn B–58 after a new bomber plane. One ad pictured a fashionably hatted woman and a beaming man soaring in a Buick among three jet bombers. The male buyer could not have failed to associate his new Buick with the Cold War rhetoric of supersonic bombers loaded with nuclear bombs to protect America's way of life.[62]

Other associations of automotive convenience with Cold War superiority were more subtle, mobilizing deep-seated associations between consumerism and freedom. An ingenious ad for the 1951 Buick pictured the gear selector for its automatic transmission along with the steering wheel held by a right hand, the customary hand for manual shifting. The ad announced this to be the "Hand of the Free," informing readers that the automatic transmission provided drivers with "freedom from physical strain," "freedom from any thought of . . . gearshifting," and "freedom from tension on a long day's drive." This polysemous ad not only promised insulation from the physical drudgery of driving but also subtly associated America's consumer technology with international superiority. The "freedom" that Americans were told distinguished their country from communism was here equated with consumer technology, not political democracy or civil liberties. Americans were superior to the communist world and consequently insulated from its threats because their consumer goods made life easy and carefree. But such subtle associations of consumer technology with Cold War supremacy would come back to haunt America in 1958.[63]

TROUBLE IN PARADISE: THE INCIPIENT REVOLT AGAINST DETROIT DREAM MACHINES

Beneath the superficial assuredness and exuberance of postwar American brewed a deep uneasiness with consumer goods in general and extravagant automobiles in particular. From the beginning of this decade there were voices that dissented from the trend of automotive America toward big, powerful, insulating dream machines. At first these criticisms came largely from bourgeois intellectuals, especially those artists, architects, planners, and designers who continued to advocate a modernist aesthetic of purism and functionalism. American purist Edgar Kaufman, director of Industrial Design at New York's Museum of

Modern Art, criticized American cars as "chromium-plated calves," and argued that their flashy, bulbous design followed the dictum of "style follows sales" rather than "form follows function." Raymond Loewy, a European-influenced American designer, denounced the typical Detroit automobile as a "jukebox on wheels," arguing that the style wars led to "a vehicle that's too big for most people, too expensive, too costly to maintain, and too gaudy."[64]

Loewy backed up his functionalist criticism with efforts to change Detroit's jukebox styling. In 1953 his styling studios designed for Studebaker the Starliner, a stunningly lithe and low beauty almost totally bereft of chrome geegaws. The car was praised by design critics and many young Detroit stylists, but poor sales signaled a lack of public acceptance. Earl and his Detroit minions gloated at the apparent failure of the functionalist aesthetic, loudly proclaiming that they gave common Americans what they wanted. They called their critics elitist, undemocratic snobs, and "gray-flannel nonconformists."[65]

There was some truth in these characterizations of Detroit's critics, whose feigned concern for the common man often masked an undercurrent of class bigotry. This was evident in *Fortune* magazine, whose editors looked down their patrician noses at Detroit jukeboxes. "Anybody who, like an up-to-date architect, believes that the honest representation of function has a great deal to do with beauty, must be mortified. The American car, which decades ago looked like a horseless wagon, now begins to resemble some comic-strip version of a moon rocket. . . . The balloon-like, chromium-encrusted bodies are designed so that middle-class wives may impress each other with their opulence." The editors expressed their preference for European sports cars, which they characterized as lean, efficient, and more exhilarating to drive.[66]

Bourgeois professionals, intellectuals, and business executives were not exposed to the worst inhumanities of Fordism. Because they exercised more decision-making power over the machinery of production than working Americans, they required less insulation from it at leisure, less forgetting and compensation. The chrome geegaws that created artificial distinction and value were less desirable to those who held distinctive, valued positions on the job. And insulation from the labors of Fordist machinery was less necessary for those not subjected to it. Soft bourgeois hands could enjoy the uncharacteristic labor of gear-jamming, as soft bourgeois bottoms could revel momentarily in slamming over bumps in a stiffly sprung sports car.

During the 1950s, this class-based disdain for Detroit's products touched off a trend which assumed a symbolic importance far beyond its numerical strength – growing sales of small European cars, especially sports cars and Volkswagens. In 1955 about 60,000 imports were sold in the United States, of which 25,000 were Volkswagens. But by 1959 sales of the European compacts and sports cars exploded to 700,000 units, 10 percent of the American market. And sales of a small American car, American Motors' Rambler, also exploded in the latter years of the decade, soaring past Buick, Olds, and Pontiac in 1959. Data revealed that these import-buyers were generally above average in income, with one survey finding that two-thirds of VW owners had incomes 40 percent higher than the average new-car buyer.[67]

Affluent small-car buyers told surveyors that their purchases were shaped by utilitarian considerations of price, economy, and quality, but many commentators detected cultural motives behind their preferences. Some contended that import owners were class snobs, displaying an unconcern for symbols of success and importance that testified to possession of the real thing. Others argued that bourgeois buyers of small and imported cars were not protesting the specifics of Detroit styling but merely rejecting its lack of individuality. Americans of all classes wanted cars that lent them some distinction in a Fordist world where the work of even bourgeois businessmen and professionals was subject to the leveling logic of rationalization. But conditions of the market denied such individuality to auto buyers during the decade.[68]

Car ownership in itself was no longer a mark of distinction, for by 1959 70.2 percent of American families owned a car. And the trend toward bigness, power, and convenience in all car classes leveled the traditional differences between cars in the price hierarchy. Most who bought smaller, more functional European cars were not thumbing their noses at automotive expressionism, but merely trying to find a different expression to distinguish themselves. Alfred Sloan, for example, wrote that the rising demand for compact cars was not motivated by economy but "was essentially a further expression of the customer's desire for greater variety." Bill Tara, an advertising agent for GM during this period, similarly argued that the trend to smaller, economy cars was mainly motivated by consumer attempts to find automotive individuality. He told Chevrolet designers that what consumers really wanted was "an automobile that has personality and *distinction* which can easily be separated in a buyer's mind from the great variety of available cars."[69]

The search for automotive individuality was not class-specific, but the direction it took was. The richest bourgeois class fraction often purchased European luxury makes like Jaguar and Mercedes–Benz to distinguish themselves. Their poorer bourgeois comrades in the intellectual fraction purchased the more moderately priced expressions of

European difference like Volkswagen, MG, Triumph, and Fiat. Their power and importance on the job probably made them more tolerant of this smaller and less powerful form of automotive distinction. The class position of working Americans determined that their grab for individuality would move to domestic cars individually modified to be more powerful, ornamented, and reified than anything Detroit had yet produced. The automotive rebellion of workers in postwar America was hot rodding, a rejection of standardization and homogenization achieved by advancing Detroit's aesthetic trends to their absurd extremes.

Hot rodding emerged in the late 1930s and early 1940s largely among working-class teenagers in Southern California. These youths were short on cash but long on time, so they expressed their commodified individuality by turning discarded copies of Detroit's products into icons of personal expression. At first these young automotive modifiers focused on the mechanicals, which were stripped apart, altered, and reassembled to squeeze every ounce of performance out of the car. This activity escalated after the war, as suburban prosperity brought hot rodding within the financial reach of lots of working-class adolescents. The proof of their mechanical prowess was racing, which was initially done illegally on streets but increasingly organized on dry lake beds and quarter-mile drag strips.[70]

The impulse behind hot rodding was resentful and rebellious. These working-class youths were critical of the standardized, loaded-down, chromed-up cars that Detroit was turning off assembly lines in the 1950s. As sociologist Reul Denney observed in an essay on hot rodders, they sought to escape from "the conformities of mass consumption" with a car that demonstrated "its freedom from the superfluous adjuncts of styling-for-obsolescence. . . ." Hot rodding also seemed driven by a class resentment of those with enough money to purchase automotive distinction. *Hot Rod Magazine* exorted its readers to "replace cubic money with hard work, talent, and integrity. Be an individual, build the car you want to build – not what the standard is." When they got hold of Detroit's "gook wagons," hot rodders irreverently stripped off all decoration and nonessential body parts to remove weight, and then "souped up" the mechanicals. To call attention to these skillful modifications, the functional parts were often chromed or painted special colors.[71]

Clearly, this hot-rod aesthetic was a reversal of Detroit's obsession with obfuscation, but was carried out for the same purpose of humanizing the alienated products of capitalist mass production. Detroit's automakers made their fragmented cars look more human by concealing the ugly, standardized parts. Hot rodders made mass-produced autos more human by using their labor to reunify the mechanical parts, which they then revealed by stripping off the obscuring body shell. Individuality was thus achieved by a display of reunifying mechanical skills rather than an obfuscation of the fragmented labor of the Fordist factory.

So however rebellious, the hot-rod aesthetic was defined by the Fordist system it sought to reject. It was a rebellion of consumption, carefully confined in the Fordist way to leisure-time pursuits which merely compensated for but did not transform the inhumanities of work. And in humanizing Fordism's products, hot rodders merely carried the stylists' aesthetics to their extremes, seeking in their mechanical alterations the same connotations of power, importance, and individuality that stylists achieved with surface ornamentation.

There was an even greater convergence of Detroit's dream makers and working-class rod makers in custom-car building, the spin-off movement of hot rodding. At first a means of attaining speed and displaying mechanical work, the low-slung, powerful, stripped-down aesthetic of hot rods soon became an end in itself. Eschewing performance-oriented modifications, the customizers concentrated on the body work. Custom-car shops, manned by working-class kids with sheet-metal and painting skills, popped up in Southern California in the late 1940s and early 1950s to cater to this automotive impulse toward individuality. And in large part, these customizers took the trends pioneered by another Californian, Harley Earl, and carried them to individualistic extremes. They pursued Earl's unified look, but instead of relying on chrome distraction and tricks to conceal the gaps and seams of mass-produced bodies, the customizers altered the surface itself. Gaps between body panels were filled with lead solder and smoothed over, and headlights and taillights were "frenched" in or recessed into fenders to eliminate the seam. Earl's aesthetic of longer, lower, and wider cars was also carried to absurd extremes by customizers, who "chopped" tops, "sectioned" bodies, and "channeled" frames to lower cars. To add the illusion of depth to the body and mask imperfections, customizers carried Detroit's glossy, colorful finishes to the limits of paint technology, applying as many as fifty coats of translucent lacquer over a reflective base and then decorating these brilliant surfaces with hand-painted flames, pinstripes, and scallops. And when it came to the addition of fantasy elements like fins to distinguish and relieve the monotony of mass production, the customizers outdid Earl and his Detroit stylists by light years.[72]

So while small-car nonconformists retreated to a functionalist aesthetic of agility and efficiency, hot-rod rebels exaggerated Detroit's aesthetic of unity, power, and fantasy. Unlike the bourgeois masters of Fordist production, its workers had more to forget and compensate for. Belittled and degraded by the class system, the sons of America's factory workers sought comfort in big, powerful cars. As one told two psychiatrists studying hot rodders: "Behind the wheel I get bigger and bigger. . . . I swell up to be just as big as the car." These two automotive rebellions from different ends of the class spectrum were harbingers of a popular revolt against American automakers. A growing proportion of all Americans who looked to the automobile for distinction were becoming dissatisfied with Detroit's standardized offerings. The escalating style competition made novelty and individuality so superficial and random that consumers began to see the mass-produced sameness beneath the bizarre surfaces.[73]

This growing skepticism about automobiles was part of a larger escalation of discontent with America's consumer society. Ever-escalating levels of consumption failed to bring satiation of displaced desires, and their rechanneled energy often found its way into guilt and aggression. Unable to recognize the real source of their malaise in the process of Fordist production, the masses of Americans began to blame those who seemed to control the process of consumption – the clever advertisers and merchandisers who manipulated unsuspecting consumers with their psychological research. Automobile salesmen and advertisers were said to be the cleverest practitioners of consumer persuasion, appealing to the impulses of buyers through hidden persuaders and subliminal messages. And auto stylists were also indicted for encoding psychological messages into the sheet metal. In his critical book of 1958, *The Insolent Chariots*, John Keats claimed that automakers hired psychologists to investigate the sounds and smells of cars, and that stylists deliberately designed sexual symbols like phallic hood ornaments and bosomlike bumpers. Vance Packard reported in his popular *Hidden Persuaders* that automakers hired motivational researchers to help them appeal to consumers' repressed desires.[74]

There is little evidence that automakers used motivational research or psychological testing to sell, style, or advertise cars. Their consumer surveys were routine queries about simple preferences and tastes. Stylists fought the influence of any extraneous tests or data on their aesthetic decisions. And they did not consciously appeal to sexual desires through visual metaphors. Stylists undoubtably and admittedly tried to make cars look "sexy" and "exciting" – Bill Mitchell was fond of saying that "Unlike a gas range, a car has sex." But they achieved the sexy look not by anatomical analogies but by symbolic references to the spatial division of work and leisure under Fordism.

As Antonio Gramsci observed, Fordist methods of mass production intensified labor to such an extent that sexual pleasure had to take place in the geographically separate home during leisure. Even at leisure, however, the sexual instinct could not be given a totally free rein, but had to be rationalized in the form of monogamous marriage to support a stable work life. The excess energy of repressed sexual desire became steered into the pleasure of consumption, and the automobile quickly became one of its commodified outlets. Stylists intuitively appealed to this desire in design by associating the car with the socially defined space of sexuality – home, leisure, vacation. The sports car was sexy because it was impractical for work and tailored to the realm of leisure extravagance and waste. The convertible was sexy because it was a leisure machine, for top-down, warm-weather drives in the country and on vacations. Cars with plush interiors reminiscent of a living room or bedroom were sexy because they looked like the site of intercourse, the home. Auto stylists thus sought to make cars look sexy by unconsciously drawing on the cultural association of sex and leisure created by Fordism.

Although Americans' discontent and anger with Fordism were real, their focus was misplaced, diverted from its source in production relations to consumption due to the latter's all-too-apparent abuses. And all of these mistargeted suspicions, fears, and projections coalesced around the most spectacular epitome of consumer extravagance of the decade, which produced the most spectacular automotive failure of the century – the Edsel.

THE EDSEL DEBACLE: THE REVOLT UNLEASHED

On August 27, 1957 the Ford Motor Company introduced to America a new line of cars that bore the name of Henry Ford's only son, Edsel. To attract attention to the car, Ford raised the promotional and visual voice of the Edsel above the already deafening din of automotive excess, launching a two-year, multimillion-dollar publicity campaign to convince consumers that the Edsel was the first really new automotive experience in at least two decades. The Edsel was indeed different, but it protested its novelty so loudly that its exhortations rang hollow. Beneath the bizarre, ballyhooed difference the public detected a standardized similarity to Detroit's other dream machines.

In 1954, when the Edsel was planned, the American market looked ripe for another middle-priced car. Rising incomes made this the fastest-growing market segment, but Ford had only one middle-priced make to compete with Chrysler's two and GM's three. So Ford executives decided to create an entirely new car division to produce a line of middle-priced cars. And the first step they took to make their new car competitive in an already crowded market was to give it a distinct "automotive personality" that would excite consumers. As David Wallace, a researcher in the Edsel Merchandising Office, wrote: "an automobile is merely a lifeless machine – until it sparks a dream in a prospect's mind. Only when the machine is seen as the means to some human ambition or desire, is it wanted." Ford merchandisers had learned from Harley Earl that to satisfy consumer dreams of individuality, cars had to be distinctive, or at least have the appearance of distinction. As Wallace wrote, what distinguishes one car from another in the consumer's mind "has nothing to do with the mechanism at all but with the car's personality, as the customer imagines it. What we wanted to do, naturally, was to give the E–car the personality that would make the greatest number of people want it."[75]

Ford executives decided to distinguish the image of the Edsel, not its underlying mechanicals, for mass-production economies dictated that the "all-new" car share mechanical parts and body shells with the Ford and Mercury Divisions. So Edsel's Merchandising Office went to work to create a "personality" to disguise the shared metal and sell the car to the largest possible market. David Wallace, director of market research, launched an extensive campaign of trendy, psychologically oriented research – the type wholly uncharacteristic of the industry – to find a name and create a marketing image for the Edsel. He assigned great importance to the name, hiring survey teams to test the psychological associations of thousands of words. But in the end top Ford manager Ernie Breech decided to name the car after his boss's father, Edsel Ford.[76]

Wallace was more successful in convincing the company to use his research on the proper "personality" for the new Edsel. Drawing on existing market data, Wallace found that Ford's middle-priced car, Mercury, appealed to younger, lower-income people, not the typically older, higher-income buyer in this market segment. Wallace then hired Columbia University's Bureau of Applied Social Research to survey car owners on their "images" of cars along three variables: youthfulness, masculinity, and social class. Based on these findings, he suggested that the Edsel be portrayed as "the smart car for the younger executive or professional family on its way up." In justification, Wallace wrote:

Smart car – recognition by others of the owner's good style and taste.
Younger – appealing to spirited but responsible adventures.

Executive or professional – millions pretend to this status, whether they can attain it or not.

Family – not exclusively masculine; a wholesome "good" role.

On Its Way Up – the E–car has faith in you, son: You will make it![77]

Foote, Cone, and Belding, Edsel's advertising agency, accepted Wallace's prescription, with one important revision – it substituted "middle-income family" for "younger professional or executive." Fairfax Cone argued, according to one Edsel executive, "that more families identified with their economic station in life than with the head-of-the-household's job." The ad executive seemed to recognize that most Americans did not want to be reminded in their leisure time of their inferior class position (as non-executives) at work. In appealing to the "middle-income family on its way up," Cone diverted attention away from the contradictory class relations of production and tapped the aspirations of millions of working Americans who used their growing incomes to achieve a higher position on the continuum of consumption.[78]

Edsel executives looked to stylists to embody this promise of indivi-duality and upward mobility in the Edsel's sheet-metal. Roy Brown, a Lincoln stylist, was selected to head the Edsel team. And he stated his design goal was "to create a vehicle which would be unique in the sense that it would be readily recognizable in styling theme from the nineteen other makes of cars on the road at the time." To produce a car that vociferously proclaimed its individuality, Edsel stylists designed a series of focal points to grab attention from every visual angle. At the rear, the Edsel had gull-like horizontal taillights, departing from the vertical-fin motif of most cars. At front, Brown gave the Edsel a vertical grille that went against the usual horizontal layout. Departing from the slab sides of other cars, the Edsel had sides with concave scallops. And in the interior of the car, stylists teamed up with engineers to offer passengers an orgy of push-button gadgetry. When Brown presented his model to the executive committee, it received a standing ovation.[79]

The Edsel was the epitome of the automotive excesses of the decade, not only in styling but also in size, horsepower, and hype. The high-priced models measured a gargantuan 219 inches in length, 2 inches longer than the biggest Oldsmobile, and were just as wide as and 2 inches lower than the Cadillac Sedan de Ville. The engine that powered the dinosaur was a huge 410 cubic inch V–8 that developed 345 horsepower, making the Edsel the most powerful production car in the United States. And the Edsel outdid all automotive competitors in outrageous publicity and engineered con-sumer excitement. Admen and publicists whipped a car-crazy public up

Figure 17 1958 Edsel Citation two-door hardtop and convertible, epitomizing the automotive excesses of the 1950s. The car's design features were so cloying in their attempt to be different that consumers began to see through the superficial style game to the underlying similarities of all Detroit's products. (Courtesy Henry Ford Museum and Greenfield Village)

into a frenzy of expectation and excitement unexcelled to this day. The strip-tease publicity campaign suggestively revealed the car's features inch by inch to a drooling press and public.[80]

Finally, on August 27, 1957 at an elaborate national press introduction, the G-string was dropped and the Edsel was revealed for all America to see. Initial critical assessments were mildly favorable, but sales were slow, and Ford officials began to worry. Then in January, *Consumer Reports* published a searing review of the car, criticizing its small brakes, small trunk space, soft, shaky ride, and sluggish steering. In April the magazine denounced the car as "epitomizing the many excesses which . . . were repulsing more and more potential car buyers," and condemned Ford executives for focusing too much on automotive status symbols and not enough on "cars as functioning machines of transportation." *Consumer Reports* was right about consumers' repulsion but wrong about its cause. The problem with the Edsel and Detroit's other cars was not their insufficient functionality but their insufficient fulfillment of the key consumer dream of individuality.[81]

Many criticized the Edsel, particularly its styling, for being too different. The focus of styling criticism fell on the upright, oval grille, which was likened to, among other things, a horse collar, a toilet seat, a vagina, and an Oldsmobile sucking a lemon. Others criticized the "slant-eyed" rear end and the scalloped sides. Taken separately, these styling elements were not that bizarre or different. But the combination of all this cloying, attention-grabbing newness was too much. The Edsel was so obviously an attempt to look different that consumers began to see its underlying similarity to other Ford products and the rest of Detroit's cars. As one Ford stylist of the day observed, the car had so much chrome ornamentation to camouflage the common body shell that "people quickly saw through that it was a Ford body coming up, and a Mercury body dropping down to be an Edsel." Especially in the context of the exaggerated promotional promises, the Edsel was not that different from Detroit's other dream machines.[82]

Many business commentators attributed the failure of the Edsel and the overall decline of middle-priced American cars to their lack of individuality. *Business Week* argued that this was the result of annual model changes, which were so expensive that manufacturers could afford them only by producing one standardized family sedan that was differentiated by options and accessories. The magazine concluded that: "Since 1955, there hasn't been enough newness in basic styling of cars to give the industry's famed 'planned obsolescence' a chance to work."[83]

Other commentators attributed the Edsel's faliure to its psychologically oriented market research. David Wallace's surveys were widely publicized before the car appeared in articles like Eric Larabee's in *Harper's*, which concluded erroneously that the Edsel was "a perfect example of how the industry – in an era of depth interviews, motivation departments, and hidden persuaders – goes about its business." When the car failed to attract consumer dollars, a wide variety of popular publications cited Wallace's motivational research as a major reason. The widely publicized research did not lead to the faulty design, which was finalized before the surveys. But it did heighten American's fears that consumer manipulation was threatening their autonomy and contributed to the atmosphere of skepticism that poisoned the Edsel.[84]

Two events that coincided with the Edsel's release in August of 1957 also contributed to this public mood: the onset of a major recession and the launch of the Sputnik. The beginning of the first major postwar recession made 1958 the worst year for new car sales since the end of the war, for it deflated the cultural exuberance and economic optimism that buoyed these dream machines. The big cars looked a bit too extravagant in a society that was beginning to feel a bit wary of and guilty about its consumer overindulgence. Contributing to these doubts was the launch of the Soviet Union's Sputnik satellite on October 4, 1957, a little over a month after the Edsel's release. As David Wallace, Edsel's market researcher, wrote: "Somebody had beaten us to an important gain in technology, and immediately people started writing articles about how crummy Detroit products were, particularly the heavily ornamented and status-symbolic medium-priced cars." The Sputnik launch shattered the myth of America's technological superiority, not only in weapons but also in the consumer goods that were stylistically associated with them. The sky now belonged to the Soviets, and the befinned automobiles that promised to take consumers there seemed silly and indulgent. Editorials chided Americans for being more concerned with their creature comforts than the defense of the nation. And these scolding voices fell on guilty ears.[85]

So consumers punished themselves for the sin of gluttony, and the Edsel was one casualty of this self-imposed austerity, selling only 34,000 units in 1958. The car survived until 1960, when it was laid to rest and went down in automotive history as a fossilized reminder of a bygone era of Detroit excess.

HARBINGER OF AUTOMOTIVE INDIVIDUALITY

In the year of the Edsel debacle, there was a ray of hope in Ford's line-up, the new four-seater Thunderbird. The addition of two tiny back seats made the Ford sports car larger than ever, but it was still smaller and sportier than just about anything else on the market. Sales shot up 50 percent over 1957, surprising Ford officials, who thought of the Thunderbird as a specialty car with limited appeal. This Thunderbird showed Detroit a way out of the woods of consumer doubt by pioneering a new automotive type called the "personal luxury car."

Ford's Thunderbird was introduced in 1955 to compete with the Corvette, GM's answer to the sporty European imports. In their early forms, neither the Corvette nor the Thunderbird was really much of a sports car. Both were American caricatures of European sports cars, with more concern for the superficial connotations of speed and maneuverability than their mechanical accomplishment. With all the inconveniences of small, cramped, convertible sports cars but with none of the performance bonuses, these cars found only limited markets, pleasing neither sports-car enthusiasts nor dream-machine fanciers. So both companies moved to reposition their sporty offerings to increase appeal. GM chose to go after the performance crowd by turning the Corvette into a real sports car. Ford, by contrast, transformed the Thunderbird into a new type of vehicle – a distinctive car catering to the luxury needs of one individual.

A four-seat Thunderbird was conceived in 1955 by Ford product planners, who realized that the two-seater's market was limited and that Ford could not, like GM, bear the costs of a money-losing prestige car. So in 1958 Ford replaced the little sports car with the expanded T-Bird, producing a dramatically different kind of car. Its 113-inch wheelbase made it shorter than the standard-sized Fords, but because it was also very low and wide, it looked a mile long. Inside the rear-seat passengers were definitely cramped, but in front the two bucket seats divided by a central console afforded great comfort and incredible room. The fixed top had extrawide or "blind" rear-quarter pillars, which lent the car the formality of classic limousines and town cars. Everything about the Thunderbird screamed plushness and luxury, and its $3,700 base price hardly made it a low-cost alternative to the increasing prices of the big sedans.

While the Edsel bit the dust in 1958, the new T-Bird soared to new heights, defying the declining sales trend of other middle-priced makes during the recession. The secret of the car's success was not price or operating economy. Nor was it the smaller size. *Business Week* noted ironically: "If a 113-inch wheelbase makes a compact car, the T-Bird is a compact car. If Ford can sell one compact car at a 'medium-price' (the T-Bird lists, bare, at $3,700), there should be room for competition." Robert Macquire, a Ford interior stylist, revealed the car's real secret, stating: "It's a distinguished car. . . . I am distinguished when I am in it." The Thunderbird sold in droves because it was different and distinctive in an increasingly homogeneous field of big, chromed-up and loaded-down family sedans. Ford promoted it as "America's most individual car" and called it a "personal luxury car," a distinctive car targeted to the needs of one individual, not an entire family. That's what America seemed to be demanding as it moved into the 1960s – real automotive individuality.[86]

There was nothing new about this demand for individuality in an auto. Since the rise of standardized, homogenized Fordist production, people had turned to their cars to lend their lives difference and distinction. But by the mid-1950s the dream machines of Americans were looking a little too standardized and homogeneous, too much like the routinized production process itself to provide them with flights of fancy. With everyone's dreams looking exactly alike, Americans began to awaken to the superficiality of consumer visions. Without another dose of dream-inducing auto opium, they threatened to awake entirely to the system of mass production lurking under the stylistically differentiated skins of their transportation machines. The Edsel debacle revealed the dangers, but the Thunderbird success showed that Detroit could rise to the demands for an entirely new type of automotive individuality – a real, designed-in diversity of cars to replace the superficially differentiated homogeneity of products.

Chapter 7

The rise and fall of auto individuality

One day late in 1965, Virgil Boyd, president of the Chrysler Corporation, paid a visit to the Dodge styling studio, where studio head Bill Brownlie was working on the 1968 Charger muscle car. The sleek, light, mid-sized coupe was equipped with a monstrous 426-cubic-inch Hemi-head engine and could compete favorably against most hot rods in a drag race. Boyd, an executive from the bean-counter mold, could not comprehend the exciting racing machine before him, especially the huge engine that could attain speeds far beyond legal limits. Boyd frankly told Brownlie that Chrysler should not sell such cars.

Maybe this frugal accountant thought it wasteful to spend corporate money on a growing array of such specialty cars with limited markets. Or maybe Boyd was worried about the signs of public discontent with Detroit's bigger, more powerful, gas-guzzling machines. But in Bill Brownlie he did not find a sympathetic ear for his practical objections to the overpowered car. Brownlie was a "with it" sort of guy who, although middle-aged, was oriented to the emerging youth subculture. Muscle cars turned him on, and he had no patience for a square like Boyd who did not understand their youthful excitement. When Boyd suggested that Chrysler stop building them, Brownlie replied: "Have you ever driven up and down Woodward Avenue? Have you ever gotten out of your chauffer-driven car, pulled into a local drive-in, ordered a hamburger . . ., and listened to the people on either side of you? You ought to try that sometime, just to sense the buying public's mood out there for Chrysler products. We're king of the street! Don't lose that!"[1]

Brownlie knew that teenaged hot rodders as well as other Americans had recently rebelled against Detroit's bland, look-alike products. He and other stylists were struggling to tap this rebellious spirit by offering a broad array of distinctive, personal cars that catered to each individual's purse and personality. Brownlie's youthful excitement carried the day over Boyd's bean-counting trepidations, and the newly designed Hemi-Charger appeared in Chrysler's 1968 line-up. But by the time this monstrous muscle car hit the streets, its heyday had passed. The American rebellion had surged over the containing walls of consumerism and begun to challenge the core of Fordist institutions. By 1971, Brownlie's turned-on muscle car had become a bad trip, and it was quietly canceled as the country moved into the sobering 1970s.

AMERICA, 1960–1970: THE ESCALATING CONTRADICTIONS OF FORDISM

The homeland of Fordism entered the decade with deepening doubts about the auto-based marriage of mass production and mass consumption. The long economic expansion between 1961 and 1969 was insufficient to suppress a rising awareness of the high costs of Fordist prosperity. The escalating civil rights struggles and the discovery of poverty revealed the seamy side of Fordism and spawned a War on Poverty that was perverted by the escalating anxiety about affluence. Projecting their own fear and guilt about consumption, affluent Americans saw in the poor not victims of a system but undisciplined individuals who surrendered to the gratifications of consumption that they feared in themselves.[2]

Gnawing doubts about the real value of America's consumer culture deepened. Not only did consumers question the individuality of their goods, but they also began to see the underlying contradiction of Fordist consumption. The attempt of everyone to find individual fulfillment through commodities led to unintended social consequences that prevented anyone from attaining fulfillment. This contradiction became manifest domestically in automotive consumption, where millions of Americans seeking escape in dream machines became trapped in a tangle of traffic that endangered not only mental fantasies but bodily security. And the countryside that was to provide individual relief from urban woes quickly turned into a collective wasteland of choking smog and environmental devastation. The social costs of Fordist consumption also escalated in the international realm, where the American dominance that ensured privileged access to the world's resources required increased military expenditures. Even greater was the cost in human lives paid in counterrevolutionary wars like that in Vietnam. By the end of the decade, a substantial proportion of Americans had decided that these public costs of privatized consumption were too high.[3]

This tumultuous decade of the 1960s exposed contradictions not only in Fordist consumption but also in Fordist production. Fordist prosperity began to undermine the incentives that induced workers to trade work-place autonomy for monetary rewards to begin with. Low rates of unemployment and increasing social-wage programs took the sting out of the threat of firing. More insulated than ever from the cost of un-employment, many workers began to reexamine the workplace issues that they had been forced to bargain away earlier. The decade saw a rising tide of worker discontent, much of which focused on non-monetary issues.[4]

These contradictions of Fordist consumption and production con-verged on America's youth. This first generation to grow up under the full sway of Fordism saw the costs of the system so increase and its benefits so decrease that to many it hardly seemed much of a bargain. These young people were consciously cultivated as consumers by merchandisers, but simultaneously pressured to prepare themselves as Fordist producers by accomodating to increasingly degraded work. For this generation, the delicate trade-off of commodified consumption for alienated production began to come apart. Because they took prosperity for granted, the rewards of a boring and standardized consumer culture hardly seemed worth the sacrifices of Fordist work. Middle-class youth rebelled against the long, degrading apprenticeship in authoritarian schools that was the price of entry into boring, standardized white-collar jobs. And working-class kids who went into the factories questioned the sacrifices required on the assembly lines for the privilege of purchasing shoddy, standardized goods. Both demanded more meaningful grati-fications and increased control over their institutions.[5]

Encumbered by Fordist institutions, America's rulers responded to these escalating revolts by offering larger doses of the same old con-sumer opium. For the excluded blacks and poor came social programs to move them toward the consumerist mainstream. For discontented workers came higher wages and benefits. And manufacturers offered these consumers with more time and money a growing array of goods, finely differentiated for the purse and personality of each individual. No longer relying on superficial diversity, companies began to differentiate their goods by essential characteristics like size and function to appeal to markets specialized by age, sex, region, and lifestyle.

Although market fragmentation is an ever-present tendency within capitalist commodity production, this tendency was hastened in the 1960s. The consumer boom of the 1950s was focused on the family, with the suburban castle and the big family car as the most prominent commodities. By the 1960s, however, the suburban idyll of family togetherness was wearing thin, as the children entered school and the growing youth subculture, and dad spent more and more time commuting to work. Increasingly isolated, family members were vulnerable to individualistic appeals of merchandisers seeking to segment their needs into market niches and sell them on distinctive products.[6]

So the more the social consequences of consumerism threatened individuality, the more Americans resorted to a stronger dose of the familiar palliative of individualistic consumption. This was the age of individuality, the do-your-own-thing decade. But this growing variety of consumer goods threatened to contradict the standardization and mechanization necessary for Fordist production. Manufacturers had to construct expensive machine and assembly lines for each product, which lowered volumes and raised costs. And on these specialized lines, the growing amount of optional equipment produced varying tasks and played havoc with precise timing and coordination. Consequently, labor productivity fell and costs rose further. Manufacturers sought to compensate for these increased costs by work speed-up and disciplinary crackdown. But these measures only exacerbated the escalating labor problems of Fordism, producing in the late 1960s the largest strike wave to hit America since the immediate postwar conflagration.

As the decade drew to a close, the contradictions of the Fordist industrial system pioneered a half-century before were coming home to roost. Individualistic consumption produced social costs it could not compensate, while alienated production was undermined by its own prosperity. And attempts to solve these problems within the confines of Fordist institutions only exacerbated these contradictions. Consequently, the 1960s exploded in a frenzy of social movements, each protesting a particular cost of Fordism.

STYLING REORGANIZES FOR AUTOMOTIVE INDIVIDUALITY

The escalating style race of the 1950s exposed the essential similarity of Detroit's dinosaurs and created a demand for truly distinctive automobiles. The ability of Americans to express their individual personalities in an automobile was facilitated by the rise of the multicar family. While only 7 percent of families owned more than one car in 1950, by 1960 that proportion had grown to 15 percent; by 1970, to 29 percent. A family's second or third car did not have to be an all-purpose family sedan, but could be tailored to the specific needs of the primary driver. For mom, engaged in the reproduction of the family and care of the home, a big station wagon would fill the bill. For dad, who commuted alone to the office or factory, an intermediate-sized but comfortable sedan seemed apropos. And for the teenaged kids driving to school and on dates, a small, sporty car was sufficient.[7]

But these different functional requirements cannot fully account for the frenzy of model proliferation during the decade, which was also caused by America's cultural definition of the car. Since at least the 1930s, the automobile was defined as a cultural outlet for the needs of individuality denied in Fordist production. It is not surprising then that as ownership expanded and lessened the practical demands of family transportation, the car increasingly became the privileged vehicle for an individual's personality and self-realization. Of course, the automakers encouraged product specialization to create new markets and expand the demand for cars. But they would not have proved so successful had not consumers been culturally predisposed to express their needs and personalities through automobile consumption.[8]

But model proliferation played havoc with a Fordist system geared to produce superficially differentiated but essentially standardized automobiles. True model diversity, as opposed to mere stylistic differentiation, was incompatible with centralized managerial control of both the design and production process. The varying tasks required could not be precisely prescribed but had to be left to the discretion of the workers themselves. This decade of increasingly varied automobiles thus created pressures to reorganize longstanding Fordist institutions.

The problem of satisfying the consumer appetite for individuality fell to the stylists, who were now primarily responsible for initiating product design. Styling organizations which had been dominated by the centralized vision of one powerful man now had to generate a plethora of truly different designs. Designers in the divisional studios, who had been cowed into aesthetic submission by the styling chief, had to be encouraged to be innovative and distinctive. The scope of reorganization was nowhere greater than at General Motors, where design was controlled by a centralized bureaucracy. But nowhere were the talents and resources necessary for reorganization in greater supply. Under Bill Mitchell's leadership, the Styling Staff loosened the bureaucratic constraints, giving designers the discretion they needed to generate a phenomenal range of different automobiles.

Coming to power late in 1958, Mitchell recognized that his main challenge was moving away from the bizarre designs induced by the fin wars while simultaneously incorporating real automotive individuality. But he knew that GM's centralized system left little room for such individuality, since all new designs were dictated by Earl's Body

Development Studio. When Chrysler leapfrogged over Earl's designs, stylists individually rushed to meet the challenge with no advanced planning, producing catastrophic results. Mitchell realized that responsibility for innovation had to be dispersed and regularized so GM would not be caught napping again.[9]

So in the late 1950s Mitchell decentralized responsibility for design innovation from the Body Development Studio to the production studios, where designers created the entire auto instead of just decorating the interchangeable body shell. Unlike Earl, he did not try to dictate aesthetics but gave his underlings the freedom to create individual designs. And to ensure the development of innovative ideas, Mitchell established alongside each production studio an advanced design studio freed from the pressures of production schedules.

The economies of mass production still required the different divisions to share body shells and other parts. But reversing Earl's procedure, Mitchell established interchangeability after the fact, sending completed divisional designs to the Body Development Studio for the creation of the shared body shells. Production designers were persuaded to modify their proposals sufficiently to allow for common parts. Although the styling chief was still the final authority, the new decentralized structure relied more on coordination and compromise than unilateral dictation of design. As Irv Rybicki, Mitchell's successor as styling chief, recognized, if one person dictated all designs, "in the end they are all going to start looking alike. . . . [But] If I let the chiefs and their teams run, we have a better chance for diversification, for creating divisional personalities that are sound. . . ."[10]

To accelerate the generation of diversity, Mitchell also altered the working procedures of the GM Styling Staff. While Earl required the development of precise orthographic drawings before modeling, Mitchell had stylists lay out merely the car's silhouette with full-scale tape drawings – half-inch tape placed on paper – which could be quickly done and altered. From these they moved directly to a full-sized clay model, bypassing the detailed orthographics. Since the tape drawings left many dimensions undefined, stylists did much designing at the model stage. Unencumbered by the rigid technical drawings, they were free to improvise and innovate, generating quicker and more varied designs.[11]

While Bill Mitchell willingly decentralized power within the Styling Staff, he adamantly refused to relinquish any control over design to corporate forces outside his organization. While Ford gave corporate product planners a large role in pioneering designs, the GM Styling Staff maintained a virtual monopoly on product innovation during the 1960s.

Market researchers at GM merely surveyed responses to new cars designed by styling. Stylists' control of innovation in this era of model proliferation meant that GM's line-up was weighted heavily toward their prejudices, especially for large cars. John De Lorean, the general manager at Chevrolet during this time, claims that in 1969 his proposal for a new compact car was killed by Mitchell, not only because it did not originate in styling but also because it "was taking the corporation into a more utilitarian design and away from the longer, lower, and sleeker look." Styling's veto power often forced GM to play catch-up during this period, scrambling to compete with innovative models pioneered by Ford product planners who did not share stylists' prejudices.[12]

Although product planners played a large role in design at Ford, the company's Styling Staff also grew in independence and importance in this decade of model proliferation. Ford designers entered the decade still subordinate, merely putting a shape on vehicles whose dimensions and architecture were dictated by engineers and product planners. But in 1961 Gene Bordinat took over as head of Ford styling, and under his leadership the department made substantial gains in organizational authority. As John Najjar, a long-time Ford stylist, recalled, "Bordinat is a pioneer in having the Design Center not only design the shapes but get in under the skin and become a part of true designing." Taking his cue from Harley Earl, his former boss, Bordinat undermined the influence of Ford Engineering by hiring his own engineers. With them he acquired Engineering's all-important section book – a set of cross-sections through important parts of the car that set dimensional requirements. Armed with this knowledge and personnel, Bordinat wrested the control of packaging away from engineers and planners.[13]

Ford executives relinquished greater power to Bordinat's Styling Staff to meet the demand for automotive diversity, but Ford designers never achieved the power of their GM counterparts. Product planners still controlled the initiation of new models and, along with top executives, held final-approval power over designs. So during this period, Ford achieved a delicate organizational balance between the traditional forces contesting design: marketing, styling, and engineering. This system of checks and balances prevented the prejudices of one group from predominating, thus yielding a record of innovation second to none in this decade.

Unlike their counterparts at either GM or Ford, the stylists at Chrysler were in retreat in the early 1960s. The corporation's powerful engineers had grudgingly conceded greater influence over design to Virgil Exner, whose cars experienced a brief success. But while Ford and GM designers rushed to subdue the design excesses on which the public soured, Exner persisted with the fins and other oddities. Chrysler sales fell, leading the corporation's engineers to move back in to regain lost territory. By the early 1960s they once again exercised decisive control over design, mandating another generation of sensible, economical cars. For 1962, Chrysler downsized its entire line-up of cars, which appeared tiny in comparison to the growing models at GM and Ford. Sales again fell disastrously, proving that even in sobering times consumers remained intoxicated with big cars. Ironically, Exner was blamed for these cars dictated largely by engineers and was fired in the managerial shake-up that followed the poor sales year.[14]

To replace Exner as styling chief Chrysler hired Elwood Engel, one of Walker's styling lieutenants at Ford. Engel took up the Sisyphean battle against Chrysler engineers, and was more successful than any of his predecessors. One Chrysler designer reported that "when Elwood came in he effected more positive change in the first month that he was here than Exner did in his entire tenure." The downsizing debacle probably persuaded Chrysler executives that stylists needed more freedom to compete successfully in this age of individuality. But Engel's success was also the result of his fiery and assertive personality, a trait lacking among previous heads of the department. He was cut from the same charismatic cloth as Walker and Earl, and was not afraid to confront and intimidate top executives over styling decisions. In one presentation of interior mock-ups, for example, Chrysler managers began to argue with him about production costs. Agitated by such nit-picking, Engel waved a disputed piece of hardware at the executives, shouting: "Ford has a department of forty guys that are just designing things like this. We've got one guy doing the same thing. We better get in it or get out of the business." He hurled the part across the floor, barely missing the feet of Chrysler president Lynn Townsend, then stomped out the door. The startled Townsend declared: "Well gentlemen, I guess we'd better build it." Chrysler styling finally got a powerful chief, but engineers and product planners retained substantial power, limiting stylists' ability to determine design.[15]

Like their competitors, the main goal of Chrysler stylists was a larger range of distinctive cars, which required organizational changes. Sometime in the mid-1960s Engel, like Mitchell, decentralized initial design decisions, giving divisional designers responsibility for completing an entire model. Efforts were then made to establish the commonality that allowed divisions to share shells. As at GM, styling decisions were decentralized to encourage the initiative required to produce truly distinctive automobiles.[16]

THE EXPLOSION OF AUTOMOTIVE DIVERSITY

Once the styling organizations were reorganized and empowered, they turned out an astounding array of distinct automobiles during this decade. In 1959 Detroit cars came in only one size – big – but by 1970 consumers could choose between subcompacts, compacts, intermediate, and full-sized cars. And within each of these categories there were dozens of models available. The number of models offered by American automakers remained virtually constant throughout the 1950s, increasing from 243 in 1950 to 244 in 1960. But by 1970 model offerings had increased over 50 percent to 370. And each of these models was available with a broad range of consumer-specified options. For example, in 1966 the Chevrolet Division of GM produced forty-six models, on which were available various combinations of thirty-two engines, twenty transmissions, thirty colors, and more than four hundred other options. One Yale physicist only half-whimsically suggested that the number of possible Chevy combinations could conceivably exceed the number of atoms in the universe. Chevy's general manager, John De Lorean, more realistically suggested that the company could build over one million different cars, so that no two buyers' cars need be alike.[17]

The point of such product diversification was just such consumer individuality. Because the ideology of individualist consumption was being undermined by its mounting social costs, Fordism required an ever-escalating amount of ostensible individuality to sustain it. As John Gordon, president of GM, declared in 1963: "Our objective is not only a car for every purse and purpose but, you might say, a car for every purse, purpose and person." Claud McCammon, an administrator in the GM Styling Staff, argued that the auto market was fragmenting into a "multi-mass market," composed of numerous markets for specific types of cars. "These new mass markets are a reflection of a kind of mass-individualism which makes everyone want to be different – exactly like everyone else is different." But could the market really be divided up almost infinitesimally without undermining the large volume necessary for mass production? This question would be answered only after nearly a decade of model proliferation.[18]

The Big Three did not enter the 1960s with a strategy of product diversification but responded to the demands of consumers. In the late 1950s, the falling sales of Detroit's automotive barges and the rising fortunes of the small imports seemed to mean that consumers wanted small economy cars. To capture this market, automakers unveiled their own compact cars in the fall of 1959. The Ford Falcon and the Plymouth

Valiant were downsized versions of uninspired Detroit engineering. But the Chevrolet Corvair was an adventuresome copy of the rear-engined, air-cooled Volkswagen. Its 6-cylinder, horizontal engine was innovative, but the suspension was deadly conventional. The independent swing axles in the rear produced dangerously unstable steering that made the Corvair a target of the budding consumer movement.

Detroit's compacts were initially successful, cutting into import sales and capturing a whopping 42 percent of the new-car market. But savvy observers of America's automotive obsession doubted that consumers were finally demanding economy and function in their cars. *Business Week* argued that compact sales were driven by demands for newness in an automotive scene that had become all too monotonous and homogeneous. Bill Tara, an advertising agent for GM, similarly told Chevrolet stylists that the trend toward small cars "does not necessarily argue that functionality will win out." Consumers still saw cars as expressions of escape and individual status, he argued, but Detroit's monotonous offerings had been unable to fulfill these desires. The greatest challenge facing automobile stylists in the 1960s, he concluded, was designing "an automobile that has personality and *distinction* which can easily be separated in a buyer's mind from the great variety of available cars."[19]

That distinction, not economy, fueled the sales of Detroit's compacts was proved by a propitious marketing move by GM in 1960. Its Corvair was introduced in two rather frugal trim lines, capitalizing on what was thought to be the economizing mood of the consumer. But at mid-year Chevrolet brought out an upscale line, the Monza. Named after a famous grand prix circuit, the car had an automatic transmission, pleated-vinyl bucket seats, loop-weave carpet, deluxe trim, and a sporty coupe body. The well-appointed Monza was an almost instant success, accounting for over half of all Corvair sales. GM chairman Alfred Sloan concluded that although small cars were designed for economy, "it soon became apparent, somewhat contradictorily, that the customer had not lost his taste for the comfort, convenience, and styling of the regular-size cars . . . it is evident that this demand [for compact cars] was essentially a further expression of the customer's desire for greater variety." The compacts were successful not because of their frugality, but because they were different from the monotonous line-up of standard family sedans.[20]

Capitalizing on this lesson, the Big Three quickly transformed their austere little compacts into distinctive automotive gems, different in size but similarly loaded down with the comforts and accessories that insulated drivers from the rigorous labors of the road. For 1961 the Corvair engine

Figure 18 1960 Chevrolet Corvair Monza coupe, the first compact with pizazz. Introduced at midyear as a deluxe model of the frugal Corvair, with bucket seats, a sporty body, and automatic transmission, the fast-selling Monza revealed that American consumers bought compacts for their distinction, not economy. (Courtesy General Motors Corporation)

was made more powerful, and by 1962 this "economy" car came in a Monza Spyder model sporting a 150-horsepower, turbocharged engine. In 1961 GM introduced another wave of compacts, of which the frugal, 4-cylinder Pontiac Tempest was most innovative in engineering. But the public preferred the conventional but upscale Olds F–85 and Buick Special, both of which came with standard V–8s and more trim. Ford entered the sporty compact market in 1961 with the Falcon Futura, which included bucket seats, plush carpet, and more trim.[21]

By 1963 it was clear that consumers of compact cars were looking not for economy but difference. *Business Week* reported that "Buyers want cars bigger, fancier," even their small ones. The article quoted Chevrolet's general manager, Semon "Bunkie" Knudsen, as saying, "A lot of people won't buy a real cheap car or a real small car today unless there is some kind of distinctive air about it, such as the Volkswagen has." Consequently, the Big Three began offering bigger and more varied compacts loaded down with a panoply of options and accessories. And these cars were not simply the result of the industry's unilateral strategy to earn the larger profits that the more accessorized cars brought, as some critics charged. Given a choice, Americans generally bought the larger, more distinctively styled and accessorized cars in their quest to achieve some individuality in an otherwise increasingly regimented society.[22]

The push for automotive individuality produced not merely smaller cars but also distinctively styled big ones. In America's automotive culture, size had always connoted the importance and luxurious excess in consumption that countered the degradation and frugalities imposed in production. So many consumers continued to demand bigness, even in cars that carried a single passenger. And the smaller passenger requirements on these big cars gave stylists a huge sheet-metal canvas on which to paint portraits of individual distinction. The automotive package that emphasized comfort and distinction for one or two passengers became known as the personal luxury car, and it was pioneered by the 1958 four-place Thunderbird. In the years after its introduction, this car grew even more excessive in size and accessories in its effort to offer consumers comfort and distinction. Even *Motor Trend*, an enthusiast's magazine with little tolerance for Detroit's boulevard barges, was forced to recognize the appeal of Ford's overgrown sports car. After faithfully recounting the mechanical shortcomings of the 1960 Thunderbird, the editors concluded that: "It is a car apart, and like royalty, rarely required to count for ordinary deficiencies. . . . The Thunderbird is different, and that is all it has ever had to be."[23]

In 1963 GM took aim at Ford's monopoly on the personal luxury market with two cars – the Buick Riviera and the Pontiac Grand Prix. The Riviera was created by Bill Mitchell to satisfy the outcry of GM dealers for a Thunderbird competitor. The elegantly unadorned car had a 117-inch wheelbase, making it a bit longer than the T-Bird but over a foot shorter than the standard Buicks. And like its competitor, the Riviera was pretentiously impractical, with most of its length given over to a long hood and front-passenger comfort. This was obviously not a family car but the selfish statement of one individual starved for distinction. Despite the rather steep price, beginning at $4,333, the Riviera sold 40,000 copies its first year.[24]

Pontiac was also itching to cash in on the emerging market in personal luxury. So in 1963 division head Pete Estes and chief engineer John De Lorean collaborated to produce an upscale version of the big Pontiac, named Grand Prix. The large, elegant car was distinctive in its virtual absence of chrome trim, giving rise to the "clean look" that reversed the previous decade's obsession with chrome encrustation. The car was a stunning sales success, selling nearly 73,000 copies, more than even the Thunderbird.[25]

By mid-decade the trend toward personal luxury had gathered enough momentum to carry it to the end of the 1960s. Even the full-sized sedans and hardtops rushed to capture the feel of individualized comfort and appointments. And the Thunderbird and Riviera grew to compete with these full-sized cars until the label "personal luxury" meant a car every bit as big as the largest family sedan but with nearly half the passenger and luggage space. In the age of individuality no one wanted to risk his or her expression of automotive freedom being pressed into service to haul the kids or household supplies.[26]

Two more types of automotive individuality emerged at mid-decade, ensuring that consumers' quest for distinction would not be drowned in a sea of loaded-down luxury barges. These were the pony car and the muscle car, both of which were targeted at the burgeoning youth market. The 1960s saw the rock-and-roll/hot-rod subculture of the 1950s spread beyond its working-class origins to coalesce into a broad youth subculture. The automakers drooled over this market of youths with discretionary cash and a urge to express their rebellious identity through the automobile. So they set out to exploit this rebellion, creating cars that incorporated the signs of youthful defiance into mass-produced sheet metal. The first such car was the 1964 Pontiac GTO, aimed at the more vigorous, masculine side of the subculture. When "Bunkie" Knudsen took over as Pontiac's general manager in 1956, he hired a

Figure 19 1964 Pontiac GTO sports coupe, John De Lorean's attempt to recapture youthful automotive rebels for Detroit automakers. This first muscle car was not merely mechanically powerful but also imitated the hot-rod aesthetic with its stripped-down no-frills look. (Courtesy General Motors Corporation)

team of young managers and engineers to create a youthful, energetic image for the stodgy division. Taking their cues from the hot-rod rebels, Knudsen's team stripped off the chrome doodads, cut the weight, lowered the body, and added bigger engines. Following this general trend, in 1963 Pontiac engineer John De Lorean stuffed the division's biggest V–8 into the timid little Tempest compact. The results were electrifying, producing "the feeling and performance of an expensive foreign sports car," De Lorean recalled. Then Pontiac engineers beefed up the brakes and suspension, and added three two-barrel carburetors, a floor shift, and dual exhausts. And to leave no one guessing about his intentions, De Lorean named the powerful new model the GTO, after a Ferrari racing coupe. But what he produced was not a lithe European sports car but a brash American brute that excelled in straight-ahead acceleration. The muscle car was born. The GTO debuted in 1964 with a $3,200 price tag, well within the reach of many seekers of automotive individuality. With a little help from a youth-oriented promotional campaign, including a manufactured hit record called "Little GTO," sales of the original automotive brute soared, reaching 84,000 by its third year.[27]

In the copy-cat world of automotive marketing, imitations of the GTO's muscle-car formula followed apace. In 1966 Ford introduced a GT performance version on its intermediate Fairlane, and Chrysler jumped into this niche by stuffing a 426-cubic-inch Hemihead engine into its mid-sized Dodge Charger. What was new about the muscle car was not just its horsepower but its individuality – it was a new category of car that advertised its difference from run-of-the-mill models. Not social superiority but being a bit different – just like everyone else – was the appeal. To stress the individuality of its AMX muscle car, American Motors set the production number in the dash, and advertised that limited production meant that "When you drive one, you won't see yourself coming and going." But to stress the democracy of such difference, the ad concluded that "possessing an AMX does not make one man better than another. Just luckier."[28]

To express such automotive individuality, muscle cars offered a wide range of options. Consumers could create almost custom-made cars by choosing from entire catalogs of performance options like engines, carburetors, transmissions, brakes, and suspensions. One ad for the Dodge Challenger listed a host of options and concluded that this "is a car you buy when you decide you don't want to be like everyone else." By cultivating connotations of difference and defiance, muscle cars sought blatantly to commodify the youthful rebellion against Fordism.

In 1966, for example, Dodge launched its "Dodge Rebellion" promotion, featuring one ad which pictured beside a Charger a young woman holding a bomb behind her back. "Charger . . . new leader of the Dodge Rebellion. This beautiful new bomb comes from the drawing board to your driveway with all the excitement left in." Also appealing to the rising tide of discontent, Buick advertised its Skylark GS as a muscle car "that would rattle your faith in the established order of sporting machinery."[29]

In 1965 another automotive milestone was released that tapped the escalating rebellion against the monotonous offerings of Fordism – the revolutionary Ford Mustang. This tamer version of youthful exuberance originated with Ford Division president Lee Iacocca, who was painfully aware that his line-up lacked appeal to the youth market. So he proposed that Ford build a new car for the 16 to 24 year-old market that was stylish and sporty, combined high performance with good handling, and was priced under $2,500. By 1963 Iacocca had a running prototype of his car, which was named after an experimental Ford sports car called Mustang. The car was displayed at shows, races, and college campuses, where it immediately generated youthful excitement. And on the cheap as well. At Iacocca's direction the Mustang was built from off-the-shelf Falcon and Fairlane components. As he recalled, "all we had to do was put a youth wrapper around it – and this was done for less than $50 million."[30]

Ford's brand of mass-produced individuality proved an enormous success, with Mustang sales reaching 417,000 in its introductory year. Although aimed at the youth market, the car had an extremely broad appeal, largely because of the wide range of options which allowed customers to create completely different types of automobiles. One automotive journalist called the Mustang the "universal multi-car." "Never before has one, simple concept car been compounded into so many variable electives to satisfy a wide range of tastes." By juggling options, the Mustang could be made into an economy car, a personal luxury car, a muscle car, or dozens of other variants. As the auto journalist concluded, late in 1964, it was evident that the 1,740 Mustangs mass-produced each day were "not so many peas in a pod, but rather a whole complex of highly distinct personalities. . . ."[31]

The success of the Mustang triggered a spate of pony-car imitations. In 1967 GM brought out its Pontiac Firebird and Chevrolet Camaro, Mustang clones with similarly long hoods, short decks, and open mouths. The GM pony cars were also built around programs of extensive options that made individual tailoring possible. In the same year, Chrysler revamped its Barracuda variant of the Valiant compact into a

Figure 20 1965 Ford Mustang 2+2 fastback, Ford's highly successful youth car. The Mustang came with a wide variety of options that allowed it to satisfy the individuality demanded by all consumers in this decade of escalating Fordist contradictions. (Courtesy National Automotive History Collection, Detroit Public Library)

separate pony car line. Like the compacts, personal luxury cars, and muscle cars, however, these pony cars grew gradually longer and heavier. By 1971 the Mustang had swollen 8 inches longer, 6 inches wider, and nearly 600 pounds heavier, leading even Iacocca to admit that "it was more like a fat pig" than a sleek horse. Sales dropped as the pony cars lost their difference from Detroit's other overgrown, over-accessorized dream boats. Automotive America seemed caught in an enigma. Consumers wanted difference, and Detroit proliferated models to accomodate them. But they also wanted the creature comforts of a big, luxurious car that insulated them from the cruel realities of Fordist America. So all the distinct new cars got bigger, heavier, and costlier, until they lost their individuality and sent consumers scampering for the newest automotive innovation to begin the cycle all over again.[32]

THE LOOK OF INDIVIDUALITY: AESTHETIC TRENDS IN THE 1960s

Automobile stylists in this decade of individuality had an easier job than in the 1950s. No longer forced to disguise shared parts, they now had a range of truly diverse automotive platforms to sculpt. So the look of difference was inherently easier to achieve. But stylists still had to give the sheet-metal skin an individual look that objectified the distinctive body shell, chassis, and components underneath. What was the proper look of distinction for such a disruptive, rapidly changing decade?

Consumers had clearly lost their tolerance for the bizarre futurism of the 1950s. By the 1960s the future was beginning to look old, for the naive belief in technological utopias had been irreparably shaken by exposure of the dark side of consumer culture. The first task of the decade's designers was to purge autos of the futuristic frivolity, especially tail fins. Ford fins were tiny in 1961, gone by 1962. The only 1961 GM make to retain them was their originator, Cadillac. Even Chrysler's Exner had let go of the nightmare by 1962. But after the fins and other oddities were shaved off, auto designers faced the troubling question of where to go from there. The answer was obvious to seasoned veterans like Bill Mitchell and Virgil Exner. If people had lost faith in the future, perhaps they could derive meaning from the past. As Americans entered a period of rapid and progressive social change, many ironically sought a sense of consolation and stability in nostalgic automotive images, giving rise to the neoclassical era.

Chrysler's Exner was the first designer to capture this trend in a production car. Struggling to save his power, Exner turned in 1961

Figure 21 1963 Buick Riviera hardtop coupe, Bill Mitchell's expression of the neoclassical aesthetic. This personal luxury car imitated the proportions and sharp-edge styling of classic cars, giving consumers a sense of tradition and security in a decade of rapid social change. (Courtesy General Motors Corporation)

desparately to classic-era ornamentation like free-standing headlights and taillights and simulated clamshell fenders. Chrysler stylists told *Motor Trend* that they imitated classic cars to get back to "honesty and integrity" in design and away from "over-ornamented Easter-eggs." In 1962 Exner tried to incorporate even more classic elements like V'd windshields, long hoods, short decks, and close-coupled passenger compartments. But on the downsized cars of this year these classic elements did not look right. Sales fell and Exner departed, leaving the neoclassical crusade to GM's Bill Mitchell.[33]

Mitchell had always loved classic cars, so when he assumed the reins of GM's Styling Staff, he pushed to incorporate their clean, lean, sculptured lines into contemporary cars. Mitchell argued: "The Mercedes, Duesenberg, and Stutz – those cars had a kind of romance, a kind of individuality; each one was a live animal. We might be able to get some of that back into our mass-produced cars." He hoped that classic-car features would bring distinction back to the mass-produced cars that had become dangerously alike in the late 1950s.[34]

In 1963 Mitchell's neoclassic aesthetic achieved its first definitive expression in the Buick Riviera, the personal luxury car that came to epitomize this styling idiom. The car was almost totally bereft of the chrome doodads. Since the Riviera had a unique chassis and body, its distinction could be established in actual form, not superficial ornamentation. One distinguishing form found on the car's belt line and roof was the sharp, sheer edge, a feature Mitchell borrowed from English classics to give his cars their formal, tailored look. He stated: "Trousers don't look any damn good without a crease in them – you've got to have an edge to accentuate form." Mitchell's sheer edges accentuated the Riviera's tight, fast forms like the flowing belt line, which deviated only slightly from the perpendicular to sensuously curve over the rear wheel. This line highlighted the long hood and short deck, proportions inspired by the impractical luxury classics. Finally, to lend the car a formal air of privacy, Mitchell gave its roof a wide rear pillar and a small rear window.[35]

Mitchell's neoclassical aesthetic of taut, razor-edged sculpting influenced the entire GM line-up of 1963, especially the smart, restrained Chevrolets. And it was not long before similarly nostalgic elements showed up on Ford and Chrysler products. Ford's new head of styling, Gene Bordinat, brought the neoclassical look to the 1962 Thunderbird with two special editions: the Sports Roadster, with wire wheels and a fiberglass tonneau; and the Landau, with a fixed vinyl top and dummy landau bars. By 1965 the entire Ford line showed sharp-edged styling and neoclassical roof lines. Under Elwood Engel, Chrysler also continued down the road toward a more restrained neoclassical aesthetic, similarly adopting squarer, straighter lines and formal roofs.[36]

Although most autos moved aesthetically backward during this decade, a countertrend appeared in the muscle-car category. Youthful aficionados of power and performance were little interested in the stability of neoclassicism, but wanted to rush defiantly ahead to new technological horizons. So technological fetishism and futurism lived on among the young, particularly those of working-class origins, who had only their mechanical skills to distinguish them. Stylists continued to create connotations of technological superiority by visually associating performance cars with the most advanced form of transportation, which during this decade was the rocket. So 1960s stylists made these cars look like rockets, not by appending superficial visual clichés, as in the 1950s, but by subtly shaping the most basic forms of the automobile.

Foremost among these stylists seeking a new form of technological expressionism was Bill Porter, who came to GM in 1957 dedicated to ridding the corporation's cars of the corny aeronautic symbolism. He sought to transform technology from a superficial to an integral influence on automobile design. "I was trying to move away from what I perceived were just the superficial symbols of aircraft in automobile designs. . . . I was interested in exploring more profound fusions of technology and design. . . ." By 1968 Porter was chief designer in the Pontiac production studio and ready to realize his more fundamental vision of technological futurism. He designed this year's GTO, which was free of chrome clichés but nonetheless bore the look of advanced jet aircraft in its subtly sculpted forms. The car's sides were rounded into a monocoque shell inspired by jet fuselages. This look was developed further in the 1970 Pontiac Firebird, on which Porter sought to achieve a "pure monocoque form." The smooth, rounded bulges gave the car not only an aircraft feel but also a "muscular look," as if the skin of the car were forced out by the mechanical strength underneath. Other muscle cars like the Dodge Charger picked up a similar idiom of muscular, technological superiority.[37]

Another influence on the youth-oriented cars of the period was the styling idiom of the customizers of California. Seeking to capture the look of youthful rebellion as well as disguise the signs of mass production, Detroit's stylists began to steal the customizers' tricks of the trade. In 1963 Ford tried to capture the image of youthful excitement by commissioning famous customizers to design a series of Ford show cars which toured teen-oriented events around the country. GM's John De

Lorean had a better idea. He incorporated the customized look into actual production cars like the 1963 Grand Prix and 1964 GTO, both of which copied the customizers' trick of "frenching in" or recessing grilles and headlights. Over the course of the decade, Detroit stylists developed a regular dialogue with the California customizers in order to incorporate their individualistic style and capture the rebellious spirit of youth for mass production. As long as this rebellion was mainly one of style, it could be and was commodified. But by the end of the decade, the youth revolt had transcended questions of style to challenge the very roots of Fordism.[38]

AMERICA'S AUTOMOTIVE DISCONTENT

Throughout the 1960s, the purveyors of auto opium sought to deaden the public's awareness of the escalating human and environmental costs of Fordism by administering an increased dose of individualized consumption. But the bigger dose only intensified the underlying sickness of the system and threatened to undermine the very foundations of Fordism.

The escalating contradictions of Fordist consumption and production

The escalation of auto individuality only exacerbated the contradictions of Fordist consumption. When each individual sought to express his or her own identity through a personally tailored vehicle, the roads became tangled in a collective traffic jam that increased breakdowns, accidents, noise, and pollution. Americans' attitudes about the car consequently became fraught with ambivalence. In the popular media for every depiction of the car as a vehicle of freedom and escape, there was a counterposing image of a menacing force, ready to consume its consumers. In Jean-Luc Godard's film *Weekend* (1968), the autos with which the bourgeois characters seek to escape the chaotic society they have created ultimately cause their undoing in a conflagration of twisted sheet metal and flesh. A similarly menacing machine turns on its human makers in Steven Spielberg's made-for-televison movie *Duel* (1971), in which an ominous tractor-trailer rig stalks an innocent driver.[39]

By the early 1970s popular automotive consciousness had undergone a revolution, with even the conservative *Wall Street Journal* noticing "a growing rebellion against cars." "Where once they viewed their cars as fun and something special to own, they currently are frustrated or bored with their cars. The novelty and status of car ownership are long gone. So they look at their auto as an appliance – to get them economically from place to place and to be replaced when it wears out." The rising consumer movement, which saw cars as utilitarian machines, "has prompted sweeping steps by the government to regulate auto designs."[40]

The automotive rebellion found its sources not only in these cultural contradictions but also in the production contradictions of Fordism. The model proliferation driven by the search for individuality threatened the foundation of automotive mass production, which still rested upon the production of a few standardized products. Model diversity drastically increased the costs of product engineering and development, according to John De Lorean, general manager of Chevrolet. And the costs of manufacturing this growing variety of vehicles also escalated rapidly. In a detailed study of the Ford Motor Company, William Abernathy found that as the number of Ford engines and models grew during the late 1950s and early 1960s, both engine and assembly plants became more specialized, producing only one or perhaps two technologically similar products. But because sales did not increase as rapidly as product variety, the specialized plants had relatively low volumes of production. Consequently, the increased costs of tooling and equipping this growing number of specialized plants were amortized over a smaller number of units in each, driving up unit production costs.[41]

But diversity of basic models was not the only production problem experienced by automakers during this age of individuality. On each of these basic models there was available to consumers a myriad of mechanical and stylistic options. It became standard practice in the 1960s for buyers to special order an automobile from a dealer, selecting from hundreds of options. To produce these individualized cars, factories had to keep huge inventories of thousands upon thousands of parts. De Lorean recalled that the Chevy parts manual had over 165,000 different material order specifications and measured a foot-and-a-half thick. Further, all these options created a nightmare of scheduling problems, for hundreds of optional parts had to be checked, routed, and transported to arrive at the assembly line at just the right time. Computerized and automated inventory and accounting systems helped some but did not solve all problems, especially those in final assembly, where people still did most of the work. There was no mechanical substitute for human labor in the complex tasks of positioning and attaching the myriad of parts to the body shell. Balancing these minutely divided tasks on the moving line required precise time and motion study, which was undermined by the increasing variety of options. Along the same assembly lines came cars of widely varying options requiring different amounts of assembly time and effort. To accomodate this variety, assembly lines had to be slowed to leave sufficient time for the most demanding tasks. And if production managers refused to lower line speeds, the rush to complete the time-consuming tasks often resulted in poor quality.[42]

These problems of product proliferation resulted in increased costs and stagnating productivity. Between 1919 and 1930, productivity in the motor vehicle industry grew at an annual rate of 8.6 percent, but between 1960 and 1971 this annual growth rate slowed to about 3 percent. The more detailed productivity figures computed by William Abernathy for Ford reveal an even bleaker picture than these aggregate industry statistics. He found that labor productivity in engine production increased sharply between 1945 and 1952, but grew only incrementally between 1952 and 1970. In final assembly, labor productivity remained relatively constant between 1929 and 1974, despite the fact that major labor-saving innovations in automatic welding were introduced during the 1960s. It is likely that any labor saved by automating welding was offset by the increased inputs required by the escalating level of product diversity.[43]

As was usual in the postwar era, the auto industry responded to these rising costs by passing them along to consumers, causing new car prices to climb steadily throughout the 1960s. But prices did not rise as steeply as costs, for manufacturers faced the restraining pressure of foreign competition. By the mid-1960s the European and Japanese automakers had captured 10.5 per cent of the American market, preventing American makers from raising prices enough to cover escalating costs. Consequently, the costs of model diversification began to hit the Big Three where it hurt – in the bottom line. Despite record sales throughout the decade, profit margins fell. At the end of 1971, GM reported that its profit per unit, when adjusted for inflation, was lower than it had been in 1965, 1955, 1950, and 1928. And the corporation's profit margin on sales was a mere 6.8 percent, lower than any year since 1958. Ford had similar problems, reporting before Price Commission hearings that its profit margin was a mere 4.1 percent of sales. These figures defied the logic of Fordism, under which higher volumes were supposed to bring higher unit profits due to decreasing unit costs. But such economies of scale were based on the presumption of product standardization, which was eroded by model proliferation. In the 1960s selling more cars required more different types of cars, which in turn required proportionally higher costs that could no longer be fully passed along to consumers.[44]

The deadly traditional Fordist responses to the crisis

Even as the foundations of Fordism crumbled, institutional inertia determined responses to the crisis that were deadly traditional. Faced with expanding costs and lower profits, auto executives responded with programs of centralization, interchangeability, and speed-up. Realizing that the divisional independence they encouraged to achieve diversity had produced a costly array of competing models, managers began in the mid-1960s to recentralize corporate power. GM's chairman, Frederic Donner, began to rein in the divisions in 1965. As John De Lorean, a young divisional executive at this time, recalled: "The divisions gradually were stripped of their decision-making power. Operating decisions were more and more being made on the Fourteenth Floor [home of top corporate executives]."[45]

GM executives saw this centralization as a crucial prerequisite to containing costs, for with this new power they launched an extensive campaign of interchangeability between their divisions. Mechanical parts like engines, which had previously been specific to divisions, were standardized and shared between them. The intent was, as De Lorean recalled, "to minimize tooling costs and increase productivity." Less component variety meant longer production runs and more standardized and closely timed assembly operations. To ensure the latter, GM also centralized control of assembly operations into the General Motors Assembly Division (GMAD), to which management of assembly plants was transferred from the car divisions. Several industry commentators and insiders suggested that this centralization program was intended to thwart antitrust proceedings by tying the divisions so closely together that GM could not be split into independent companies. Although this may have formed part of the motive, the main impetus for centralization, as others suggested, was cutting the costs of model proliferation.[46]

Ford also moved in the middle of the decade to cut costs by standardizing major component parts like frames and engines across its divisions. And to accomplish this the company similarly centralized operational management away from the divisions. But Ford's recentralization started earlier than GM's, around 1960. When the Edsel Division collapsed, the company reorganized its remaining divisions, transferring all the assembly, purchasing, and engineering operations of Lincoln–Mercury to the Ford Division. This centralized structure facilitated the cost-cutting standardization and coordination of components necessitated at mid-decade. Similarly, Chrysler's divisionalization attempt collapsed by 1960, leaving only a consolidated Chrysler–Plymouth

Division and the Dodge Division. In 1961 President Townsend centralized control over these divisions into the hands of a new, top-level
Administrative Committee, which sought to contain costs in ways
similar to Ford and GM.[47]

Another cost-cutting policy adopted by automakers during the
decade was slowing down the cycle of annual model change. Realizing
in the early 1960s that consumers wanted real automotive difference,
not superficial newness, automakers slowed planned obsolescence as
they increased model diversification. Many new models experienced no
major appearance changes for four years, and major body-shell changes
were also stretched out. Between 1961 and 1974 the average body-shell
production life at Ford was 6.1 years, up substantially from the 3.8 years
of the 1934 through 1960 period. As the costs of model proliferation
climbed toward the end of the decade, corporate executives stepped on
the style-cycle brakes even harder. By 1970 *Time* magazine wondered
whether the industry was moving toward "An end to obsolescence?,"
citing executives' attempts to stretch out changes to save on tooling and
marketing costs.[48]

Since Henry Ford's day, auto executives faced with escalating production costs resorted to the panacea of speed-up, using their mechanical
control of work pace to force workers to work harder. So when model
proliferation began to cut into corporate profits, they administered a large
dose of this bitter medicine, transferring more work to machines and using
these to intensify the human labor that remained. The plant built by GM at
Lordstown, Ohio in 1970 to produce its new minicar, Vega, well illustrates
this new speed-up regime. Touted as one of the most modern, automated
plants in the world, the Lordstown facility was actually built around the old
Fordist principle of intensified labor. Some skilled work was transferred to
robots, but automation left behind lots of manual jobs whose pace was set
by the speeding machines. On assembly lines old-fashioned time and
motion study so intensified labor that an unprecedented 102 cars were
produced in an hour. And to compel workers to submit to the inhuman pace,
plant management was turned over to the tough-minded GMAD, which
immediately fired 700 assembly-line workers and cracked down on
discipline.[49]

But these traditionally Fordist solutions to declining profits and
productivity – centralization, interchangeability, speed-up – only made
the industry's problems worse. Increased interchangeability made corporate models look more alike, undermining the individuality that sold
cars. And with cars changing little from year to year, consumers could
not find excitement in new cars either. The quality of automobiles also

suffered under the new regime of cost-cutting and speed-up. De Lorean recalls that when GMAD took over Pontiac assembly plants, the first areas cut were inspection and quality control. Speed-up in plants also allowed workers less time to do their jobs right, resulting in proliferating defects in parts and assembly. And attempts to cut material and labor costs resulted in designed-in defects and weaknesses. For example, the Chevrolet Vega, designed and produced under stringent cost restraints, was notoriously unsafe and unreliable, with a muffler that set fire to the gas tank, an idling mechanism that jammed the car's accelerator, and a rear axle that caused wheels to fall off.[50]

The victims fight back: growth of popular anti-Fordist movements

Escalating problems of product safety and reliability spawned the automobile industry's biggest enemy, the consumer movement. Although not new to this decade, consumer discontent with high-priced, unreliable, and unsafe autos rose in the mid-1960s and was given impetus by the dramatic confrontation between GM and consumer crusader Ralph Nader. This Harvard Law School graduate and mild-mannered son of Lebanese immigrants had a profound dislike for corporate power and arrogance, which he focused on the automobile manufacturers. Nader worked in Washington, DC as a free-lance consultant, lecturer, and researcher on auto safety. So when Senator Abraham Ribicoff opened hearings in March of 1965 to address this rising public concern, Nader was recruited as an unpaid adviser.

The Ribicoff committee called to testify the top officers of GM, Fred Donner and James Roche. Their testimony revealed not only corporate arrogance and unconcern for consumer safety but also a bungling ineptitude. Donner and Roche were uninformed and evasive about automotive safety. Donner hid behind the ideology of consumer sovereignty, proclaiming that safety features should be optional equipment to ensure "the basic freedom of the customer to pay the cost of tailoring a car to his own specifications. . . ." Unimpressed with this excuse, the committee pressed harder, with Senator Robert Kennedy proving a particularly pesky interrogator. When he asked about the corporation's contributions to auto safety, Roche replied that door locks had been improved. The committee's staff then produced a Cornell University study showing that GM doors were torn off in accidents six times more frequently than those of other makes. Kennedy then asked Roche how much GM spent on collision-safety research. After much conferring with his staff, Roche pronounced he did not know, since such research was not segregated from other engineering programs, but that GM spent about $1.25 million on safety research by outside consultants. Kennedy bristled and closed in on the wounded automotive moguls. "What was the profit of General Motors last year?" he demanded. Another round of head-scratching and whispered conferring ensued, at the end of which Roche replied, "One-thousand seven-hundred million dollars." Kennedy was indignant. "You made $1.7 billion last year? . . . And you spent $1 million of this [on safety research]?"[51]

But the epitome of corporate callousness and arrogance was yet to be revealed. In November of 1965, when the hearings were in recess, Ralph Nader published his scathing attack on American automakers, *Unsafe At Any Speed*, which charged that their obsession with sales and styling prevented them from building safe, economical cars. The lead chapter drove home this theme with a case study of the Chevrolet Corvair, which, Nader documented, was dangerously unstable at high speeds due to the design of its rear suspension system. More damaging still was the revelation that GM executives knew of the problem prior to production but refused to approve the remedy – a $15 stabilizing bar – because it was too expensive.

Nader's book made GM executives so livid that they hired private investigators to dig up discrediting information on its author. Finding none, the investigators tried to harrass and intimidate Nader, but their clumsy efforts backfired. GM officials went back before the Ribicoff committee in March of 1966 and were forced to account not only for the Corvair but also for their harrassment of Nader. The mighty moguls of GM were humbled into issuing a public apology to Nader, and ultimately handed him $425,000 in a civil-suit settlement. This exposure of corporate abuses added fuel to the fire of public rage over the escalating human and environmental costs of America's automobility. By the end of the year Congress had passed the landmark National Traffic and Motor Vehicle Safety Act, which empowered a federal agency to set safety standards for new cars beginning in 1968. Congress had already responded in 1965 to the mounting public concern over automobile pollution by passing the Motor Vehicle Air Pollution and Control Act, which set emission standards for automobiles. The Federal Clean Air Act of 1970 got even tougher on this diasatrous side-effect of auto opium, mandating a further reduction of 90 percent in three pollutants.[52]

The automobile industry fought these regulation claiming that they infringed on the right of individ choose their products. In the past, this contention h among American consumers seeking to express thei cars. But by the mid-1960s the social costs of auto consumption had so undermined the ideology of consumer individualism that most Americans were demanding social solutions to the problems of safety, congestion, and pollution.

The 1960s' revolt against Fordism was not, however, confined to the realm of consumption. As consumers rejected their dream machines due to rising social costs, many rechanneled their desires back to the original site of displacement, the Fordist workplace. This decade also brought a rebellion against the minutely divided, monotonous, Fordist work led by those closest to the heart of Fordism, automobile workers. Largely quiescent throughout the 1950s, auto workers began to show signs of renewed activism in the 1960s. As the opium of mass consumption wore off under the strain of rising social costs, they felt the pain of mass production more acutely and were aroused to action. Workplace issues like work pace, safety, and discipline came to the fore once again. Protected from the threat of firing by social spending programs and tight labor markets, workers felt the freedom to press these issues on management.

The result was an epidemic in American factories known popularly as the "blue-collar blues." Disaffection with work became widespread and took the forms of absenteeism, turnover, strikes, and stoppages. Quit rates among manufacturing employees rose steadily and by 1969 reached levels unknown since the postwar labor turmoil. Absenteeism also skyrocketed in the decade, doubling or tripling in auto plants, according to Ford officials. And strikes and stoppages rose sharply, with many in the auto industry unauthorized by the union. By 1970, labor relations in the industry were so strained that GM complained in a position paper that worker discipline had broken down and production was "disrupted repeatedly by 'crisis' situations and strikes."[53]

This rebellious activity was exacerbated in the late 1960s to early 1970s by corporate programs of speed-up and crackdown. The struggle was particularly intense at GM, where disaffected auto workers struck eight of the ten plants taken over by the hard-nosed GMAD. The strike that attracted the most public attention and came to epitomize the new militancy occurred at Lordstown in 1971. When GMAD took over the Vega plant, slashing the workforce and intensifying discipline, the union local struck, demanding concessions on control issues like line speed and unilateral managerial authority. The national media focused on the youth of Lordstown strikers, with many interpreting their actions as another manifestation of the period's youthful revolt. These young workers did seem less willing to make the trade-offs their fathers had. Growing up in prosperous times, they put less stock in the economic security so important to the Depression-era generation. And many young people entered factories with high-school diplomas and college experience, and demanded what they had been taught to expect from an educational credential – meaningful, challenging, autonomous work. When they encountered only the mindless monotony of Fordism, they did not consider high wages and benefits sufficient compensation for their thwarted expectations. But the generational component of the period's escalating labor struggles was probably exaggerated. Since the inception of Fordism, many workers – young and old, schooled and unschooled – fought the indignities of such work, taking advantage of favorable labor-market and political conditions. Here was another instance, fanned by the generally rebellious tenor of the times. As John De Lorean, general manager of Chevrolet at the time, stated: "What was taking place was a classical confrontation of union and management over the oldest issue in the history of auto-labor relations – a work speed-up."[54]

But this time the age-old struggle assumed monumental proportions, for it combined with the discontent of consumers to shake the foundations of the Fordist system. Escalating consumer demands for individuality generated by the contradictions of Fordist consumption led to changes that contradicted Fordist production and gave workers both the motivation and the power to struggle against its abuses. Fordism, the shotgun marriage of mass production and mass consumption consummated by the intercourse of class conflict, had reached its limits, and attempts to revive the union only drove the partners further apart. The only issue now to be settled was who would benefit from the slow demise of the system.

Epilogue
Design in the wake of Fordism

The history of America after 1970 is one of the progressive dismantling of the system of Fordism whose construction began a half-century before. Yet, trendy conceptions about post-Fordism aside, there have emerged no viable institutional alternatives, no new social regimes to regulate the relation between production and consumption. The measures undertaken to solve the crisis of Fordism have been largely dictated by the logic of Fordism itself. Even as the employment and wage foundation of mass production has eroded, consumerism has remained the major focus of popular solutions to Fordism's problems. Consequently, the mainstay of American consumerism, the automobile, has maintained its importance as a cultural icon. But despite concerted efforts by automakers and their designers, the car has yet to regain the cultural significance it achieved during the heyday of Fordism.

THE GREAT REPRESSION, CONSUMER SALVATION, AND THE DEMISE OF STYLING SUPREMACY

The popular discontent that spilled over into the mass-production foundation of Fordism was quickly dispatched by a concerted program of workplace repression in the early 1970s. Major corporations like the automakers tightened managerial surveillance and control of workers on the shop floor, hiring more supervisors to enforce intensified labor. And to undermine workers' ability to combat these repressive measures, corporations began to dismantle the system of collective bargaining that had previously underwritten mass consumption. They launched an anti-union drive that decertified hundreds of unions and viciously opposed new attempts at organization. And to badger workers into concessions on work rules and wages, American employers began to use the threat and actual implementation of plant closures and relocations to the more accomodating business climates of right-to-work states and under-developed countries with few labor protections. At the macroeconomic level, these policies were supported by restrictive fiscal policies that slowed down the economy and created higher levels of unemployment and job insecurity.[1]

As so often in America's past, the workplace repression mounted by the major corporations left only one outlet for popular discontent – consumption. Channeled away from the foundation in production, criticisms of Fordism were unleashed against its consumer products. Americans demanded products more efficient, safe, and reliable than the purveyors of consumer dreams had been accustomed to offering, convincing themselves once again that the system's contradictions could be solved if only they consumed in the right, "socially responsible" way. And once again, the automobile – the symbol of all that was wrong with American consumerism – became the focus of the discontent. Pressure mounted in the early 1970s for the government to mandate changes in Detroit's dinosaurs, reaching a fever pitch after 1973.

In this year the oil embargo by the Organization of Petroleum Exporting Countries forced Americans to confront the real costs of automobility. Gasoline prices skyrocketed, consumers waited with short tempers in long lines at gas stations, and gas-guzzling cars became defined as socially irresponsible. Under public pressure, Congress passed the Energy Policy and Conservation Act of 1975, mandating that automakers achieve a corporate average fuel economy (CAFE) of 27.5 miles per gallon by 1985. And to ensure both the safety of passengers and their bank accounts against the devastatingly high costs of collisions, Congress mandated the production of bumpers that could withstand 5-mile-per-hour crashes without damage. This massive public intervention was the culmination of a shift in America's automotive consciousness away from fantastic dreams of escape and individuality toward the sober reality of efficiency and functionality. But this consciousness was still trapped within the Fordist assumption that merely altering consumption, without changing the system of production, could solve the country's problems.[2]

As a result of these government regulations, for the first time since the founding of Fordism a public representative stepped into the automobile market between individual consumers and private corporations to influence automobile design. And this undermined the supremacy of the stylists. Their fantastic freedom to appeal to consumers' displaced desires was restricted by legislative requirements of safety, economy, and emissions.

As one designer bitterly recalled: "Car design came to a screaming halt in 1973, and it stopped for an entire decade. . . . People began to pull back from fantasy cars and now they were into reality." So publicly maligned did the entire profession become in the sobering days of social consciousness that it sought to side-step criticism by changing its name. In 1966 the Ford Styling Office became the Ford Design Staff, "partly because," one automotive journalist noted, "Ralph Nader lambasted the stylists for what he said was their mindlessness about safety." A similarly cosmetic name change was adopted by the General Motors organization in 1972, transforming it into the General Motors Design Staff. Although the erstwhile stylists liked to portray this change in appellation as reflecting their increased responsibilities – designing the entire car and not merely cosmetically styling the surface – the truth was that it was indicative of a diminution of their power within automotive corporations.[3]

The trend in consumer demand in the 1970s toward safety, efficiency, and environmental responsibility shifted the balance of power over design to the stylists' historic enemy, the engineers. Since they had the technical expertise to design autos that met the requirements of government regulators, engineers gained more and more influence on design as the 1970s progressed. As one Ford designer recalled: "The designers were calling the shots through the sixties. Then in the seventies, the cars that were designed were very much controlled by engineering . . . not only engineers, but the government and all the other external forces. The designers were playing a very subordinate role." The stylists' other traditional rival, marketing personnel, also moved back in during this decade to regain influence previously lost to the pretty-picture boys. When the costs of unrestrained consumerism came home to roost in the public consciousness, rational demands for safety and economy predominated over nonrational wish fulfillment. Market researchers used this resurgence of automotive rationality to argue successfully that more influence be accorded to their market surveys, which better tapped consumers' utilitarian demands. The comeback of marketing experts was particularly strong at Ford, where they had always been a strong force in the powerful Product Planning Office. But even at GM, where they had exercised little influence, the marketing office gained power at the expense of stylists during the 1970s, prompting styling head Bill Mitchell to become very outspoken against it and its surveys. In response to questions about the auto industry's problems, he told *Car and Driver* in 1974: "The first instinct is to try some cockamamie market research. But that's a cop-out – the truth of the matter is most consumers don't know what they want. . . . The idea that the industry is an obedient servant to public wishes is bull."[4]

Top corporate officials may have been willing to tolerate such insensitive arrogance by stylists in the 1950s, when their cars were selling hand over fist. But declining sales of Detroit's big cars in the 1970s and the public's desertion to smaller, more efficient imports made them extremely sensitive to consumer wishes and public criticism. So the high-flying stylists, who thought they knew what consumers wanted better than they themselves, got their wings clipped. Corporations forced designers to cooperate with engineers and marketing personnel to give people the smaller, safer, more efficient cars they were demanding. And when recalcitrant old-timers like Bill Mitchell stood in the way, they paid the price. When he retired at the mandatory age of sixty-five in 1977, Mitchell, unlike Earl, was not allowed to choose his own successor. In the words of a top Ford designer, the executives at GM "had had it up to here with these guys [the stylists]." They passed over several of Mitchell's headstrong protégés to select Irv Rybicki, a mild-mannered diplomat who worked well with other corporate units. Although lacking the strong aesthetic vision of his GM predecessors, Rybicki had a talent for budgeting, organization, and cooperation which, in the words of one GM designer, helped "to adjust aesthetics into systems of control, legislation, the world economy."[5]

At Ford the power of stylists was similarly deflated in 1980 upon the retirement of its domineering head from the golden days, Gene Bordinat. Top executives took this opportunity to divide and conquer the design staff, splitting it into two parts. Ford Design continued to hold the vice-president's office, which was filled by a long-time Ford stylist, Don Kopka. But its former responsibilities were now divided between it and the newly created North American Design Staff, which reported not to Ford Design but to Ford Engineering. In this way Ford executives ensured a closer coordination between designers and engineers. And to head the engineering-subordinated North American Design group they chose Jack Telnack, who formerly headed Ford Design of Europe. At Chrysler, where styling never had been very strong, no such organizational downgrading was necessary. But there too a more equitable sharing of design responsibilities with engineering and marketing emerged in the mid- to late 1970s.[6]

With the designers and their car-as-entertainment philosophy now subordinated, automakers began to offer cars that emphasized function and efficiency, at least in appearance if not in reality. The Big Three did make concerted efforts to give consumers smaller, lighter, more efficient cars in the mid-1970s, increasing their offerings in the compact and intermediate classes. And in 1977 GM, the pioneer of the longer-lower-wider direction, took the drastic step of downsizing its entire car line-up, with even the big sedans stepping down a notch in self-important size. But as many designers and auto executives stressed in retrospect, these 1970s cars often gave consumers the appearance rather than the reality of efficiency and functionality. One Chrysler designer stated: "These cars [of the 1970s] looked like more European, fuel-efficient machines, and they really weren't. It was a cosmetic treatment."[7]

Designers achieved the look of functionality by copying the square, boxy designs of European cars, especially those from Germany. The country that produced the Bauhaus school of stark, modernist design had always produced cars that emphasized rectilinear lines. Mercedes–Benz was the epitome of this functionalist aesthetic, with its upright grille and three-box architecture – one box each for the trunk, passenger compartment, and engine. But during the 1970s another purveyor of the Germanic box aesthetic emerged in the small-car field, Volkswagen. In 1975 the German automaker abandoned the streamlined Beetle it had produced for thirty years and introduced a new small car with a decidedly boxy design, the Golf (sold in the United States as the Rabbit). Although the car was designed by an Italian, Giorgetto Giugiaro of Ital Design, it reflected the same severe German functionalism.

The quickest way for American automakers to convince consumers that they were coming down from the clouds and offering efficient, functional machines was to append this functionalist look to the surface of their cars. So, for example, in 1975 Ford brought out a new car, the Granada, whose upright and square lines shamelessly imitated the Mercedes sedan. Ads for this Ford with the European-sounding name even portrayed passers-by mistaking it for a Mercedes. The downsized 1977 offerings from GM also had square, Teutonic lines. But wholesale design felony by the corporation awaited 1982, when GM offered its new A–bodied intermediates. The chrome was gone, the lines were sharp, the grilles were square, and the interiors were muted. In an obvious reference to the German cars they copied, one Pontiac ad declared: "The Road Kings have a new rival." Chrysler also caught the European bug in 1975 and introduced the small luxury Cordoba, with an upright grille, straight lines, and an actor with a heavy accent touting its "rich Corinthian leather." The rest of the corporation's cars were soon infected with this pseudofunctionalism copied from Europe. And when the Big Three finally got around to introducing real economy subcompacts in the early 1980s, nearly all were exact copies of Giugiaro's "econobox" design for the Golf.[8]

So the degraded stylists were forced for the first time in the history of their profession to present the car as a machine, a means of functional transportation for getting here to there. But this functionalist aesthetic reminiscent of German modernism was no less ideological than the fantastic–entertainment aesthetic that Harley Earl pursued throughout his career. For even though the body shell of the auto took on simpler, squarer shapes, it still was a unified whole that obscured the fragmented ugliness of the mass-produced mechanicals underneath. The scaled-down efficiency presented to people was an efficiency of consumption, saving fuel, operating costs, and the environment, rather than an efficiency of production, saving time, effort, and material in manufacturing. Americans still did not want to be reminded of the cruel efficiencies of mass production with the sight of exposed mechanicals, especially in this era of the disciplinary crackdown, speed-up, and lay-offs in American industry. They continued to seek salvation through consumption, believing that the country's problems could be solved if only they consumed in a responsible, frugal, efficient way. The square, stern lines of the cars of the late 1970s to early 1980s assured Americans that they could consume themselves out of the indulgent excesses of the 1950s and 1960s and back to a more "natural" lifestyle without altering the structure of Fordist production that gave rise to the notion of salvation through consumption to begin with.

THE BIFURCATED BOOM, OVERCONSUMPTION, AND UPSCALE FUNCTIONALISM

The superficial functionalism offered by American automakers in the late 1970s and early 1980s was unable, however, to bring back the masses of consumers that previously underwrote Fordism. Many Americans during this period seemed unmoved by the enticements of Detroit's *faux* functionalism, opting instead for the real economy of small, fuel-efficient imports from Germany and Japan. By the time a Detroit constitutionally committed to the big car finally got into small-car competition, its products seemed shoddy copies of the higher-quality imports. And Detroit found it very difficult to compete in price also. Used to the huge profit margins on the big cars, the anemic returns on econoboxes were disheartening. The higher wages and benefits of American workers, especially relative to the Japanese, was a big part of the problem. Still relatively protected by union contracts and social welfare benefits, the incomes of Americans remained relatively high despite rising levels of unemployment during this period. But the inefficiency of American automakers was also to blame. Long used to merely incremental productivity innovation and passing increased costs along to consumers, the Big Three were hit hard by foreign makers with innovative technology, whose tough competition prevented them from merely jacking up prices. So American automakers rapidly lost market share to their German and Japanese competitors during this period, throwing the industry into an unprecedented crisis, a position shared by many other American manufacturers.

These conditions led automakers and other corporations to look for a political solution, which they found in the reactionary economic program of the new president who took office in 1981. Elected on the promise of bringing back America's economic and geopolitical strength, Reagan launched an economic program that irreparably shattered the foundations of Fordism in the United States. The main thrust of his "supply-side economics" was an attack on the Fordist institutions that underwrote the demands of the working class. First, Reaganomics slashed back social welfare programs – unemployment insurance, food stamps, aid to families with dependent children – which had traditionally provided workers with nonmarket income and empowering alternatives to employment. Second, the administration launched a frontal assault on unions, firing the air traffic control strikers, packing the National Labor Relations Board with antiunion ideologues, and generally sending a message to corporations that union-busting was tolerated in Washington. Third, and decisively, Reaganomics's restrictive monetary policies engineered a devastating recession that disciplined labor by driving unemployment to unprecedented postwar levels. Accompanied by American corporations' own campaign of union-busting, concession demands, and plant closings, this program did indeed restore corporate profits, but on a much narrower, unstable foundation.

A major consequence of Reaganomics was a fall in the real wages of American workers and a rise in the inequality of incomes. While the working class's share of income and wealth declined beginning in the mid-1970s, the share held by the upper and professional-managerial classes rose. This created an increasingly polarized class structure that undermined the mass market and created a bifurcated consumer market. While the inexpensive goods, including automobiles, sold to the working class were increasingly produced offshore in low-wage countries, American manufacturers concentrated on the upscale markets for expensive, distinctive goods produced in lower volumes. As Mike Davis wrote, the economic recovery of the 1980s depended largely on the overconsumption of the Reagan-enriched layer of managers, professionals, entrepreneurs and rentiers, or as some pundits preferred to label them, the Yuppies. Many of these young urban professionals who so benefitted from the income-revolution of the 1980s were the rebellious children of the 1960s and to some extent still imbued with this generation's critical attitude toward socially and environmentally destructive consumption. But during this period these impulses that once struck at the roots of the American system were steered, perhaps by their own affluent self-interest, into merely responsible, healthy, and environmentally sound consumerism.[9]

Beginning in the mid-1980s, the American automobile industry experienced a comeback based on the bifurcated consumer marketplace. Relenting to their foreign competitors, the Big Three largely gave up on the domestic production of small economy cars for the increasingly impoverished working class, choosing to produce whole vehicles or major components offshore or merely to import and place their nameplate on the vehicles of their erstwhile foreign competitors. They began to focus their efforts on the growing and more profitable market of upscale autos for the class of overconsumers. But in order to do so, they had to change aesthetic directions from the severe, downsized functionalism of the 1970s and early 1980s. This aesthetic of austerity no longer captured the exuberant, expansive mood of the professional-managerial class enriched by the bifurcated boom. Nor did it meet the Yuppie demand for distinction that symbolized their growing social and economic distance from the masses of downsliding Americans. As many designers noted, the downsizing of cars and the accompanying aesthetics of austere functionality on all makes had a dangerous homogenizing effect on design. One Chrysler designer stated of the period: "Cars were losing their distinctness, with each make becoming part of a herd of econoboxes. You have all of these appliances running around with different names on them, and whether you buy a Westinghouse or Frigidaire doesn't make much difference." The design dilemma faced by American automakers in the mid-1980s was to capture the optimistic mood of this obsessively successful class and its demand for distinction without going to the extreme of a decadent overindulgence that was anathema to a group that prided itself on its lean, healthy, nonpolluting lifestyle.[10]

American automakers found two solutions to this dilemma – one pirated from Europe and the other more authentically home-grown. The borrowed solution was actually a refurbished automotive ideology from the 1930s – streamlining – that entered America through its European incarnation of aerodynamics. Once again, the sleek, slippery shape of automobiles connoted a promise of salvation through the application of the latest science and technology. But in the 1980s the salvation promised was no longer to be achieved through expanded mass production, as in the 1930s, but through sober but distinctive conservation.

In contrast to the American purveyors of aesthetic streamlining as a symbol of expansive progress, European streamlining had always been driven by the circumstances of more precious fuel and resources to privilege the conservationist advantages of shapes functionally engineered to offer less resistance to the wind. In the late 1970s and early 1980s, with gasoline and material prices escalating again, European manufacturers like Mercedes–Benz, Audi, and BMW took a renewed interest in aerodynamically engineered shapes that lowered the car's coefficient of drag. On these upscale examples of Germanic functionalism, the austere three-box designs turned into sensuously rounded but frugally decorated shapes. The large radiuses of the curves seemed to convey substance and durability – as if the metal was so thick that it could not be bent tighter – as well as wind-cheating efficiency. And their frugally functional interiors, with matte-black fixtures and bench-hard seats, were the opposite of the self-indulgent plushness of *faux* walnut panels and thick velour. Here was an aesthetic of distinction, substance, and efficiency that exited the hearts of many upscale entrepreneurs and professionals, making these German marques the badge of Yuppiedom.

American automakers began to copy the European aerodynamic aesthetic in the mid-1980s as a way of courting upscale consumers. And the pioneer of the American "aero" trend was Ford. The new head of its North American Design section, Jack Telnack, had served a stint as head of Ford's European design staff and was known as an advocate of aerodynamics. When the young turk returned to Dearborn, he instituted a revitalization of design and designers not only at Ford but in the industry as a whole. Telnack's first attempt at the new aero aesthetic was on the 1983 model of Ford's personal luxury car, Thunderbird. Developed in more than 500 hours of wind-tunnel tests, the new T-Bird had gently rounded contours everywhere and a steeply raked windshield. And to show it was serious about performance achieved by smart engineering, not brute force, Ford offered the car with a turbocharged 4-cylinder engine that could outperform most V-8s. Telnack and the other designers must have been elated when *Road and Track* wrote of the car: "You could close your eyes and think you're in Germany – in a German car. . . ."[11]

The next model year Telnack's technophiles gave the aero look to Ford's compact line with the new Tempo and its Mercury cousin, Topaz. These cars were scaled-down versions of the T-Bird's sloped-nose, bustle-tail design and were generally well-received. But Ford's biggest gamble came in 1986, when it brought aero to the standard family sedan in the form of Ford Taurus and Mercury Sable. It was definitely aiming at the upscale market of young, well-educated buyers to whom the BMW appealed. Although marketing clinics were generally unfavorable to the radical design, in a show of faith in its revived design team Ford executives produced the car regardless. And when it hit the market, it was a rousing success, marking Ford as a pioneer in high-tech aero design and setting off a spate of copy-cat cars in the other American makers. The success of these new aero designs enhanced the relative status of designers within the corporations, demonstrating that they could cooperate with engineers to build efficient, smart, high-tech cars that were also exciting and attractive.[12]

Just why did aero seize designers and the automotive market in the mid- to late 1980s? Was this reincarnation of the streamlining craze merely a "look" as it was in the 1930s, or was it now authentically functional? There were differences of opinion, even among automobile designers themselves. Several told me bluntly in interviews that aero was a fad, a functionally irrelevant sales gimmick. But others resolutely insisted that modern aero was driven by the functional necessity of lowering wind resistance and improving fuel economy. Federally mandated increases in the corporate average fuel economy could be achieved either by making the running gear more efficient or by reducing the wind resistance of the moving car. One Ford designer claimed that while it could cost $200 to $300 million to achieve a one-tenth mile-per-gallon increase by engineering "under the hood," aero design achieved a three- to four-tenths m.p.g. increase for almost nothing. And such arguments were backed by the results of wind-tunnel tests. But the most astute designers admitted that the aero trend was both aesthetics and function. Improving fuel economy was important, but probably more important was the fact that the aero look became associated in the consumer's mind with high-tech, efficiently engineered automobiles. As another Ford designer stated, it was "a new look . . . that identified us with the new era."[13]

The aero aesthetic gave designers not only a new grip on the market, especially of upscale professional-managerial types, but also a new claim on power within auto corporations. For the first time in the history of the profession, designers had an objective, technical rationale for their work, which in the past had rested solely on subjective judgment or taste. The rather imprecise, uncalculable nature of aesthetic decisions had initially served auto stylists well, for it prevented the engineers and corporate executives from subordinating them with bureaucratic rules. Those who controlled the variable and mysterious realm of style had to be given discretion over their own tasks. But with the growing demand for efficiency and safety, the stylists' expertise in superficial aesthetics seemed a luxury, a waste of resources. The precision engineering of cars to technical specifications of fuel economy, safety, performance, and emissions was required, so power shifted to the technical professions. Aerodynamics gave designers control of a precise, technical expertise that yielded measurable, functional increases in fuel economy. For the first time, they could point to the technical results of wind-tunnel tests to legitimate their styling decisions. As one Ford designer stated of aerodynamics: "It became a very useful tool for the designers. . . . We've been able to justify a design with something that was factual, rather than just saying, well, we like it, and it should be this way."[14]

Designers proudly paraded their coefficients of drag before the public and their corporate bureaucracies, as if to say: "We are no longer merely pretty-picture boys. We are responsible automotive technicians seeking to improve automobile efficiency." Most designers recognized that aerodynamics was and still is far from a precise science – more of a black art, one stated – and that their aerodynamic experiments were more trial-and-error tinkering than precise application of a body of principles. Nevertheless, aero gave designers a foothold in the brave new world of automotive engineering, serving as a professionally legitimating ideology in an era in which the public and the automakers became weary of the stylists' sophomoric superficialities. The Ford designer stated that aero gave them a grounds for cooperation with engineers who controlled design. "We have learned how to back up our designs with really reasonable objectives – we haven't really lost control of design [to the engineers]."[15]

In the mid- to late 1980s there was, however, another trend in automotive design that appealed to the upscale demands for functionality and distinction, one more authentically American than the European import of aerodynamics. It emerged in the exploding market for what the industry called sports/utility vehicles, which included pickup trucks, vans, jeeps, and other automotive hybrids. There was nothing particularly new about these types of autos – all had been around for decades, but mainly as specialty vehicles tailored to the needs of small markets for work or sport transport. What was new to the 1980s was the entrance of these vehicles into the mainstream automobile market. The pickup truck, once a special vehicle for the hauling needs of working people, entered the mainstream in the form of small, sporty trucks, many of whose beds were rarely marred by the insult of actual cargo. Big bulky vans that once were used for mundane delivery and cargo transport were transformed into trendy minivans by making them smaller, lower, and easier to handle. The humble jeep, that general purpose vehicle designed for use in World War Two, was transformed into a variety of sporty all-terrain vehicles. The inspiration for some of these vehicles came from a growing auto sport know as off-roading. As the freeways, highways, and surface streets of America became increasingly crowded, polluted, and regulated, many Americans took their automotive fantasies off the roads into the countryside and wilderness, conjuring up nostalgic fantasies of an American frontier of unbounded space and opportunities. Once again, the automobile became a mobile means of escape from the escalating problems of urban and suburban America. As one California off-roader told writer Peter Steinhart: "Listen, I work all week at a meaningless job that I hate. My children are growing up to be weaklings and the country is going to hell. All I want to do is ride my motorcycle in the desert." For the purpose of racing or cruising in the desert, on the beach or mountain trails, off-roaders modified jeeps, small trucks, and motorcycles by jacking them up off the ground and adding oversized, knobby tires, roll bars, special lights, and other equipment. Those engaged in such raucous, masculine, often environment-destroying activities were, I suspect, much like hot rodders – that is, working-class men who viewed the automobile as a powerful machine for the compensatory conquering of nature and people.[16]

What is puzzling, perhaps, was the spread of this brand of functional autos, whether of utility or sport, to the genteel classes in the 1980s, especially the upwardly striving Yuppies, many of whom probably belonged to the Sierra Club or Audubon Society and objected to the automotive destruction of America's wilderness. These high, square, rugged, often four-wheel-drive vehicles began showing up not only at the job site or on the off-road expedition but also at the country club and the symphony. Most of these erstwhile hauling and off-road vehicles could be seen whining along freeways and suburban surface roads, their engines struggling to maintain speed with absurdly low gearing and to overcome the resistance of high, square bodies and knobby, super-traction tires. Increasingly these rugged Yuppie pioneers betrayed their real intentions by demanding on these vehicles with names like Blazer, Explorer, Bronco, and Ranger all the comforts and conveniences of urban living: automatic transmissions, leather seats, sun roofs, air conditioning, sophisticated stereos, and, of course, cellular car phones.

The fascination of upscale consumers for rugged-looking off-road vehicles was more symbolic than functional. Of course, as this group discovered parenthood and turned child-rearing trendy, these spacious cars did provide ample room for hauling kids to school and after-school ballet and violin lessons. So did the station wagon, but it was stigmatized as the frumpy old vehicle of suburban mass consumption and would never do to express the distinction of America's newly enriched professional-managerial elite. These jeep-like autos were not only distinctive but also expressed this environmentally correct group's penchant for natural, healthy lifestyles. Like the working-class people from which these vehicles were appropriated, these Yuppies were symbolically escaping back to nature, not in desert-rutting, hill-eroding dominance but in the genteel communing of back-packing and rock climbing.

The aesthetics of these functional "off-road" vehicles were dominated by the look of utility, substance, and power. Square, upright lines revealed a practical concern for hauling people and sporting equipment. Jacking up the chassis high off the ground telegraphed the need for transport over rugged terrain. And bulging bulkiness, as opposed to svelte sophistication, said these were vehicles of substance and power. One styling trick that emerged in the late 1980s to symbolize substance was the fender bulge, a rounded protrusion above the wheel opening that gave trucks and jeep-like vehicles the look of broad-shouldered brawn.

As the upscale vehicles of the late 1980s went to either aero or off-road aesthetics to symbolize an exuberant yet responsible, healthy consumerism, the cheaper autos remained in a plain-jane econobox mold. The small Yugos, Escorts, Civics, and Corollas clearly revealed in their unadorned, largely flat surfaces that these were cheap, mass-produced vehicles, despite the designers' best attempts to conceal the signs of mass production. They betrayed their origins and the social standing of those who drove them, much in the way that the Model T did in an earlier automotive era. So in the late 1980s autos began to aesthetically register the class polarization of America. Cars once again symbolized class, eroding the ideology of mass consumption that underwrote the now-decaying system of mass production.

The automobiles of the early 1990s seem to extend this bifurcation of consumption that symbolizes America's socioeconomic polarizarion. The 1980s' emphasis on efficiency and conservation, however, is giving way to the reemergence of size and brute force as automotive values, at least at the high end of the market where most American automakers are focusing their efforts. An aesthetic of size and substance is taking hold, especially at GM, where its big Chevies, Buicks, Olds, and Cadillacs are showing the bulky, tubby proportions reminiscent of the bathtub cars of the immediate postwar years. For most makers, svelte aero is giving way to protective bulk, perhaps symbolizing the nervous determination of the nouveau riche to protect their wealth against the encroaching albeit unorganized unrest of the lower orders. Size and power is back under the hood as well, with big V–8s packing 200 plus horsepower and a few V–12s appearing again for the first time since the extravagant 1930s. And nose-thumbing, mind-numbing exclusivity is making a reappearance in the form of superexpensive special automobiles. For example, Jaguar, now owned by Ford, recently introduced a $600,000 542-horsepower limited edition sports car, arrogantly asserting that only 350 privileged individuals will be able to purchase one. At the lower end of the market, small imports are catching the aero bug, now largely yesterday's fashion, to try to conceal their mass-produced monotony. But they can hardly match the visual and real size and power of their automotive betters.[17]

Some pundits see in the concentration of American automakers, as well as other manufacturers, on the production of varied, upscale goods by more flexible and less specialized production processes the emergence of a new system of post-Fordism, destined to save stagnating industrial powers like the United States.[18] But can entire industrial nations sustain themselves by producing trendy products for the world's wealthy, while abandoning mass-produced goods? Unless the rich can expand their overconsumption at exponential rates, surely this strategy of industrial recovery is futile. And the obstacle of class conflict must also be taken into account. Workers in advanced capitalist countries can hardly remain content for long to slave at downscale wages producing upscale products that they have no hope of purchasing. As the class-obscuring ideology of mass consumption breaks down and exposes the dirty secret of an increasingly polarized society, perhaps America's working people will once again organize and fight for their own interests, as they did in similar circumstances some sixty years ago. And what sort of social order are they likely to construct on the ruins of a failed Fordism? Only history – that is, the strivings and struggles of humans for freedom – will tell.

Notes

1 THE AESTHETICS OF FORDISM

1 A. Gramsci, "Americanism and Fordism," in Q. Hoare and G. Smith (eds and trans.), *Selections from the Prison Notebooks*, New York, International Publishers, 1971, pp. 302–13.

2 On the basic premises of the Regulation School, see M. Aglietta, *A Theory of Capitalist Regulation: The US Experience*, London, New Left Books, 1979; and A. Lipietz, *Mirages and Miracles*, London, Verso, 1987.

3 Aglietta, *Capitalist Regulation*, pp. 151–61.

4 A. Chandler, *The Visible Hand: The Managerial Revolution in American Business*, Cambridge, Mass., Harvard University Press, 1977, pp. 285–376; M. Piore and C. Sabel, *The Second Industrial Divide*, New York, Basic Books, 1984, pp. 49–104; Aglietta, *Capitalist Regulation*, pp. 179–208, 328–79; M. Davis, *Prisoners of the American Dream: Politics and Economy in the History of the US Working-Class*, London, Verso, 1986, pp. 102–53.

5 For a critique of the functionalism of two characteristic works in the field, see D. Gartman, "Structuralist marxism and the labor process: where have the dialectics gone?" *Theory and Society*, 1983, vol. 12, pp. 659–69.

6 For an analysis of consumption which reduces individual needs to system needs in this way, see E. Preteceille and J.-P. Terrail, *Capitalism, Consumption and Needs*, Oxford, Basil Blackwell, 1985.

7 Aglietta, *Capitalist Regulation*, pp. 160–1. On the functionalist aesthetic of Fordism, see also D. Harvey, *The Condition of Postmodernity*, Oxford and Cambridge, Mass., Basil Blackwell, 1989, pp. 135–6, 156.

8 This Frankfurt School theory is developed in H. Marcuse, *One-Dimensional Man*, Boston, Beacon Press, 1964; Marcuse, *The Aesthetic Dimension*, Boston, Beacon Press, 1978; Marcuse, "The affirmative character of culture," in *Negations*, Boston, Beacon Press, 1968, pp. 88–133; T. Adorno, "Cultural criticism and society," in *Prisms*, Cambridge, Mass., MIT Press, 1981, pp. 17–34; Adorno, *Aesthetic Theory*, London, Routledge & Kegan Paul, 1984.

9 M. Horkheimer and T. Adorno, "The culture industry: enlightenment as mass deception," in *Dialectic of Enlightenment*, New York, Herder & Herder, 1972, p. 137.

10 Adorno, *Aesthetic Theory*, p. 102.

11 T. Adorno, *Introduction to the Sociology of Music*, New York, Continuum, 1976, pp. 21–70; Adorno, "On the fetish-character in music and the regression of listening," in A. Arato and E. Gebhardt (eds), *The Essential Frankfurt School Reader*, Oxford, Basil Blackwell, 1978, pp. 270–99.

12 Horkheimer and Adorno, "Culture industry," pp. 121–4, 154–6; T. Adorno, "Perennial fashion – jazz," in *Prisms*, Cambridge, Mass., MIT Press, 1981, pp. 119–32.

13 T. Adorno, "Culture industry reconsidered," *New German Critique*, 1975, no. 6, p. 14.

14 H. Marcuse, *An Essay on Liberation*, Boston, Beacon Press, 1969, p. 11; Marcuse, *One-Dimensional Man*, pp. 4–9.

15 See esp. Marcuse, *One-Dimensional Man*, pp. 19–34, 256–7.

16 D. Kellner, "Critical theory and the culture industries," *Telos*, 1984–85, no. 62, pp. 196–206; M. Gottdiener, "Hegemony and mass culture: a semiotic approach," *American Journal of Sociology*, 1985, vol. 90, pp. 979–1001.

17 G. Lukács, *History and Class Consciousness*, Cambridge, Mass., MIT Press, 1971; Lukács, "Idea and form in literature," in E. San Juan Jr (ed.), *Marxism and Human Liberation*, New York, Dell, 1973, pp. 109–31; Lukács, "The ideology of modernism," in ibid., pp. 277–307.

18 K. Marx, "Economic and philosophical manuscripts," in T. Bottomore (ed.), *Karl Marx: Early Writings*, New York, McGraw-Hill, 1963, pp. 120–34; Marx, "Contribution to the critique of Hegel's Philosophy of Right. Introduction," in ibid., pp. 55–9. See also A. Heller, *The Theory of Need in Marx*, New York, St Martin's, 1976.

19 H. Marcuse, *Eros and Civilization*, Boston, Beacon Press, 1966; Marcuse, *Essay on Liberation*.

2 EARLY DEVELOPMENT OF THE AUTOMOTIVE FORM

1 Wilson quoted in "Motorists don't make socialists, they say," *New York Times*, March 4, 1906, p. 12; Hitler quoted in J. Flink, *The Automobile Age*, Cambridge, Mass., MIT Press, 1988, p. 113.

2 The following account of the industrial struggles of the period is based on these works: D. Gordon, R. Edwards, and M. Reich, *Segmented Work, Divided Workers*, Cambridge, Cambridge University Press, 1982; R. Edwards, *Contested Terrain: The Transformation of the Workplace in the Twentieth Century*, New York, Basic Books, 1979; D. Montgomery, *The Fall of the House of Labor*, Cambridge, Cambridge University Press, 1986; Montgomery, *Workers' Control in America*, Cambridge, Cambridge University Press, 1979; H. Braverman, *Labor and Monopoly Capital*, New York, Monthly Review Press, 1974; J. Weinstein, *The Corporate Ideal in the Liberal State: 1900–1918*, Boston, Beacon Press, 1968; R. Wiebe, *The Search for Order: 1877–1920*, New York, Hill & Wang, 1967.

3 J. Lears, "From salvation to self-realization: advertising and the therapeutic roots of the consumer culture, 1880–1920," in R. Fox and J. Lears (eds), *The Culture of Consumption: Critical Essays in American History, 1880–1980*, New York, Pantheon, 1983, pp. 1–38; W. Susman, *Culture as History: The Transformation of American Society in the Twentieth Century*, New York, Pantheon, 1984, pp. xx–xxx.

4 R. Rosenzweig, *Eight Hours For What We Will: Workers and Leisure in an Industrial City, 1870–1920*, Cambridge, Cambridge University Press, 1983.
5 S. Brandes, *American Welfare Capitalism*, Chicago, University of Chicago Press, 1976; R. Goldman and J. Wilson, "The rationalization of leisure," *Politics and Society*, 1977, vol. 7, pp. 157–87.
6 J. Rae, *The American Automobile*, Chicago, University of Chicago Press, 1965, pp. 7–12; Flink, *Automobile Age*, pp. 10–14.
7 C. Glasscock, *The Gasoline Age*, Indianapolis, Bobbs–Merrill, 1937, pp. 46–9; J. Rae, *American Automobile Manufacturers*, Philadelphia, Chilton Books, 1959, pp. 8, 18–19, 24; D. Hounshell, *From the American System to Mass Production: 1800–1932*, Baltimore, Johns Hopkins University Press, 1984, pp. 189–215; J. Flink, *America Adopts the Automobile, 1895–1910*, Cambridge, Mass., MIT Press, 1970, pp. 242–8.
8 Flink, *America Adopts Automobile*, pp. 238–42; G. Georgano, *Cars, 1886–1930*, New York, Beekman House, 1985, pp. 35–8; V. Scharff, *Taking the Wheel: Women and the Coming of the Motor Age*, New York, Free Press, 1991, pp. 36–50.
9 P. Wilson, *Chrome Dreams: Automobile Styling Since 1893*, Radnor, Penn., Chilton Books, 1976, pp. 5–8, the *Horseless Age* quote is on p. 8.
10 Rae, *American Automobile Manufacturers*, p. 57; Wilson, *Chrome Dreams*, pp. 13–14.
11 Flink, *America Adopts Automobile*, pp. 12–15; Wilson, *Chrome Dreams*, pp. 14–17.
12 Quote from Flink, *America Adopts Automobile*, pp. 243–4; Georgano, *Cars*, p. 64.
13 Flink, *America Adopts Automobile*, pp. 244–78.
14 General Motors Corporation, *Styling: The Look of Things*, Detroit, Public Relations, Styling Staff, General Motors Corporation, 1955, p. 30; P. Roberts, *Any Color So Long As It's Black: Fifty Years of Automobile Advertising*, New York, William Morrow, 1976, pp. 13–15; E. Cray, *The Chrome Colossus: General Motors and Its Times*, New York, McGraw-Hill, 1980, pp. 37–8.
15 A. Bird, *Antique Automobiles*, London, Treasure Press, 1984, pp. 141–2; G. Oliver, *Cars and Coachbuilding*, London, Sotheby Parke Bernet, 1981, pp. 43–4; J. Mclellan, *Bodies Beautiful: A History of Car Styling and Craftsmanship*, Newton Abbot, David & Charles, 1975, pp. 19–21.
16 G. Oliver, *A History of Coachbuilding*, London, Cassell, 1962, pp. 24–5, 73–4, the quote is on p. 39.
17 Ibid., p. 42; S. Brams, "The styling staff," manuscript in the Historic Files of the General Motors Design Staff, Design Library, General Motors Technical Center, Warren, Mich., p. 8.
18 W. Baunard, "The future car: how car bodies have developed at home and abroad," *Scientific American*, 1913, vol. 108, pp. 28–30, the quote is on p. 29; Mclellan, *Bodies Beautiful*, pp. 43, 47; Oliver, *Cars*, p. 118.
19 Bird, *Antique Automobiles*, pp. 135–6; Baunard, "Future car," pp. 28–30.
20 Bird, *Antique Automobiles*, pp. 136–42; Georgano, *Cars*, pp. 79–82; Oliver, *History*, pp. 31–4; Wilson, *Chrome Dreams*, pp. 31–43.
21 S. MacMinn, "American automobile design," in G. Silk (ed.), *Automobile and Culture*, New York, Harry Abrams, 1984, p. 214; L. Mandel, *American Cars*, New York, Stewart, Tabori & Chang, 1982, pp. 67–74.

22 R. Carson, *The Olympian Cars*, New York, Knopf, 1976, p. 54; Mclellan, *Bodies Beautiful*, pp. 22–5, 40, 47–8; J. Day, *The Bosch Book of the Motor Car*, New York, St Martin's, 1976, p. 137; J. Shepherd, *Motor-Body Building*, London, Cassell, 1923, pp. 169–71.

23 Mclellan, *Bodies Beautiful*, p. 24; Oliver, *History*, p. 52; Overland advertising supplement to *The Automobile*, 1911, vol. 25, no page (following 288); Georgano, *Cars*, p. 204.

24 Oliver, *History*, p. 99. See also p. 115.

25 D. Gartman, *Auto Slavery: The Labor Process in the American Automobile Industry, 1897–1950*, New Brunswick, NJ, Rutgers University Press, 1986, pp. 24–38.

26 Baunard, "Future car," pp. 29–30; Mclellan, *Bodies Beautiful*, pp. 29, 47; D. Haskell, "From automobile to road-plane," *Harper's*, July 1934, vol. 169, p. 175; Bird, *Antique Automobiles*, pp. 138–40.

27 Oliver, *Cars*, p. 57; Oliver, *History*, pp. 74, 93; Wilson, *Chrome Dreams*, pp. 63–7; R. Langworth and J. Norbye, *The Complete History of General Motors, 1908–1986*, New York, Beekman House, 1986, pp. 46–8; Haskell, "From automobile," pp. 175–6.

28 Flink, *America Adopts Automobile*, pp. 252–5, 88–95, 70–1.

29 Mandel, *American Cars*, pp. 14–15; F. Donovan, *Wheels for a Nation*, New York, Thomas Crowell, 1965, pp. 1–14, the *New York Times* quote is on p. 1.

30 R. Flower and M. Jones, *One Hundred Years on the Road*, New York, McGraw-Hill, 1981, pp. 80, 90, the *Automobile Topics* quote is on p. 90.

31 Flink, *America Adopts Automobile*, pp. 70–4; the quote is from an ad reproduced in F. Clymer, *Treasury of Early American Automobiles, 1877–1925*, New York, McGraw-Hill, 1950, p. 68.

32 F. Munsey, "Impressions by the way," *Munsey's Magazine*, May 1903, vol. 29, p. 108, quoted in Flink, *America Adopts Automobile*, p. 106.

33 L. McKilvin, "Keeping the land yacht shipshape," *Harper's Weekly*, Jan. 2, 1909, vol. 53, p. 10, quoted in Flink, *America Adopts Automobile*, pp. 101–2.

34 W. Belasco, *Americans on the Road: From Autocamp to Motel, 1910–1945*, Cambridge, Mass., MIT Press, 1979, pp. 3–68, the quote is on p. 3.

35 J. Smith, "A runaway match: the automobile in the American film, 1900–1920," in D. Lewis and L. Goldstein (eds), *The Automobile and American Culture*, Ann Arbor, University of Michigan Press, 1983, pp. 180–3; G. Silk, "The automobile in art," in Silk (ed.), *Automobile and Culture*, p. 47. For an example of a critical cartoon, see Donovan, *Wheels*, p. 8.

36 Flink, *America Adopts Automobile*, pp. 66–8; Flower and Jones, *One Hundred Years*, pp. 36–41; M. Berger, *The Devil's Wagon in God's Country: The Automobile and Social Change in Rural America, 1893–1929*, Hamden, Conn., Archon, 1979, pp. 14–31, the quote is on p. 29.

37 Flink, *America Adopts Automobile*, pp. 68–70, 83–5; Berger, *Devil's Wagon*, pp. 31–52; R. Wik, "The early automobile and the American farmer," in Lewis and Goldstein (eds), *Automobile and American Culture*, pp. 37–47.

38 The *Horseless Age* report is in Flink, *America Adopts Automobile*, pp. 65–6; Bird, *Antique Automobiles*, p. 151; J. Pettifer and N. Turner, *Automania: Man and the Motor Car*, Boston, Little, Brown, 1984, p. 43, the quote is on this page.

3 DIVERGING PATHS OF DESIGN: MASS AND CLASS PRODUCTION

1 The following account of the general labor struggles of this period is based upon these works: D. Montgomery, *The Fall of the House of Labor*, Cambridge, Cambridge University Press, 1987; Montgomery, *Workers' Control in America*, Cambridge, Cambridge University Press, 1979; D. Gordon, R. Edwards, and M. Reich, *Segmented Work, Divided Workers*, Cambridge, Cambridge University Press, 1982. The detailed account of the auto industry is based upon D. Gartman, *Auto Slavery: The Labor Process in the American Automobile Industry, 1897–1950*, New Brunswick, NJ, Rutgers University Press, 1986; S. Meyer, *The Five Dollar Day: Labor Management and Social Control in the Ford Motor Company, 1908–1921*, Albany, State University of New York Press, 1981.

2 J. Weinstein, *The Corporate Ideal in the Liberal State, 1900–1918*, Boston, Beacon Press, 1968; R. Wiebe, *The Search for Order: 1877–1920*, New York, Hill & Wang, 1967.

3 R. Rosenzweig, *Eight Hours for What We Will*, Cambridge, Cambridge University Press, 1983, pp. 168–228; F. Couvares, "The triumph of commerce: class, culture, and mass culture in Pittsburgh," in M. Frisch and D. Walkowitz (eds), *Working-Class America*, Urbana, University of Illinois Press, 1983, pp. 142–7; N. Harris, "The drama of consumer desire," in O. Mayr and R. Post (eds), *Yankee Enterprise: The Rise of the American System of Manufactures*, Washington, DC, Smithsonian Institution Press, 1981, pp. 198–205; S. Ewen, *Captains of Consciousness: Advertising and the Social Roots of the Consumer Culture*, New York, McGraw-Hill, 1976.

4 R. Lynd and H. Lynd, *Middletown: A Study in Contemporary American Culture*, New York, Harcourt, Brace, 1929, pp. 103, 251–61; L. Rainwater, R. Coleman, and G. Handel, *Workingman's Wife: Her Personality, World and Life Style*, New York, Oceana Publications, 1959, pp. 174–5.

5 Lynd and Lynd, *Middletown*, pp. 80–1.

6 D. Boorstin, *The Americans: The Democratic Experience*, New York, Random House, 1973, pp. 89–160; L. Lowenthal, "The triumph of mass idols," in *Literature, Popular Culture, and Society*, Palo Alto, Calif., Pacific Books, 1961, pp. 109–36.

7 A. Nevins and F. Hill, *Ford: The Times, the Man, the Company*, New York, Scribner's, 1954, pp. 240–1, 260, 332–4; J. Rae, *The American Automobile*, Chicago, University of Chicago Press, 1965, p. 62.

8 M. La Fever, "Workers, machinery, and production in the automobile industry," *Monthly Labor Review*, Oct. 1924, vol. 19, pp. 15–17; E. Schipper, "Quantity production of sheet metal bodies," *Automotive Industries*, 1918, vol. 38, pp. 1188–93; W. Carver, "Straight line production attained in wooden body building," *Automotive Industries*, 1925, vol. 53, pp. 946–9, 982–5.

9 J. Mclellan, *Bodies Beautiful: A History of Car Styling and Craftsmanship*, Newton Abbot, David & Charles, 1975, pp. 48–50; E. Thum, "Many advantages realized in body of 5-piece all-steel design," *Automotive Industries*, 1928, vol. 59, pp. 370–2.

10 P. Wilson, *Chrome Dreams: Automobile Styling Since 1893*, Radnor, Penn., Chilton Books, 1976, pp. 90–103; A. Sloan, *My Years with General Motors*, Garden City, NY, Anchor Books, 1972, pp. 174, 182–6; E. Schipper, "Closed body production costs minimized in Essex coach," *Automotive Industries*, 1921, vol. 45, pp. 956–7.

11 La Fever, "Workers, machinery, production," pp. 17–19; Sloan, *My Years*, pp. 271–2; H. Arnold and F. Faurote, *Ford Methods and the Ford Shops*, New York, Arno Press, 1972, pp. 360–83; "Why the 1916 cars are cheaper," *The Automobile*, 1915, vol. 33, p. 596.

12 G. Oliver, *A History of Coachbuilding*, London, Cassell, 1962, p. 115.

13 The Mitchell quote is a composite from two sources: J. Flint, *The Dream Machine: The Golden Age of American Automobiles, 1946–1965*, New York, Quandrangle, 1976, p. 2, and B. Mitchell and K. Wilfert, "Is romantic styling dead? pro and con forum," *Motor Trend*, Sept. 1973, vol. 25, p. 113; K. Forbes, *The Principles of Automobile Body Design*, Philadelphia, Ware Brothers, 1922, p. 11.

14 "Growing demand for low priced closed car," *Automotive Industries*, 1921, vol. 45, p. 1002; N. Shidle, "'How to reduce body production costs' topic of body session," *Automotive Industries*, 1923, vol. 48, pp. 112–15; "Reminiscences of John Najjar," Automotive Design Oral History Project, Edsel B. Ford Design History Center, Henry Ford Museum and Greenfield Village, Dearborn, Mich., 1981, 1984, pp. 48–9.

15 "Reminiscences of Gordon Buehrig," Automotive Design Oral History Project, Edsel B. Ford Design History Center, Henry Ford Museum and Greenfield Village, Dearborn, Mich., 1984, pp. 5–6.

16 W. Chrysler, *Life of an American Workman*, New York, Dodd, Mead, 1937, p. 134.

17 Quote is from Engineering Staff, Technical Information Section, Chrysler Corporation, *Story of the Airflow Cars, 1934–1937*, Detroit, Chrysler Corporation, 1963, p. 6.

18 "Reminiscences of John Najjar," p. 48; "Reminiscences of Gordon Buehrig," pp. 4–5.

19 Oliver, *History*, pp. 103–5, 114.

20 R. Carson, *The Olympian Cars: The Great American Luxury Automobiles of the Twenties and Thirties*, New York, Knopf, 1976, pp. 7–10; Wilson, *Chrome Dreams*, pp. 118–20; G. Borgeson and E. Jaderquist, *Sports and Classic Cars*, New York, Bonanza Books, 1955, pp. 158–63.

21 J. Geschelin, "Packard's 88 acres of production efficiency," *Automotive Industries*, 1936, vol. 74, p. 636; E. Schipper, "Individual engine assembly method gets greater accuracy," *Automotive Industries*, 1923, vol. 48, pp. 773–4.

22 Carson, *Olympian Cars*, pp. 11–13, 54–6; Mclellan, *Bodies Beautiful*, pp. 92–4; T. Hibbard, "Early days in GM Art and Colour," *Special-Interest Autos*, 1974, no. 23, p. 41.

23 Carson, *Olympian Cars*, pp. 14–21; S. Bayley, *Harley Earl and the Dream Machine*, New York, Knopf, 1983, pp. 19–23.

24 Carson, *Olympian Cars*, pp. 20–5.

25 Borgeson and Jaderquist, *Sports and Classic Cars*, pp. 161–2; Carson, *Olympian Cars*, p. 56; Wilson, *Chrome Dreams*, pp. 68–79, 109, 121, 134.

26 W. Belasco, "Motivatin' with Chuck Berry and Frederick Jackson Turner," in D. Lewis and L. Goldstein (eds), *The Automobile and American Culture*, Ann Arbor, University of Michigan Press, 1983, pp. 262–4; J. Flink, *America Adopts the Automobile, 1895–1910*, Cambridge, Mass., MIT Press, 1970, p. 101.

27 J. Smith, "A runaway match: the automobile in the American film, 1900–1920," in Lewis and Goldstein (eds), *Automobile and American Culture*, pp. 184–7.

28 C. Vanderbilt, "The democracy of the motor car," *Motor*, Dec. 1921, vol. 37, p. 21, quoted in J. Flink, *The Car Culture*, Cambridge, Mass., MIT Press, 1975, p. 156; W. Dix, "The automobile as a vacation agent," *Independent*, 1904, vol. 56. pp. 1259–60, quoted in Flink, *America Adopts Automobile*, p. 109; Lynd and Lynd, *Middletown*, pp. 64–5, 251–61; W. Belasco, *Americans on the Road*, Cambridge, Mass., MIT Press, 1979, pp. 96–8,105–13.

29 Flink, *Car Culture*, pp. 156–7; advertisement for the Chevrolet Motor Company, 1924, reprinted in J. Stern and M. Stern, *Auto Ads*, New York, Random House, 1978, p. 21.

30 R. Lynd and H. Lynd, *Middletown in Transition*, New York, Harcourt, Brace, 1937, p. 245.

31 P. Frankl, *Machine-Made Leisure*, New York, Harper & Bros., 1932, pp. 12–13. See also W. Susman, *Culture as History: The Transformation of American Society in the Twentieth Century*, New York, Pantheon, 1984, pp. 105–21, 186–92.

32 Frankl, *Machine-Made Leisure*, pp. 25, 27; W. Teague, *Design This Day: The Technique of Order in the Machine Age*, London, Studio Publications, 1947, p. 23.

33 On the English Arts and Crafts movement, see J. Heskett, *Industrial Design*, New York and Toronto, Oxford University Press, 1980, pp. 19–26; R. Loewy, *Never Leave Well Enough Alone*, New York, Simon & Schuster, 1951, p. 11; Teague, *Design This Day*, pp. 37–8.

34 Heskett, *Industrial Design*, p. 49; A. Forty, *Objects of Desire*, New York, Pantheon, 1986, p. 101.

35 E. Calkins, "Beauty the new business tool," *Atlantic Monthly*, Aug. 1927, vol. 140, p. 146; Model T jokes from D. Lewis, *The Public Image of Henry Ford*, Detroit, Wayne State University Press, 1976, pp. 121–5.

36 On class cultures symbolizing relative distance from necessity, see P. Bourdieu, *Distinction: A Social Critique of the Judgement of Taste*, Cambridge, Mass., Harvard University Press, 1984. For an appreciation and critique of Bourdieu, see D. Gartman, "Culture as class symbolization or mass reification?" *American Journal of Sociology*, 1991, vol. 97, pp. 421–47.

37 Calkins, "Beauty," p. 146; S. Lewis, *Babbitt*, New York, New American Library, 1961, p. 63; Harris, "Drama of consumer desire," pp. 206–10.

38 M. Frostick, *Advertising and the Motor Car*, London, Lund Humphries, 1970, pp. 64, 73–84; the Duesenberg ad is reproduced in Stern and Stern, *Auto Ads*, p. 27.

39 G. Georgano, *Cars, 1886–1930*, New York, Beekman House, 1985, p. 210; Kissel ad reproduced in F. Clymer, *A Treasury of Early American Automobiles, 1877–1925*, New York, McGraw-Hill, 1950, p. 185; Roamer ad reproduced in Georgano, *Cars*, p. 218.

40 Carson, *Olympian Cars*, p. 30; letter sent to a British motor publication in 1920, quoted in Lewis, *Public Image*, p. 124.

41 Joke quoted in R. Wik, *Henry Ford and Grass-roots America*, Ann Arbor, University of Michigan Press, 1972, p. 48; song quoted in R. Ames, "Cars in song," *Special-Interest Autos*, 1977, no. 38, p. 43.

42 Le Corbusier (C.E. Jeanneret), *Towards a New Architecture*, London, Architectural Press, 1946, p. 96.

43 L. Cohen, "Embellishing a life of labor: an interpretation of the material culture of American working-class homes, 1885–1915," in T. Schlereth (ed.), *Material Culture Studies in America*, Nashville, American Association for State and Local History, 1982, pp. 289–305; Heskett, *Industrial Design*, pp. 78–104; Forty, *Objects of Desire*, pp. 156–60.

44 C. Jordan, "The automobile stylist – a partner of the engineer," SAE Paper No. 474B, presented at the 1962 Society of Automotive Engineers International Congress and Exposition, Detroit, Mich., p. 6.

45 Flink, *America Adopts Automobile*, p. 103.

46 Flink, *Car Culture*, pp. 142–3, 167–81; J.-P. Bardou, J.-J. Chanaron, P. Fridenson, and J. Laux, *The Automobile Revolution: The Impact of an Industry*, Chapel Hill, University of North Carolina Press, 1982, pp. 94–6; E. Kefauver, *In a Few Hands: Monopoly Power in America*, Baltimore, Penguin, 1965, pp. 80–9.

47 M. Bird, "The 1922 car," *Scientific American*, Mar. 1922, vol. 126, p. 161; "Art in bodies," *Automotive Industries*, 1925, vol. 52, p. 201.

48 Stern and Stern, *Auto Ads*, pp. 16ff.; Model T ad reproduced in F. Clymer, *Henry's Wonderful Model T, 1908–1927*, New York, McGraw-Hill, 1955, p. 159; Hibbard, "Early days," p. 42.

49 Sloan, *My Years*, p. 313; Wilson, *Chrome Dreams*, pp. 68–79.

50 Kettering quoted in E. Wheeler, "Tomorrow's motor car," *World's Work*, May 1927, vol. 54, p. 85; General Motors Corporation, *Styling: The Look of Things*, Detroit, Public Relations, Styling Staff, General Motors Corporation, 1955, pp. 33–4.

51 Sloan, *My Years*, pp. 271–4; Mclellan, *Bodies Beautiful*, p. 85.

52 Maxwell ad reproduced in Clymer, *Treasury*, p. 148.

53 Sloan, *My Years*, pp. 176–7; Wilson, *Chrome Dreams*, pp. 111–12; R. Langworth and J. Norbye, *The Complete History of Chrysler Corporation*, New York, Beekman House, 1985, p. 22.

54 Clymer, *Henry's Wonderful Model T*, pp. 107–30, ads quoted are reproduced on pp. 200, 216; D. Hounshell, *From the American System to Mass Production, 1800–1932*, Baltimore, Johns Hopkins University Press, 1984, pp. 273–6.

55 Sloan, *My Years*, pp. 184–5, 310–11; E. Cray, *Chrome Colossus: General Motors and Its Times*, New York, McGraw-Hill, 1980, pp. 243–4; Carson, *Olympian Cars*, pp. 57–8; H. Pfau, "The master craftsmen: the golden age of the coachbuilder in America," in *Automobile Quarterly* (ed.), *The American Car Since 1775*, New York, E.P. Dutton, 1971, pp. 145–6.

4 THE STRUGGLE FOR STYLING I: THE 1920s AND THE BIRTH OF AUTOMOBILE STYLING

1 This story is pieced together from A. Fleming, "The Earl of design,"

Automotive News, Sept. 16, 1983, p. 232; and B. Holliday, "Harley Earl, the original car stylist," *Detroit Free Press, Detroit* magazine, May 25, 1969, p. 13. I have inserted characteristic expletives.

2 I. Bernstein, *The Lean Years: A History of the American Worker, 1920–1933*, Boston, Houghton Mifflin, 1972, pp. 63–71; R. Edsforth, *Class Conflict and Cultural Consensus: The Making of a Mass Consumer Society in Flint, Michigan*, New Brunswick, NJ, Rutgers University Press, 1987.

3 R. Lynd and H. Lynd, *Middletown*, New York, Harcourt, Brace, 1929, pp. 81, 87.

4 Ibid., p. 82n.; R. Fox, "Epitaph for Middletown: Robert S. Lynd and the analysis of consumer culture," in R. Fox and J. Lears (eds), *The Culture of Consumption*, New York, Pantheon, 1983, p. 103. On consumption as class compensation, see S. Ewen, *Captains of Consciousness*, New York, McGraw-Hill, 1976, esp. 77–109; Ewen, *All Consuming Images: The Politics of Style in Contemporary Culture*, New York, Basic Books, 1988, esp. pp. 57–108.

5 S. Cheney and M. Cheney, *Art and the Machine: An Account of Industrial Design in 20th-Century America*, New York, Whittlesey House, 1936, pp. 7–14; J. Meikle, *Twentieth Century Limited: Industrial Design in America, 1925–1939*, Philadelphia, Temple University Press, 1979, pp. 10–18.

6 Meikle, *Twentieth Century Limited*, pp. 19–38; A. Pulos, *American Design Ethic: A History of Industrial Design to 1940*, Cambridge, Mass., MIT Press, 1983, pp. 295–316.

7 P. Frankl, *Machine-Made Leisure*, New York, Harper & Bros., 1932, pp. 13–14, the final Frankl quote is from Meikle, *Twentieth Century Limited*, p. 153; R. Loewy, *Never Leave Well Enough Alone*, New York, Simon & Schuster, 1951, pp. 210, 219.

8 W. Teague, *Design This Day: The Technique of Order in the Machine Age*, London, Studio Publications, 1947, pp. 26, 89; R. Sheldon and E. Arens, *Consumer Engineering: A New Technique for Prosperity*, New York, Arno Press, 1976, originally 1932, p. 150.

9 H. Dreyfuss, *Designing for People*, New York, Simon & Schuster, 1951, pp. 59–60; Ewen, *All Consuming Images*, pp. 233–58; S. Ewen and E. Ewen, *Channels of Desire: Mass Images and the Shaping of American Consciousness*, New York, McGraw-Hill, 1982, pp. 159–225; D. Boorstin, *The Americans: The Democratic Experience*, New York, Random House, 1973, pp. 434–5.

10 E. Lucie-Smith, *A History of Industrial Design*, New York, Van Nostrand Reinhold, 1983, pp. 145, 151; Meikle, *Twentieth Century Limited*, pp. 77–9; Pulos, *American Design Ethic*, p. 403.

11 J.-P. Bardou, J.-J. Chanaron, P. Fridenson, and J. Laux, *The Automobile Revolution*, Chapel Hill, University of North Carolina Press, 1982, pp. 93–6; J. Flink, *The Automobile Age*, Cambridge, Mass., MIT Press, 1988, pp. 229–31.

12 E. Cray, *The Chrome Colossus: General Motors and its Times*, New York, McGraw-Hill, 1980, p. 137; A. Sloan, *My Years with General Motors*, Garden City, NY, Anchor Books, 1972, pp. 67–8, the quote is on p. 76.

13 Sloan, *My Years*, pp. 63–77, 171–5, the quote is on p. 172.

14 Ibid., pp. 79–106, the quotes are on pp. 70, 175.

15 Ibid., p. 72.
16 Ibid., pp. 176, 311.
17 Sloan quoted in Ibid., p. 190.
18 Ibid., pp. 72–3, 295–7, 178–82, the quotes are on pp. 73, 181; GM executive quoted in Cray, *Chrome Colossus*, p. 248; R. Langworth and J. Norbye, *The Complete History of General Motors, 1908–1986*, New York, Beekman House, 1986, pp. 93–5.
19 Sloan, *My Years*, pp. 207–8.
20 D. Hounshell, *From the American System to Mass Production, 1800–1932*, Baltimore, Johns Hopkins University Press, 1984, pp. 278–301; W. Abernathy, *The Productivity Dilemma*, Baltimore, Johns Hopkins University Press, 1978, pp. 30–3.
21 D. Lewis, M. McCarville, and L. Sorensen, *Ford: 1903 to 1984*, New York, Beekman House, 1983, pp. 75–81; "Reminiscences of Eugene T. Gregorie," Automotive Design Oral History Project, Edsel B. Ford Design History Center, Henry Ford Museum and Greenfield Village, Dearborn, Mich., 1985, pp. 14, 17, 23–5; song reproduced in F. Clymer, *Treasury of Early American Automobiles, 1877–1925*, New York, McGraw-Hill, 1950, p. 196.
22 Sloan, *My Years*, pp. 178, 312–13, the quote is on p. 313; Langworth and Norbye, *General Motors*, pp. 95–9; J. Geschelin, "Cadillac production keyed to quality products at lower costs," *Automotive Industries*, 1937, vol. 78, pp. 389–403.
23 Holliday, "Harley Earl," pp. 9–10; S. Bayley, *Harley Earl and the Dream Machine*, New York, Knopf, 1983, pp. 19–25; Fisher–Earl conversation quoted in C. Armi, *The Art of American Car Design*, University Park, Pennsylvania State University Press, 1988, pp. 5–6; M. Lamm, "Harley Earl's California years, 1893–1927," *Automobile Quarterly*, 1982, vol. 20, no. 1, pp. 34–44.
24 Holliday, "Harley Earl," pp. 10–11; Sloan, *My Years*, pp. 312–13; Bayley, *Harley Earl*, pp. 43–4.
25 Earl quoted in Holliday, "Harley Earl," p. 9; P. Wilson, *Chrome Dreams: Automobile Styling since 1893*, Radnor, Penn., Chilton Books, 1976, pp. 123–4; S. MacMinn, "American automobile design," in G. Silk (ed.), *Automobile and Culture*, New York, Harry Abrams, 1984, p. 223; Sloan, *My Years*, p. 313.
26 Sloan, *My Years*, p. 313.
27 C. Borth, "Harley J. Earl," *Ward's Auto World*, June–July 1969, vol. 5, pp. 33–5; Bayley, *Harley Earl*, pp. 19–25; H. Earl, "I dream automobiles," *Saturday Evening Post*, Aug. 7, 1954, vol. 227, p. 82; Earl quoted in S. Brams, "The styling staff," manuscript in the Historic Files of the General Motors Design Staff, Design Library, General Motors Technical Center, Warren, Mich., 1957, p. 1.
28 Sloan, *My Years*, p. 314.
29 On the general principles of organizational control, see R. Collins, *Conflict Sociology*, New York, Academic Press, 1975, pp. 286–347.
30 Sloan, *My Years*, p. 19; Holliday, "Harley Earl," pp. 7–9; Armi, *American Car Design*, pp. 31–2.
31 "Reminiscences of Frank Q. Hershey," Automotive Design Oral History Project, Edsel B. Ford Design History Center, Henry Ford Museum and

Greenfield Village, Dearborn, Mich., 1985, pp. 80–1; "Reminiscences of William L. Mitchell," in ibid., 1984, p. 2.

32 Earl, "I dream automobiles," p. 19; Sloan, *My Years*, p. 317.
33 Sloan, *My Years*, pp. 315–16; "Reminiscences of William L. Mitchell," p. 55.
34 Armi, *American Car Design*, pp. 17, 24–34.
35 H. Earl, "The look of things," booklet based on a film prepared by Earl for the General Motors Executive Conference in Lake Placid, NY, Oct. 6, 1952, in the Historic Files of the General Motors Design Staff, Design Library, General Motors Technical Center, Warren, Mich.; Earl, "Setting the style," in General Motors Corporation, *Opportunities Unlimited – Meeting Tomorrow's Challenge*, published speeches delivered at the General Motors Executive Conference in White Sulphur Springs, WV, Sept. 26–8, 1955, in ibid., p. 86; "Reminiscences of Paul W. Gillan," Automotive Design Oral History Project, Edsel B. Ford Design History Center, Henry Ford Museum and Greenfield Village, Dearborn, Mich., 1985, pp. 45–6; "Reminiscences of Richard Teague," in ibid., 1985, p. 45.
36 Bayley, *Harley Earl*, pp. 12–13; Fleming, "Earl of design," p. 225; "Reminiscences of Frank Q. Hershey," p. 172; Armi, *American Car Design*, pp. 19–21, 24–34.
37 Personal interview with C. Gale, Senior Designer, Chrylser Corporation, Aug. 27, 1987, Highland Park, Mich.; "Reminiscences of Frank Q. Hershey," pp. 90, 92, 179.
38 "Reminiscences of Paul W. Gillan," pp. 40, 49–50; "Reminiscences of George Walker," Automotive Design Oral History Project, Edsel B. Ford Design History Center, Henry Ford Museum and Greenfield Village, Dearborn, Mich., 1985, pp. 9–11.
39 "Reminiscences of Frank Q. Hershey," p. 15; "Reminiscences of Gordon Buehrig," Automotive Design Oral History Project, Edsel B. Ford Design History Center, Henry Ford Museum and Greenfield Village, Dearborn, Mich., 1985, pp. 1, 6; S. MacMinn quoted in Armi, *American Car Design*, p. 204; "Reminiscences of William L. Mitchell," pp. 2–3, 20; Earl quoted in Holliday, "Harley Earl," pp. 12–13.
40 H. Earl, "Styling in General Motors," *General Motors Engineering Journal*, May–June 1956, vol. 3, p. 79; Sloan, *My Years*, pp. 308, 318.
41 Mitchell quoted in Armi, *American Car Design*, p. 223; "Reminiscences of Strother MacMinn," Automotive Design Oral History Project, Edsel B. Ford Design History Center, Henry Ford Museum and Greenfield Village, Dearborn, Mich., 1986, p. 26; "Reminiscences of Richard Teague," pp. 42–5.
42 Mitchell quoted in Armi, *American Car Design*, p. 224; "Reminiscences of Paul W. Gillan," p. 48; Gene Garfinkle quoted in Armi, *American Car Design*, pp. 174–5, 178; "Reminiscences of Irvin W. Rybicki," Automotive Design Oral History Project, Edsel B. Ford Design History Center, Henry Ford Museum and Greenfield Village, Dearborn, Mich., 1985, p. 35.
43 "The story of GM styling," manuscript in the Historic Files of the General Motors Design Staff, Design Library, General Motors Technical Center, Warren, Mich., 1962, p. 1; Earl, "Setting the style," p. 86; "Reminiscences of Frank Q. Hershey," p. 81.
44 Armi, *American Car Design*, pp. 6-7, 27–9; Brams, "The styling staff," pp. 51–2.

Notes 237

45 "Reminiscences of Gordon Buehrig," pp. 5–7; "Reminiscences of Strother MacMinn," pp. 51–7; Brams, "The styling staff," pp. 52–4.

46 N. Shidle, "'Beauty doctors' take a hand in automotive design," *Automotive Industries*, 1927, vol. 57, p. 218.

47 Lewis *et al.*, *Ford*, pp. 84–8.

48 R. Langworth and J. Norbye, *The Complete History of Chrysler Corporation: 1924–1985*, New York, Beekman House, 1985, pp. 40–5; Brams, "The styling staff," p. 12.

49 S. MacMinn and M. Lamm, "A history of American auto design, 1930–1950," in *Detroit Style: Automotive Form, 1925–1950*, Detroit, Detroit Institute of Arts, 1985, pp. 59–62; "There are no automobiles," *Fortune*, Oct. 1930, vol. 2, p. 75; Langworth and Norbye, *History of Chrysler*, p. 45, the quote is on p. 27.

50 H. Pfau, "The master craftsmen: the golden age of the coachbuilder in America," in *Automobile Quarterly* (ed.), *The American Car Since 1775*, New York, E.P. Dutton, 1971, pp. 144–6; MacMinn and Lamm, "History of American auto design," pp. 62–5.

51 A. Sloan, *Adventures of a White-Collar Man*, New York, Doubleday, Doran, 1941, p. 177; L. Mandel, *American Cars*, New York, Stewart, Tabori & Chang, 1982, p. 213.

52 Personal interview with C. Gale, Senior Designer, Chrysler Corporation, Aug. 27, 1987, Highland Park, Mich.; Earl quoted in Sloan, *My Years*, p. 324.

53 K. Gross, "Never carry a package by the string: the inside story of Jordan advertising," *Special-Interest Autos*, 1975, no. 31, pp. 20–2, 52.

54 D. Holls, "The disciplines of design," manuscript of a speech delivered to the Society of Automotive Engineers, May 25, 1978, Oshawa, Ont., in the Historic Files of the General Motors Design Staff, Design Library, General Motors Technical Center, Warren, Mich., pp. 3–4.

55 Quote from Earl, "I dream automobiles," p. 18; General Motors Corporation, *Styling: The Look of Things*, Detroit, Public Relations, Styling Staff, General Motors, 1955, p. 36; Mitchell quoted in Armi, *American Car Design*, p. 216; interview with Bill Porter, in ibid., pp. 268–9; J. Mitarachi, "Harley Earl and his product: the styling section," *Industrial Design*, Oct. 1955, vol. 2, p. 58.

56 Sloan, *My Years*, p. 313; Mandel, *American Cars*, pp. 161–6; the quote is from Shidle, "'Beauty doctors,'" p. 219.

57 Personal interview with W. Brownlie, automobile designer for Chrysler Corporation (retired), Aug. 30, 1987, Dearborn, Mich.

58 "Reminiscences of Strother MacMinn," p. 7; personal interview with D. Turner, Director, Advanced Concepts and Industrial Design, Ford Motor Company, Aug. 29, 1988, Dearborn, Mich.

59 Langworth and Norbye, *General Motors*, pp. 80–111; Cray, *Chrome Colossus*, p. 276; Bardou *et al.*, *Auto Revolution*, pp. 209–11.

60 Sloan, *My Years*, p. 308; Earl quoted in Mitarachi, "Harley Earl," p. 52; Earl, "Styling in General Motors," p. 79.

61 R. Bach, "Design and style as selling factors," *Journal of the Society of Automotive Engineers*, Apr. 1928, vol. 22, p. 471; Mitchell quoted in Armi, *American Car Design*, p. 221.

62 Jordan quoted in P. Roberts, *Any Color So Long As It's Black*, New York, William Morrow, 1976, p. 107; "Automobiles with sex appeal," *Literary Digest*, March 2, 1929, vol. 100, p. 64.

63 GM designer quoted in Armi, *American Car Design*, p. 18. On the ideology of separate spheres, see E. Zaretsky, *Capitalism, the Family, and Personal Life*, New York, Harper & Row, 1976. On the way this ideology complexly influenced the automobile, see V. Scharff, *Taking the Wheel*, New York, Free Press, 1991.

5 THE STRUGGLE FOR STYLING II: THE DEPRESSION AND THE DECADE OF STREAMLINING

1 S. MacMinn and M. Lamm, "A history of American automobile design, 1930–1950," in Detroit Institute of Arts, *Detroit Style: Automotive Form, 1925–1950*, Detroit, Detroit Institute of Arts, 1985, pp. 65–8; and J. Fenster, "World's Fair '33: the promise of progress," *Automobile Quarterly*, 1987, vol. 25, no. 1, pp. 54–69.

2 See W. Pretzer, "The ambiguities of streamlining: symbolism, ideology, and cultural mediator," in *Streamlining America*, Dearborn, Mich., Henry Ford Museum and Greenfield Village, 1986, pp. 86–97.

3 R. Sheldon and E. Arens, *Consumer Engineering*, New York, Arno Press, 1976, pp. 17, 19.

4 D. Bush, *The Streamlined Decade*, New York, Braziller, 1975, pp. 21–6; J. Meikle, *Twentieth Century Limited*, Philadelphia, Temple University Press, 1979, passim.

5 S. Cheney and M. Cheney, *Art and the Machine*, New York, Whittlesey House, 1936, p. 139, the quote is on p. 291; N. Geddes, *Horizons*, New York, Dover, 1977, pp. 250–4; Meikle, *Twentieth Century Limited*, pp. 101–10; A. Forty, *Objects of Desire*, New York, Pantheon, 1986, pp. 156–60, 179.

6 Bush, *Streamlined Decade*, pp. 176–82. This critique of the aesthetics of flow and continuity as irrationalism is based on the philosophy of G. Lukács, especially his *The Destruction of Reason*, Atlantic Highlands, NJ, Humanities Press, 1980.

7 Bush, *Streamlined Decade*, pp. 63–96; Meikle, *Twentieth Century Limited*, pp. 84–110, 155–65; J. Law, "Designing the dream," in *Streamlining America*, Dearborn, Mich., Henry Ford Museum and Greenfield Village, 1986, pp. 18–31.

8 R. Lynd and H. Lynd, *Middletown in Transition*, New York, Harcourt, Brace, 1937, p. 265.

9 On the collectivization of consumption during this period, see M. Aglietta, *A Theory of Capitalist Regulation*, London, New Left Books, pp. 162–9, 179–208; E. Preteceille and J.-P. Terrail, *Capitalism, Consumption, and Needs*, Oxford and New York, Basil Blackwell, 1985, pp. 120–49.

10 The quote is from R. Carson, *Olympian Cars*, New York, Knopf, 1976, p. 52; M. Sedgwick, *Cars of the Thirties and Forties*, New York, Beekman House, 1979, pp. 127–38.

11 Carson, *Olympian Cars*, pp. 27, 32–4, 49, 53, 185–8.

12 A. Sloan, *My Years With General Motors*, New York, Anchor Books, 1972, pp. 205–6; R. Langworth and Norbye, *The Complete History of Chrysler Corporation, 1924–1985*, New York, Beekman House, 1985, pp. 51–9.

13 Sloan, *My Years*, pp. 198, 204, 207.
14 Langworth and Norbye, *History of Chrysler*, pp. 52–9, 75–6; R. Langworth and J. Norbye, *The Complete History of General Motors, 1908–1986*, New York, Beekman House, 1986, pp. 139–60; Sloan, *My Years*, p. 206.
15 Kaptur quoted in A. Fleming, "The Earl of design," *Automotive News*, Sept. 16, 1983, p. 226; see also MacMinn and Lamm, "History of American auto design," pp. 75–8.
16 J. Flink, *The Car Culture*, Cambridge, Mass., MIT Press, 1975, pp. 174–5; P. Wilson, *Chrome Dreams: Automobile Styling since 1893*, Radnor, Penn., Chilton Books, 1976, pp. 144–5.
17 The quote is from "Reminiscences of Irvin W. Rybicki," Automotive Design Oral History Project, Edsel B. Ford Design History Center, Henry Ford Museum and Greenfield Village, Dearborn, Mich., 1985, p. 13. See also "Reminiscences of Paul W. Gillan," in ibid., 1985, p. 42; "Reminiscences of Strother MacMinn," in ibid., 1986, p. 24.
18 "Reminiscences of Frank Q. Hershey," Automotive Design Oral History Project, Edsel B. Ford Design History Center, Henry Ford Museum and Greenfield Village, Dearborn, Mich., 1985, pp. 73–4; "What the public wants," *Business Week*, Aug. 19, 1933, p. 14; T. MacGowan, "How do buyers feel about today's cars . . . today?" *Automotive Industries*, 1938, vol. 79, pp. 86–90, 140–4.
19 First and last quotes from a personal interview with W. Brownlie, auto designer, Chrysler Corporation (retired), Dearborn, Mich., Aug. 30, 1987; personal interview with W. Porter, Chief Designer, Buick Studio, General Motors Corporation, Warren, Mich., Aug. 26, 1986.
20 "Reminiscences of Richard Teague," Automotive Design Oral History Project, Edsel B. Ford Design History Center, Henry Ford Museum and Greenfield Village, Dearborn, Mich., 1985, p. 214.
21 "Reminiscences of Strother MacMinn," p. 31; S. MacMinn, "Inside the prewar Olds studio," *Special-Interest Autos*, 1977, no. 40, p. 40.
22 "Reminiscences of Paul W. Gillan," pp. 25–9; J. Mitarachi, "Harley Earl and his product: the styling section," *Industrial Design*, Oct. 1955, vol. 2, p. 57.
23 The quote is from S. MacMinn, "Chief Pontiac and the Silver Streak," *Special-Interest Autos*, 1978, no. 43, p. 21. See also "Reminiscences of Frank Q. Hershey," pp. 62–6; MacMinn and Lamm, "American auto design," pp. 78–83.
24 The quotes are from S. MacMinn, "Inside prewar Olds," p. 41; and "Reminiscences of Strother MacMinn," p. 49.
25 C. Armi, *The Art of American Car Design*, University Park, Pennsylvania State University Press, 1988, p. 30; "Reminiscences of William L. Mitchell," p. 4.
26 MacMinn and Lamm, "American auto design," pp. 56–7; B. Holliday, "Harley J. Earl, the original car stylist," *Detroit Free Press*, Detroit magazine, May 25, 1969, the Sloan quote is on p. 13.
27 Mitarachi, "Harley Earl," p. 52; Armi, *American Car Design*, pp. 19, 31.
28 "Reminiscences of Strother MacMinn," p. 18; Ford Motor Company, *The Ford Book of Styling*, Dearborn, Mich., Public Relations, Styling Office, Ford Motor Company, 1963, p. 64; H. Crane, "The car of the future,"

Journal of the Society of Automotive Engineers, April 1939, vol. 44, p. 141; Earl quoted in Holliday, "Harley Earl," p. 16.

29 Earl quoted in Holliday, "Harley Earl," p. 16.

30 "Reminiscences of Richard Teague," pp. 7–21; "Reminiscences of Eugene Bordinat," Automotive Design History Project, Edsel B. Ford Design History Center, Henry Ford Museum and Greenfield Village, Dearborn, Mich., 1984, 1986, pp. 1–2. On socialization into norms and values as a method of controlling organizational inferiors, see R. Collins, *Conflict Sociology*, New York, Academic Press, 1975, pp. 300–7.

31 D. Lewis, M. McCarville, and L. Sorensen, *Ford: 1903 to 1984*, New York, Beekman House, 1983, pp. 90–8.

32 Armi, *American Car Design*, pp. 34–7, 233–46; "Reminiscences of Eugene T. Gregorie," Automotive Design Oral History Project, Edsel B. Ford Design History Center, Henry Ford Museum and Greenfield Village, Dearborn, Mich., 1985, passim.

33 "Reminiscences of Eugene T. Gregorie," pp. 18, 78; B. Gregorie interview in Armi, *American Car Design*, p. 238.

34 B. Gregorie interview in Armi, *American Car Design*, p. 238; "Reminiscences of Eugene T. Gregorie," pp. 23, 83.

35 "Reminiscences of Arnott 'Buzz' Grisinger," Automotive Design Oral History Project, Edsel B. Ford Design History Center, Henry Ford Museum and Greenfield Village, Dearborn, Mich., 1985, pp. 3–21; Carson, *Olympian Cars*, p. 59; Langworth and Norbye, *History of Chrysler*, pp. 34–5, 92–3, 101.

36 Art director quoted in L. Peat, "Looking ahead a few years at the SAE body session," *Automotive Industries*, 1931, vol. 64, p. 153; K. Ludvigsen, "Automobile aerodynamics: form and fashion," *Automobile Quarterly*, 1967, vol. 6, no. 2, pp. 146–61; Meikle, *Twentieth Century Limited*, pp. 141–4; A. Klemin, "Streamlining and your automobile," *Scientific American*, Feb. 1934, vol. 150, pp. 76–9.

37 E. Smith, "Buckminster Fuller's Dymaxion car," in G. Silk (ed.), *Automobile and Culture*, New York, Harry Abrams, 1984, pp. 248–51; W. Stout, "The new terranautics," *Scientific American*, March 1934, vol. 150, pp. 126–7.

38 Carson, *Olympian Cars*, pp. 35–8, 59.

39 "Body design of Reo Royale Eight has custom-built features," *Automotive Industries*, 1930, vol. 63, pp. 442–4, 445; Wilson, *Chrome Dreams*, pp. 145–6.

40 J. Andrade, "Wind-tunnel tests and body design," *Journal of the Society of Automotive Engineers*, July 1931, vol. 29, pp. 31, 56.

41 The quote is from MacMinn and Lamm, "American auto design," p. 62. See also Wilson, *Chrome Dreams*, p. 147.

42 Sloan, *My Years*, pp. 319, 321, the quote is on p. 319; "Brave new model world," *Business Week*, Jan. 11, 1933, p. 3.

43 H. Irwin, "The history of the Airflow car," *Scientific American*, Aug. 1977, vol. 237, p. 99; A. Klemin, "How research makes possible the modern motor car," *Scientific American*, Aug. 1934, vol. 151, pp. 61–3; Chrysler Corporation, Engineering Staff, Technical Information Section, *Story of the Airflow Cars, 1934–1937*, Detroit, Chrysler Corporation, 1963, pp. 1–2.

44 Langworth and Norbye, *History of Chrysler*, pp. 71–2, 77, 92; MacMinn and Lamm, "American auto design," pp. 68–70; Chrysler Corporation, *Story of Airflow*, pp. 2–3.

45 Klemin, "How research," p. 108; Irwin, "History of Airflow," p. 101; Chrysler Corporation, *Story of Airflow* p. 6; MacMinn and Lamm, "American auto design," pp. 69–72.

46 Quoted Chrysler advertisement of 1934, reprinted in J. Stern and M. Stern, *Auto Ads*, New York, Random House, 1978, p. 44; *Chrysler News*, vol. 1, no. 1 (no date), promotional newspaper published by Chrysler Sales Corporation; "How the Airflows were designed," *Automotive Industries*, 1934, vol. 70, pp. 766–7, 769.

47 *Chrysler News*, vol. 1, no. 1, p. 1; Chrysler ad in the *Saturday Evening Post*, Dec. 6, 1933, p. 31.

48 Langworth and Norbye, *History of Chrysler*, pp. 72–3, 92; "Reminiscences of Arnott 'Buzz' Grisinger," p. 8; M. Lamm, "Magnificent turkey," *Special-Interest Autos*, 1973, no. 16, p. 56.

49 Dreyfuss quoted in Langworth and Norbye, *History of Chrysler*, p. 73; Allen quoted in ibid.; Wilson, *Chrome Dreams*, pp. 157–61.

50 *Chrysler News*, vol. 1, no. 1, p. 1.

51 H. Earl, transcript of press conference, March 25, 1958, Historic Files, General Motors Design Staff, Design Library, General Motors Technical Center, Warren, Mich., p. 2.

52 Langworth and Norbye, *History of Chrysler*, pp. 65–6, 77–82; Lamm, "Magnificent turkey," p. 56.

53 Sloan letter quoted in Meikle, *Twentieth Century Limited*, p. 151; Klemin, "Streamlining and your automobile," pp. 76–9; Crane, "Car of the future," pp. 141–4, 153.

54 Personal interview with R. Gale, Senior Designer, Exterior Fit and Finish, Chrysler Corporation, Aug. 27, 1987, Highland Park, Mich.; R. Loewy, *Never Leave Well Enough Alone*, New York, Simon & Schuster, 1951, p. 219.

55 Carson, *Olympian Cars*, p. 255.

56 "Reminiscences of Eugene T. Bordinat," p. 556; MacMinn and Lamm, "American auto design," pp. 66, 68; Wilson, *Chrome Dreams*, pp. 166–8.

57 Holls quote is a combination of comments made in a personal interview on Aug. 14, 1986, and D. Holls, "Disciplines of Design," transcript of a speech given to the Society of Automotive Engineers, Oshawa, Ont., May 25, 1978, Historic Files, General Motors Design Staff, Design Library, General Motors Technical Center, Warren, Mich., p. 5.

58 G. Buehrig interview in Armi, *American Car Design*, pp. 227–32; "Reminiscences of Gordon Buehrig," passim; L. Mandel, *American Cars*, New York, Stewart, Tabori & Chang, 1982, pp. 208–14.

59 M. Lamm, "1941 Cadillac styling development," *Special-Interest Autos*, 1976, no. 36, p. 57; L. Houff and F. Whiting, "Design of this year's cars," *Magazine of Art*, 1937, vol. 30, p. 720; "Reminiscences of Strother MacMinn," p. 23.

60 B. Gregorie interview in Armi, *American Car Design*, p. 245. See also B. Mitchell interview in ibid., pp. 222–3.

61 D. Holls and M. Lamm, "The revolutionary 1934 La Salle," *Special-Interest Autos*, 1977, no. 40, pp. 12–17, 60–1; Sedgwick, *Cars of the Thirties and Forties*, p. 97.

62 MacMinn and Lamm, "American auto design," pp. 86–8; S. Bayley, *Harley Earl and the Dream Machine*, New York, Knopf, 1983, pp. 49–55; S. Brams, "The styling staff," manuscript in Historic Files, General Motors Design Staff, Design Library, General Motors Technical Center, Warren, Mich., pp. 31–2.
63 W. Boyne, *Power Behind the Wheel*, New York, Stewart, Tabori & Chang, 1988, p. 145; Langworth and Norbye, *History of General Motors*, p. 158.
64 MacMinn and Lamm, "American auto design," pp. 83, 88; Langworth and Norbye, *History of General Motors*, p. 165; Brams, "The styling staff," p. 31; Armi, *American Car Design*, pp. 68–71.
65 "Reminiscences of Eugene T. Gregorie," pp. 60, 80, 82; "Reminiscences of Frank Q. Hershey," p. 99.
66 Armi, *American Car Design*, p. 71; M. Lamm, "What Chryler Corp. cars could have looked like," *Special-Interest Autos*, 1971, no. 2, pp. 10–15; Lewis *et al.*, *Ford*, pp. 129–33.
67 Buick ad reproduced in Stern and Stern, *Auto Ads*, pp. 62–3.
68 R. Loewy and W. Teague, "What of the promised post-war world – is it just a dream or will it come true?" *New York Times*, Sept. 26, 1943, sec. 6, p. 34; B. Crandell, "Dreams unlimited," *Collier's*, June 28, 1947, vol. 119, pp. 14–15; E. Grace, "Your car after the war," *Saturday Evening Post*, Nov. 14, 1942, vol. 215, p. 13.
69 Mitchell quoted in R. Langworth, "Of tail fins and V–8s," *Automobile Quarterly*, 1975, vol. 13, no. 3, p. 311. See also "Reminiscences of Frank Q. Hershey," pp. 115–16; H. Earl, "I dream automobiles," *Saturday Evening Post*, Aug. 7, 1954, vol. 227, p. 82.

6 1950s' FINS AND THE TRIUMPH OF FANTASTIC STYLING

1 The quotes are from the F. Hershey interview in C. Armi, *The Art of American Car Design*, University Park, Pennsylvania State University Press, 1988, p. 195.
2 The following account of postwar political economy is based largely on M. Davis, *Prisoners of the American Dream*, London, Verso, 1986, pp. 85–8; M. Piore and C. Sabel, *The Second Industrial Divide*, New York, Basic Books, 1984, pp. 79–91; D. Gordon, R. Edwards, and M. Reich, *Segmented Work, Divided Workers*, Cambridge, Cambridge University Press, 1982, pp. 185–215.
3 R. Nixon, *Six Crises*, Garden City, NY, Doubleday, 1962, pp. 256, 259–60.
4 On suburbanized workers, see B. Berger, *Working Class Suburb*, Berkeley, University of California Press, 1960; D. Halle, *America's Working Man*, Chicago, University of Chicago Press, 1984.
5 S. Freud, *Civilization and its Discontents*, New York, Norton, 1962. For a revisionist interpretation relevant to capitalism and consumerism, see H. Marcuse, *Eros and Civilization*, Boston, Beacon Press, 1966.
6 W. Susman, "Did success spoil the United States? Dual representations in postwar America," in L. May (ed.), *Recasting America: Culture and Politics in the Age of Cold War*, Chicago, University of Chicago Press, 1989, pp. 19–37; J. Lears, "A matter of taste: corporate cultural hegemony in a mass-consumption society," in ibid., pp. 38–57.

7 G. Price, "Arguing the case for being panicky," *Life*, Nov. 18, 1957, vol. 43, pp. 126, 128.
8 D. Carter, *The Final Frontier: The Rise and Fall of the American Rocket State*, London, Verso, 1988, pp. 120–52.
9 A. Sloan, *My Years with General Motors*, Garden City, NY, Anchor Books, 1972, pp. 516–17; J.-P. Bardou, J.-J. Chanaron, P. Fridenson, and J. Laux, *The Automobile Revolution*, Chapel Hill, University of North Carolina Press, 1982, p. 175.
10 Sloan, *My Years*, pp. 323, 516–18; "A new kind of car market," *Fortune*, Sept. 1953, vol. 48, p. 98; T. Hine, *Populuxe*, New York, Knopf, 1986, pp. 98–9.
11 "Industry studies auto styling as key to sell new engineering," *Business Week*, Nov. 10, 1956, pp. 123–4; J. Flink, *The Automobile Age*, Cambridge, Mass., MIT Press, 1988, pp. 240, 277–9; Bardou *et al.*, *The Automobile Revolution*, pp. 208–17.
12 Flink, *Auto Age*, pp. 277–9; E. Kefauver, *In a Few Hands: Monopoly Power in America*, Baltimore, Penguin, 1965, pp. 89–93; Sloan, *My Years*, pp. 159–69;
13 Flink, *Auto Age*, pp. 245–50; D. Halberstam, *The Reckoning*, New York, William Morrow, 1986, pp. 204–23, 242–60; J. Wright, *On A Clear Day You Can See General Motors*, Grosse Pointe, Mich., Wright Enterprises, 1979, pp. 184–92, 205–10.
14 G. Walker interview in Armi, *American Car Design*, pp. 250–1; "Reminiscences of Eugene T. Gregorie," Automotive Design Oral History Project, Edsel B. Ford Design History Center, Henry Ford Museum and Greenfield Village, Dearborn, Mich., 1985, pp. 90–5; "Reminiscences of George Walker," in ibid., 1985, pp. 4–6, 30–9, 49.
15 Personal interview with C. Gale, Senior Designer, Soft Trim, Chrysler Corporation, Highland Park, Mich., Aug. 27, 1987; "Reminiscences of Eugene Bordinat," Automotive Design Oral History Project, Edsel B. Ford Design History Center, Henry Ford Museum and Greenfield Village, Dearborn, Mich., 1984, 1986, pp. 5–9, 33–41; "Reminiscences of John Najjar," in ibid., 1981, 1984, pp. 90, 95–6; "Reminiscences of Joseph Oros and Betty Thatcher Oros," in ibid., 1985, pp. 20–30, 46–9.
16 H. Ford II quoted in G. Walker interview in Armi, *American Car Design*, p. 249.
17 "Reminiscences of John Najjar," pp. 105–9, the quote is on p. 108; Ford Motor Company, *Styling at Ford Motor Company* Dearborn, Mich., Ford Motor Company, 1957, pp. 7–8.
18 "Reminiscences of George Walker," pp. 1–20, the quote is on p. 9; "The Cellini of chrome," *Time*, Nov. 4, 1957, vol. 70, pp. 102–4.
19 "Cellini of chrome," pp. 100–2; "Reminiscences of Eugene Bordinat," pp. 75, 99–100.
20 "Reminiscences of John Najjar," p. 265; Ford Motor Company, *The Ford Book of Styling*, Dearborn, Mich., Public Relations, Styling Office, Ford Motor Company, 1963, pp. 55–6, 63; "Reminiscences of Joseph Oros and Betty Thatcher Oros," pp. 63, 72–3.
21 Keller quoted in H. Whitman, "The shape of cars to come," *Collier's*, Nov. 13, 1948, vol. 122, p. 22; R. Langworth and J. Norbye, *The Complete History of Chrysler Corporation, 1924–1985*, New York, Beekman House,

1985, pp. 109–12, 129, 137–49; "Reminiscences of Arnott 'Buzz' Grisinger," Automotive Design Oral History Project, Edsel B. Ford Design History Center, Henry Ford Museum and Greenfield Village, Dearborn, Mich., 1985, pp. 19–22.

22 Langworth and Norbye, *History of Chrysler*, pp. 144–5, 155–60; personal interview with T. Bertsch, Senior Designer, Soft Trim, Chrysler Corporation, Highland Park, Mich., Aug. 27, 1987.

23 Langworth and Norbye, *History of Chrysler*, pp. 144–5, 155–6; R. Langworth, "SIA profile: Virgil Exner," *Special-Interest Autos*, 1982, no. 72, pp. 20–5; personal interview with R. Gale, Senior Designer, Exterior Fit and Finish, Chrysler Corporation, Highland Park, Mich., Aug. 27, 1987; personal interview with C. Gale.

24 Personal interview with C. Gale. For an example of Exner's writings, see V. Exner, "Styling of Chrysler K–310," *Journal of the Society of Automotive Engineers*, May 1962, vol. 60, pp. 23–5.

25 Personal interview with T. Bertsch; personal interview with W. Brownlie, auto designer, Chrysler Corporation (retired), Dearborn, Mich., Aug. 30, 1987.

26 "Reminiscences of William L. Mitchell," Automotive Design Oral History Project, Edsel B. Ford Design History Center, Henry Ford Museum and Greenfield Village, Dearborn, Mich., 1984, p. 58; Sloan, *My Years*, pp. 300–5; W. Mitchell, "Styling Staff facilities," *General Motors Engineering Journal*, May–June 1956, vol. 3, pp. 80–4.

27 Personal interview with D. Holls, Executive Designer, North American Passenger Car Group, General Motors, Warren, Mich., Aug. 14, 1986.

28 Sloan, *My Years*, pp. 277–80; J. Mitarachi, "Harley Earl and his product," *Industrial Design*, Oct. 1955, vol. 2, pp. 53–6; A. Fleming, "The Earl of design," *Automotive News*, Sept. 16, 1983, p. 226.

29 C. Arnold, "The interrelationship of styling and basic chassis design," *General Motors Engineering Journal*, May–June 1954, vol. 1, pp. 2–7, the quote is on p. 4.

30 Personal interview with C. Jordan, Director of Design Staff, General Motors, Warren, Mich., Aug. 14, 1986. See also personal interview with D. Holls.

31 "Reminiscences of David R. Holls," pp. 9–10; personal interview with D. Holls; Armi, *American Car Design*, pp. 90–1.

32 P. Wilson, *Chrome Dreams: Automobile Styling since 1893*, Radnor, Penn., Chilton Books, 1976, pp. 191–5; Mandel, *American Cars*, pp. 243–53; R. Loewy, *Never Leave Well Enough Alone*, New York, Simon & Schuster, 1951, pp. 305–7.

33 Armi, *American Car Design*, pp. 77–80; G. Walker interview in ibid., p. 252; J. Flint, *The Dream Machine*, New York, Quadrangle, 1976, pp. 46–50; Mandel, *American Cars*, pp. 262–4.

34 D. Lewis, M. McCarsville, and L. Sorensen, *Ford: 1903 to 1984*, New York, Beekman House, 1983, pp. 137–9, 145–6.

35 Walker interviewed in "Why do our cars look the way they do?" *Popular Mechanics*, Jan. 1959, vol. 111, pp. 282–4.

36 L. Rainwater, R. Coleman, and G. Handel, *Workingman's Wife: Her Personality, World and Life Style*, New York, Oceana Publications, 1959, p. 210. See also Hine, *Populuxe*, pp. 37–8.

37 Mitchell quoted in Flint, *Dream Machine*, p. 96. On abandoned small-car programs, see Langworth and Norbye, *History of GM*, pp. 174–5; E. Cray, *The Chrome Colossus: General Motors and its Times*, New York, McGraw-Hill, 1980, pp. 352–3; Lewis *et al.*, *Ford*, pp. 130–3.

38 "The big change coming in autos," *US News and World Report*, March 9, 1959, vol. 46, p. 51; Cole quoted in "The Chevrolet story: styling," *Business Week*, Oct. 30, 1954, p. 46.

39 F. Bello, "How strong is GM research?" *Fortune*, June 1956, vol. 53, p. 194.

40 W. Teague, "Detroit in 1965: renaissance or old hat," *Automobile Quarterly*, Winter 1965, vol. 3, p. 422; M. Sedgwick, *Cars of the Fifties and Sixties*, New York, Beekman House, p. 89; J. Flink, *The Car Culture*, Cambridge, Mass., MIT Press, 1975, pp. 195–6; Flink, *Auto Age*, p. 287.

41 W. Whyte, "The Cadillac phenomenon," *Fortune*, Feb. 1955, vol. 51, pp. 106–9, 174–84.

42 Hine, *Populuxe*, pp. 1–10.

43 H. Earl, "Styling unlimited," manuscript in the Historic Files of the General Motors Design Staff, Design Library, General Motors Technical Center, Warren, Mich., 1958, p. 2.

44 "GM's Motoramas," *Special-Interest Autos*, 1974, no. 21, pp. 24–9; S. MacMinn, "American auto design," in G. Silk (ed.), *Automobile and Culture*, New York, Harry Abrams, 1984, pp. 237–8; J.-R. Piccard, *The Automobile Year Book of Dream Cars*, New York, Norton, 1981, p. 197.

45 H. Earl, "Styling in General Motors," *General Motors Engineering Journal*, May–June 1956, vol. 3. p. 78; personal interview with T. Bertsch.

46 "Reminiscences of Alex Tremulis," Automotive Design Oral History Project, Edsel B. Ford Design History Center, Henry Ford Museum and Greenfield Village, Dearborn, Mich., 1984, pp. 73, 104; H. Earl, "Setting the style," General Motors Corporation, *Opportunities Unlimited – Meeting Tomorrow's Challenge*, published speeches delivered at the 1955 GM Executive Conference held at the Greenbrier, White Sulphur Springs, WV, September 26–28, 1955, in the Historic Files of the General Motors Design Staff, Design Library, General Motors Technical Center, Warren, Mich., pp. 86–8.

47 K. Ludvigsen, "Le Sabre and XP-300," *Special-Interest Autos*, 1973, no. 16, pp. 22–7; General Motors Corporation, *Le Sabre: An Experimental Laboratory on Wheels*, pamphlet distributed at the Chicago Automobile Show, March 14–22, 1953, in the Cadillac Division file, National Automotive History Collection, Detroit Public Library, Detroit, Mich.

48 Piccard, *Dream Cars*, pp. 72, 81, 97.

49 "Reminiscences of Eugene Bordinat," pp. 84–5.

50 M. Lamm, "1948 and 1949 Cadillac fastbacks," *Special-Interest Autos*, 1972, no. 11, pp. 10–17, 56; R. Langworth, "Of tail fins and V-8s," *Automobile Quarterly*, 1975, vol. 13, pp. 309–21; H. Earl, "I dream automobiles," *Saturday Evening Post*, August 7, 1954, vol. 227, p. 82.

51 Langworth and Norbye, *History of GM*, pp. 185–6; A. Brown, "1949 Buick Riviera," *Special-Interest Autos*, 1985, no. 89, pp. 16–23; Mandel, *American Cars*, p. 232.

52 Langworth and Norbye, *History of GM*, pp. 186–7; General Motors Corporation, *Styling: The Look of Things*, Detroit, Public Relations, Styling Staff, General Motors Corporation, 1955, pp. 42–3; Ant Farm (C. Lord),

Automerica: A Trip Down US Highways From World War II to the Future,
New York, E.P. Dutton, 1976, pp. 75–7.
53 Personal interview with C. Jordan; Wilson, *Chrome Dreams*, pp. 198, 206.
54 Langworth and Norbye, *History of Chrysler*, pp. 164–70; V. Exner, "How
    does a designer style an automobile," *Gentry*, otherwise unidentified maga-
    zine article in the Historic Files of the General Motors Design Staff, Design
    Library, General Motors Technical Center, Warren, Mich.
55 Exner quoted in Langworth and Norbye, *History of Chrysler*, p. 176; on
    shortening style cycles, see the chart in A. Brown, "1956 Hudson Hornet
    Special," *Special-Interest Autos*, 1983, no. 77, p. 57.
56 V. Exner, "Fins improve automobile stability," *Journal of the Society of
    Automotive Engineers*, Jan. 1958, vol. 66, p. 122; Earl quoted in "I dream
    automobiles," p. 19; D. Cole, "Designer's dilemma," *Saturday Evening
    Post*, Nov. 1976, vol. 248, p. 30.
57 "Styling assignment in GM," *General Motors Engineering Journal*, Oct.–
    Nov. 1957, vol. 4, inside back cover.
58 "Reminiscences of John Najjar," p. 88; "The story of GM styling," manu-
    script in the Historic Files of the General Motors Design Staff, Design
    Library, General Motors Technical Center, Warren, Mich., 1962, p. 3;
    "Reminiscences of Suzanne E. Vanderbilt," Automotive Design Oral
    History Project, Edsel B. Ford Design History Center, Henry Ford Museum
    and Greenfield Village, Dearborn, Mich., 1986, passim; "Reminiscences of
    Joseph Oros and Betty Thatcher Oros," passim.
59 Both quotes are from "Reminiscences of Suzanne E. Vanderbilt," pp. 36,
    38; S. Bayley, *Harley Earl and the Dream Machine*, New York, Knopf,
    1983, pp. 99, 103–4, 108; H. Earl, transcript of a press conference held
    March 25, 1958 at General Motors Technical Center with thirty women
    writers, in the Historic Files of the General Motors Design Staff, Design
    Library, General Motors Technical Center, Warren, Mich.
60 Quoted ads are reproduced in J. Stern and M. Stern, *Auto Ads*, New York,
    Random House, 1978, pp. 65, 94.
61 Rainwater *et al.*, *Workingman's Wife*, p. 181; Bordinat quoted in R.
    Atcheson, "Gasoline in their blood: the Detroit designers," *Show*, Dec.
    1963, p. 157.
62 Buick B–58 ad reproduced in Stern and Stern, *Auto Ads*, pp. 98–9.
63 Buick Dynaflow ad reproduced in Lord, *Automerica*, p. 30.
64 E. Kaufmann, "Borax, or the chromium-plated calf," *Architectural Review*,
    Aug. 1948, vol. 104, pp. 88–93, quotes are on pp. 88, 89; R. Loewy,
    "Jukebox on wheels," *Atlantic Monthly*, Apr. 1955, vol. 195, pp. 36–8,
    quotes are on p. 36.
65 Flint, *Dream Machine*, pp. 96, 118–20, 220; Wilson, *Chrome Dreams*, pp.
    207–9; "Why do our cars look the way they do?" p. 286.
66 "Jukeboxes, F.O.B. Detroit," *Fortune*, Sept. 1947, vol. 36, pp. 48b, 184.
67 J. Rae, *The American Automobile*, Chicago, University of Chicago Press,
    1965, pp. 211–12; Flint, *Dream Machine*, pp. 211–13; "Why smaller cars
    are coming," *Business Week*, Jan. 17, 1959, p. 30; VW survey reported in
    Cray, *Chrome Colossus*, p. 402.
68 R. Banham, "The end of insolence," in *Design by Choice*, New York,
    Rizzoli, 1981, p. 121.

69 Sloan, *My Life*, p. 517; B. Tara, "Personal relationships with the automobile," transcript of a speech delivered to GM designers, in the Historic Files of the General Motors Design Staff, Design Library, General Motors Technical Center, Warren, Mich., n.d., pp. 2–3.

70 H. Robert, "Hot rods and customs," in Silk (ed.), *Automobile and Culture*, pp. 181–7; R. Boyle, "The car cult from Rumpsville," *Sports Illustrated*, Apr. 24, 1961, pp. 70–2, 77–9, 83–6; H. Moorhouse, *Driving Ambitions: An Analysis of the American Hot Rod Enthusiasm*, Manchester, Manchester University Press, 1991.

71 R. Denny, "The plastic machines," in *The Astonished Muse*, Chicago, University of Chicago Press, 1964, pp. 154–5; *Hot Rod Magazine* quoted in Moorhouse, *Driving Ambitions*, p. 161.

72 Robert, "Hot rods," pp. 189–95; F. Basham, B. Ughetti, and P. Rambali, *Car Culture*, New York, Delilah, 1984, pp. 96–127; T. Wolfe, *The Kandy-Kolored Tangerine-Flake Streamline Baby*, New York, Noonday Press, 1965, pp. 79–105.

73 Hot rodder quoted in Boyle, "Car cult," p. 86.

74 J. Keats, *The Insolent Chariots*, Philadelphia, J.B. Lippincott, 1958, pp. 70–1, 75; V. Packard, *Hidden Persuaders*, New York, Pocket Books, 1980, pp. 82–3.

75 C. Warnock, *The Edsel Affair*, Paradise Valley, Ariz., Pro West, 1980, pp. 5, 39; D. Wallace, "The personalities of eight makes of cars," Marketing Research Department, Merchandising and Product Planning Office, Edsel Division, in Ford Motor Company Archives, Accession no. 633, Box E–1, Dearborn, Mich., 1957, p. 1; second Wallace quote in J. Brooks, *The Fate of the Edsel and Other Business Adventures*, New York, Harper & Row, 1963, pp. 27–8.

76 Warnock, *Edsel Affair*, pp. 55–7, 75–6, 100–1; M. Lamm, "E–Bomb! The Edsel's aim was right, but the target moved," *Special-Interest Autos*, 1973, no. 19, p. 14; Brooks, *Fate of Edsel*, p. 34.

77 "The market and personality objectives of the E–Car," Marketing Research Department, Merchandising and Product Planning Office, Special Products Division, Ford Motor Company, in Ford Motor Company Archives, Accession no. 633, Box E–1, Dearborn, Mich., 1956, the quote is on p. 52; "Personalities of eight makes;" E. Larabee, "The Edsel and how it got that way," *Harper's*, Sept. 1957, vol. 215, pp. 72–3.

78 Warnock, *Edsel Affair*, p. 143. See also Brooks, *Fate of Edsel*, p. 37.

79 Brown quoted in Brooks, *Fate of Edsel*, p. 23. See also R. Brown, *Prelude to Production*, Ford Motor Company Archives, Accession no. 795, Dearborn, Mich., 1956.

80 Brooks, *Fate of Edsel*, pp. 55–6; Warnock, *Edsel Affair*, passim.

81 "The new Edsel," *Consumer Reports*, Jan. 1958, vol. 23, pp. 30–3; "The Edsel story," *Consumer Reports*, Apr. 1958, vol. 23, p. 218.

82 "Reminiscences of John Najjar," Automotive Design Oral History Project, Edsel B. Ford Design History Center, Henry Ford Museum and Greenfield Village, Dearborn, Mich., 1981, 1984, p. 253.

83 "Detroit makes an about-face on design," *Business Week*, Feb. 28, 1959, p. 25.

84 Larrabee, "Edsel," pp. 67, 71; Brooks, *Fate of Edsel*, pp. 65–8.

85 Wallace quoted in Brooks, *Fate of Edsel*, p. 71.

86 Lewis *et al.*, *Ford*, pp. 153–5, 159–60, 175–8; T. Hawley, "1958–60 Ford Thunderbird: misunderstood masterpiece," *Collectible Automobile*, Sept. 1984, vol. 1, pp. 52–69; "Detroit makes an about-face on design," p. 25; Macquire quoted in "Why do our cars look the way they do?" p. 282.

7 THE RISE AND FALL OF AUTO INDIVIDUALITY

1 Personal interview with W. Brownlie, auto designer, Chrysler Corporation (retired), Dearborn, Mich., Aug. 30, 1987.
2 B. Ehrenreich, *Fear of Falling: The Inner Life of the Middle Class*, New York, HarperCollins, 1989, pp. 42–56.
3 J. O'Connor, *Accumulation Crisis*, New York, Basil Blackwell, 1984, pp. 179–87; M. Bosquet, *Capitalism in Crisis and Everyday Life*, Hassocks, Harvester, 1977, pp. 20–6; S. Bowles, D. Gordon, and T. Weisskopf, *Beyond the Wasteland*, London, Verso, 1984, pp. 79–84.
4 Bowles *et al.*, *Beyond the Wasteland*, pp. 84–91; S. Aronowitz, *False Promises*, New York, McGraw-Hill, 1973.
5 Ehrenreich, *Fear of Falling*, pp. 57–96.
6 On consumerism and the disintegration of the family, see B. Ehrenreich, *The Hearts of Men*, Garden City, NY, Anchor Books, 1984.
7 E. Rothschild, *Paradise Lost: The Decline of the Auto-Industrial Age*, New York, Vintage, 1973, p. 44; E. Cray, *The Chrome Colossus: General Motors and its Times*, New York, McGraw-Hill, 1980, p. 435; "Autos: the new generation," *Time*, Oct. 5, 1959, vol. 74, pp. 94–5.
8 T. Hine, *Populuxe*, New York, Knopf, 1986, p. 91; L. Mandel, *American Cars*, New York, Stewart, Tabori & Chang, 1982, pp. 295–6.
9 Mitchell interview in F. Coates, "Auto outlook: fuel shortage dictates future design," *Industrial Design*, Sept. 1977, vol. 24, pp. 56–60.
10 C. Armi, *The Art of American Car Design*, University Park, Pennsylvania State University Press, 1988, pp. 38–43, Rybicki quoted on p. 294; "Reminiscences of D. Holls," Automotive Design Oral History Project, Edsel B. Ford Design History Center, Henry Ford Museum and Greenfield Village, Dearborn, Mich., 1985, p. 21.
11 Armi, *American Car Design*, pp. 39–40.
12 Ibid., p. 43; "Reminiscences of David R. Holls," p. 23; De Lorean quoted in J. Wright, *On a Clear Day You Can See General Motors*, Grosse Pointe, Mich., Wright Enterprises, 1979, p. 182.
13 "Reminiscences of Arnott 'Buzz' Grisinger," Automotive Design Oral History Project, Edsel B. Ford Design History Center, Henry Ford Museum and Greenfield Village, Dearborn, Mich., 1985, p. 78; "Reminiscences of John Najjar," in ibid., 1981, 1984, pp. 167, 272; "Reminiscences of David C. Turner, Jr," in ibid., 1984, pp. 25–6.
14 R. Langworth and J. Norbye, *The Complete History of Chrysler Corporation, 1924–1985*, New York, Beekman House, 1985, pp. 186–90; personal interview with W. Brownlie; personal interview with R. Gale, Senior Designer, Exterior Fit and Finish, Chrysler Corporation, Highland Park, Mich., Aug. 27, 1987.
15 Engel quoted in a personal interview with T. Bertsch, Senior Designer, Soft Trim, Chrysler Corporation, Highland Park, Mich., Aug. 27, 1987.

16 Personal interview with R. Gale.
17 J.-P. Bardou, J.-J. Chanaron, P. Fridensen, and J. Laux, *The Automobile Revolution*, Chapel Hill, University of North Carolina Press, 1982, pp. 177–9; J. Flint, *The Dream Machine: The Golden Age of American Automobiles, 1946–1965*, New York, Quadrangle, 1976, p. 278; R. Langworth and J. Norbye, *The Complete History of General Motors, 1908–1986*, New York, Beekman House, 1986, p. 272; Wright, *On a Clear Day*, p. 104.
18 Gordon quoted in A. Sloan, *My Years With General Motors*, Garden City, NY, Anchor, 1972, p. 520; C. McCammon, "Styling – the crossroads of corporate creativity," transcript of a speech delivered to Campbell–Ewald Co., in the Historic Files of the General Motors Design Staff, Design Library, General Motors Technical Center, Warren, Mich., April, 1959, p. 6.
19 Langworth and Norbye, *History of GM*, p. 236; "Detroit makes an about-face on design," *Business Week*, Feb. 28, 1959, p. 25; B. Tara, "Personal relationships with the automobile," transcript of a speech delivered to GM designers, in the Historic Files of the General Motors Design Staff, Design Library, General Motors Technical Center, Warren, Mich., n.d., pp. 2–3.
20 Langworth and Norbye, *History of GM*, pp. 234–5; S. MacMinn, "American automobile design," in G. Silk (ed.), *Automobile and Culture*, New York, Harry Abrams, 1984, pp. 241–2; Sloan, *My Years*, pp. 517, 518–19.
21 Langworth and Norbye, *History of GM*, pp. 237–40, 243; D. Lewis, M. McCarville, and L. Sorensen, *Ford: 1903 to 1984*, New York, Beekman House, 1983, pp. 190–1.
22 "Buyers want cars bigger, fancier," *Business Week*, May 4, 1963, p. 33; "Autos get longer for 1964," *Business Week*, June 22, 1963, pp. 32–3; Cray, *Chrome Colossus*, pp. 435–6.
23 *Motor Trend* quoted in Lewis *et al.*, *Ford*, p. 184.
24 Langworth and Norbye, *History of GM*, p. 250; Armi, *American Car Design*, pp. 218–19; "Reminiscences of William L. Mitchell," Automotive Design Oral History Project, Edsel B. Ford Design History Center, Henry Ford Museum and Greenfield Village, Dearborn, Mich., 1984, pp. 12–13.
25 Langworth and Norbye, *History of GM*, p. 254; Wright, *On a Clear Day*, pp. 91–2, Armi, *American Car Design*, p. 218.
26 Langworth and Norbye, *History of Chrysler*, p. 200; Lewis *et al.*, *Ford*, p. 215; Langworth and Norbye, *History of GM*, pp. 269–70.
27 De Lorean quoted in Wright, *On A Clear Day*, p. 92; Mandel, *American Cars*, pp. 298–305; Langworth and Norbye, *History of GM*, pp. 257–8.
28 AMX ads reproduced in M. Frumpkin, *Muscle Car Mania: An Advertising Collection, 1964–1974*, Osceola, Wis., Motorbooks International, 1981, pp. 7, 10.
29 Dodge Challenger and Buick Skylark ads reproduced in ibid., pp. 22, 32, 106.
30 L. Bailey, "Mustang rides the market," *Automobile Quarterly*, Fall 1964, vol. 3. pp. 322–3; personal interview with G. Halderman, Director, North American Design, Ford Motor Company, Dearborn, Mich., Aug. 30, 1988; Iacocca quoted in Mandel, *American Cars*, p. 308.
31 Bailey, "Mustang rides the market," p. 323.
32 Flint, *Dream Machine*, p. 339; Iacocca quoted in J. Flink, *The Automobile Age*, Cambridge, Mass., MIT Press, 1988, p. 155.

33 S. Lanson, "Will the classic look return?" *Motor Trend*, Sept. 1960, vol. 12. pp. 30–1; personal interview with W. Brownlie; Langworth and Norbye, *History of Chrysler*, pp. 183–90.
34 Mitchell quoted in J. Mitarachi, "Harley Earl and his product," *Industrial Design*, Oct. 1955, vol. 2, p. 60.
35 Mitchell quoted by Irv Rybicki in A. Fleming, "The Earl of design," *Automotive News*, Sept. 16, 1983, p. 233; Armi, *American Car Design*, pp. 39–40, 91–2, 215, 218–19.
36 N. Thimmesch, "The metaphysics of automotive design," *Esquire*, Dec. 1967, vol. 68, pp. 291–2; Lewis *et al.*, *Ford*, pp. 194–5, 215–17; Langworth and Norbye, *History of Chrysler*, p. 190; "The change is gradual: slabs, cubes and some curves," *Time*, Sept. 25, 1964, vol. 84, pp. 88–9.
37 B. Porter interview in Armi, *American Car Design*, pp. 259–68, the quote is on p. 260; personal interview with B. Porter, Chief Designer, Buick Studio II, General Motors Corporation, General Motors Technical Center, Warren, Mich., Aug. 26, 1986.
38 J. Lawlor, "The customizer and the car maker," *Motor Trend*, Apr. 1966, vol. 18, pp. 28–9; T. Wolfe, *The Kandy-Kolored Tangerine-Flake Streamline Baby*, New York, Noonday Press, 1965, pp. 76–107; Wright, *On A Clear Day*, p. 91; F. Basham, B. Ughetti, and P. Rambali, *Car Culture*, New York, Delilah, 1984, pp. 105–9.
39 K. Brougher, "The car as star," in Silk (ed.), *Automobile and Culture*, pp. 172–3; S. Bayley, *Sex, Drink, and Fast Cars*, New York, Pantheon, 1985, pp. 5, 27–30.
40 W. Mossberg and L. O'Donnell, "End of the affair," *Wall Street Journal*, March 30, 1971, pp. 1, 17.
41 Wright, *On A Clear Day*, pp. 104, 118–19; W. Abernathy, *The Productivity Dilemma*, Baltimore, Johns Hopkins University Press, 1978, pp. 93–9, 131–5.
42 Wright, *On A Clear Day*, pp. 102–4, 107; personal interview with G. Halderman; Rothschild, *Paradise Lost*, pp. 87–9.
43 A. Herman, "Rapid productivity gains reported for selected industries for 1971," *Monthly Labor Review*, Aug. 1972, vol. 95, pp. 41–3; Abernathy, *Productivity Dilemma*, pp. 156–9.
44 Rothschild, *Paradise Lost*, pp. 3–5, 27–9, 55–64; A. Altshuler, M. Anderson, D. Jones, D. Roos and J. Womack, *The Future of the Automobile*, Cambridge, Mass., MIT Press, 1984, p. 25.
45 Wright, *On A Clear Day*, pp. 6–7.
46 Ibid., pp. 130, 210–12, the quote is on p. 130; Cray, *Chrome Colossus*, pp. 448–9; Langworth and Norbye, *History of GM*, pp. 313–14; Rothschild, *Paradise Lost*, pp. 113–14.
47 Abernathy, *Productivity Dilemma*, pp. 94–5, 123, 127n.; "The Edsel dies, and Ford regroups survivors," *Business Week*, Nov. 28, 1959, pp. 26–8; Langworth and Norbye, *History of Chrysler*, pp. 181, 190, 215.
48 Abernathy, *Productivity Dilemma*, pp. 123, 131; "An end to obsolescence?" *Time*, May 18, 1970, vol. 95, p. 83; L. O'Donnell, "Ford says it's soft-pedaling style change because of costs and less buyer interest," *Wall Street Journal*, March 26, 1971, p. 3.
49 Rothschild, *Paradise Lost*, pp. 97–118; Wright, *On a Clear Day*, pp. 168–9.

50 Langworth and Norbye, *History of GM*, pp. 113–14; Wright, *On A Clear Day*, pp. 129–30, 211; Rothschild, *Paradise Lost*, pp. 85–91.
51 Roche and Kennedy exchange quoted in R. Nader, *Unsafe At Any Speed*, New York, Bantam, 1973, pp. 264, 267. See also B. Yates, *The Decline and Fall of the American Automobile Industry*, New York, Empire, 1983, pp. 255–9; Mandel, *American Cars*, pp. 391–4.
52 Nader, *Unsafe*, pp. 1–34; Wright, *On a Clear Day*, pp. 42, 53–7; Langworth and Norbye, *History of GM*, p. 264; Flink, *Auto Age*, pp. 382–8.
53 Quit rates reported in US Bureau of Labor Statistics, *Handbook of Labor Statistics, 1972*, Bulletin no. 1735, Washington, DC, Government Printing Office, 1972, p. 117; Ford and GM officials quoted in Rothschild, *Paradise Lost*, pp. 124–5.
54 De Lorean quoted in Wright, *On A Clear Day*, p. 169. On the Lordstown strike, see also Rothschild, *Paradise Lost*, pp. 113–67; B. Garson, *All the Livelong Day*, Harmondsworth and New York, Penguin, 1975, pp. 86–98; S. Terkel, *Working*, New York, Avon, 1975, pp. 256–65; Aronowitz, *False Promises*, pp. 21–50.

EPILOGUE   DESIGN IN THE WAKE OF FORDISM

1 S. Bowles, D. Gordon, and T. Weisskopf, *Beyond the Wasteland*, London, Verso, 1984; B. Bluestone and B. Harrison, *The Deindustrialization of America*, New York, Basic Books, 1982; M. Davis, *Prisoners of the American Dream*, London, Verso, 1986.
2 J. Flink, *The Auto Age*, Cambridge, Mass., MIT Press, 1988, pp. 388–91.
3 Personal interview with J. Godshall, Senior Project Designer, Interior Studio III, Chrysler Corporation, Highland Park, Mich., Aug. 27, 1987; N. Thimmesch, "The metaphysics of automotive design," *Esquire*, Dec. 1967, vol. 68, p. 188.
4 Personal interview with D. Turner, Director, Advanced Concepts and Industrial Design, Ford Motor Company, Dearborn, Mich., Aug. 29, 1988; Mitchell quoted (anonymously) in B. Yates, "Detroit's shattered love affair," *Car and Driver*, Oct. 1974, pp. 51, 91.
5 Personal interview with G. Halderman, Director, North American Design, Ford Motor Company, Dearborn, Mich., Aug. 30, 1988; GM designer quoted in M. Tremont and M. Lamm, "Jordan: bringing the fun back," *Car Styling*, Apr. 1987, no. 58, p. 25.
6 "Reminiscences of William Clay Ford," Automotive Design Oral History Project, Edsel B. Ford Design History Center, Henry Ford Museum and Greenfield Village, Dearborn, Mich., 1986, p. 64; "Reminiscences of Fred 'Fritz' Mayhew," in ibid., 1984, pp. 15–16, 57–9; personal interview with C. Gale, Senior Designer, Soft Trim, Chrysler Corporation, Highland Park, Mich., Aug. 27, 1987.
7 Personal interview with J. Godshall.
8 B. Yates, *The Decline and Fall of the American Automobile Industry*, New York, Empire, 1983, pp. 176–8, 193–6; C. Armi, *The Art of American Car Design*, University Park, Pennsylvania State University, 1988, pp. 96–8.
9 Davis, *Prisoners*, pp. 181–230; B. Harrison and B. Bluestone, *The Great U-Turn: Corporate Restructuring and the Polarizing of America*, New

York, Basic Books, 1988; B. Ehrenreich, *Fear of Falling: The Inner Life of the Middle Class*, New York, HarperCollins, 1989, pp. 196–243.

10 Personal interview with J. Godshall.
11 *Road and Track* quoted in D. Lewis, M. McCarville and L. Sorensen, *Ford: 1903 to 1984*, New York, Beekman House, 1983, p. 371.
12 Personal interviews with Ford designers D. Turner, G. Halderman, and P. Shivani, Dearborn, Mich., Aug. 29 and 30, 1988.
13 Personal interview with D. Turner; the quote is from a personal interview with G. Halderman.
14 "Reminiscences of Fred 'Fritz' Mayhew," p. 21.
15 Ibid., p. 59.
16 Quote is from P. Steinhart, "Our off-road fantasy," in D. Lewis and L. Goldstein (eds), *The Automobile and American Culture*, Ann Arbor, University of Michigan Press, 1983, p. 350.
17 For the increased emphasis on bulk, see J. Healey, "Auto design: reflection of the times," *USA Today*, Oct. 1, 1992.
18 On post-Fordism, see M. Piore and C. Sabel, *The Second Industrial Divide*, New York, Basic Books, 1984.

Index

Abernathy, W. 204, 205
accessories 75, 141, 193
accidents 125, 208, 213; *see also*
    safety
accountants 142–3, 182
accumulation, regime of 2
Adorno, T. 6–8
advertising 42, 173; of automobiles
    23, 59–60, 63, 65, 94, 134, 168,
    176, 178, 197, 216
aerodynamics 116, 218–22; *see also*
    streamlining
aesthetics: of automobiles *see*
    automobile aesthetics; of
    continuums 102; of democracy
    72–3; of Fordism 5; functionalist
    4, 168–9, 172; machine, of
    modernism 61; of mass-produced
    goods 4, 6–8, 11, 57, 61, 71–3;
    organic 7–8, 61, 72; reified 7; of
    revelation 100–1; of streamlining
    115–33
air conditioning 162
airplanes: influence on automobile
    aesthetics 116, 130, 133–5, 151–2,
    159–63, 168, 202; P–38 Lightning
    135, 136, 162; *see also*
    aerodynamics
Allen, F. L. 124
American Motors Corporation 170,
    196
"Americanism and Fordism"
    (Gramsci) 2
AMX (automobile) 196
annual model change 87, 109, 112,

113; acceleration of 142, 163,
    165; costs of 93–4, 142, 178;
    ideology of 96–7; origins of 23,
    75–6; slowing of 207
anxiety, and consumerism 139–40,
    183
Apple Tree Girl, The 54
Art and Color Department (Chrysler
    Corporation) 93, 114–15; *see also*
    Styling Department (Chrysler
    Corporation)
Art and Color Section (General
    Motors Corporation) 68; Body
    Development Studio of 109, 112,
    187; body interchangeability in
    106–7; corporate position of 82–4,
    111; creation of studio system in
    110–11; Design Committee of
    109, 111, 166; design process in
    89, 92; engineers in 107–8;
    founding of 81; organization of
    87–9; personnel of 87; renamed
    Styling Staff 111; rise to
    supremacy 107–13; *see also*
    Styling Staff (General Motors
    Corporation)
Arts and Crafts movement 57
Art Deco 123, 130
Art Nouveau movement 27
assembly line 1, 2, 40, 204–5, 207–8
assembly plants 204–8
automation 205, 207
Audi (automobile) 116, 220
automobile: cost of operation 155; as
    entertainment 82; as furthering

automobile design 214
Graham (automobile): 1932 Blue
    Streak 119-20
Gramsci, A. 2, 174
Gray and Brass (Sloan) 36
Gregorie, B. 113–14, 130, 143–4
grille 119, 123, 124, 125, 127, 129,
    132, 162, 176, 178
guilt, and consumerism 139–40, 179
Gutherie, W. 101, 103

hardtop convertible 162–3
Harper's Weekly 35, 124, 179
headlights 119, 124, 129, 130, 172,
    201
Henderson, H. 93
"Henry's made a lady out of Lizzie"
    77
Hershey, F. 86, 87, 110, 136
Hibbard, T. 50, 63
Hidden Persuaders, The (Packard)
    139, 173
Hispano–Suiza (automobile) 81
Hitchcock, A. 139
Hitler, A. 15
Holls, D. 127, 150
Hollywood (California) 79, 82, 159
home ownership 42, 137
hood 22, 31, 53, 65, 124, 125, 127,
    129, 130, 194, 201
Horkheimer, M. 6
Horseless Age 37
horsepower 153, 155
hot rodding 182, 196; aesthetic of
    171–2; class basis of 171, 173
Hot Rod Magazine 171
Hudson (automobile): 1922 Essex
    coach 45
Hudson Company 93, 151
human nature 10–11

Iacocca, L. 197, 199
identification cues 110
ideology: automobile as 14, 15,
    117–18, 159; of consumer
    sovereignty 208; consumption as
    6, 8, 224, 225; of irrationalism
    102–3; nationalist, of Cold War
    137–8, 162, 167–8; of progress

56, 116, 117; religion as 14, 160;
    of separate gender spheres 98, 167
individualism 17, 18, 35, 56, 190,
    209–10
individuality: age of 185; in
    automobiles 97, 106, 109–10,
    170–3, 175, 176, 178–81, 184,
    186, 190–9, 203; in consumer
    goods 8, 71, 72, 139;
    reorganization of automobile
    design for 185–9
industrial design 71–3, 101–3
industrial designers 71–3, 101–3
Industrial Workers of the World 41
Insolent Chariots, The (Keats), 173
insulation, technology of 152, 160,
    162, 165–8, 199
interchangeability 76–7, 87, 106,
    206–7; of body 106–7, 109–10,
    114–15, 187
interior 123, 129, 166, 174, 176, 180
Interstate Highway Act 137
irrationality: of automotive
    purchases 108; of consumer
    desires 109, 163; and streamlining
    102–3, 127
Ital Design 216

Jaguar (automobile) 225
Japanese automobiles 217–18
Jaray, P. 116
Jeep (automobile) 222–3
Jordan (automobile) 94
Jordan, N. 94, 97–8
Jordan Motor Car Company 94
*Journal of the Society of Automotive
    Engineers* 119

Kaiser–Frazer Company 151
Kamm, W. 116
Kaptur, V. 106
Kaufmann, E. 168–9
Keats, J. 173
Keller, K. T. 115, 146
Kennedy, J. F. 140
Kennedy, R. 208–9
Kettering, C. 64, 74
Kissel (automobile) 59–60
Klemin, A. 116

standardization of products 43–4, 71, 72, 76, 77, 204, 205
state: in Fordism 3; economic intervention of 104, 137
station wagon 224
Steinhart, P. 223
Stout, W. 117
streamlining: aesthetic 118–21, 125–33, 221–2; of automobiles 53, 100, 115–33, 219–22; as corporate program 101–2, 118; functional 116–17, 119, 121–5, 221–2; as ideology 101– 3, 116, 117–19, 123, 126, 222; and irrationality 102–3, 127
strikes 137, 185, 210–11, 218
Studebaker (automobile): 1947 Champion 152; 1953 Starliner 169
Studebaker Corporation 147
studios, of automobile styling 109, 145, 147; centralized control of 109–10, 111, 150–1; decentralized control of 186–7; separation of 110–11
style: in automobiles 5, 62–7, 77–81, 92, 141–2; in consumer goods 69–73; reconciliation of, with mass production 81–2, 107; *see also* aesthetics
styling cycle 96, 112, 141, 163, 165
Styling Department (Chrysler Corporation) 146–8, 163, 188–9; subordination to engineers 146, 148, 189; *see also* Art and Color Department (Chrysler Corporation)
Styling Office (Ford Motor Company) 163, 166; competition within 144; founding of 113; organization of 114, 144–6, 188, 215; postwar growth of 143–6; renamed Design Staff 214; subordination to engineers 113, 144
Styling Staff (General Motors Corporation) 129, 133, 166; Advanced Design Studio of 112, 135, 187; Body Development Studio of 109, 112, 187; bureaucratization of 148, 150–1;

corporate position of 111, 150, 187–8; decline in power 214–15; Design Committee of 150; dominance during 1950s 149; founding of 111; organization of 111, 186–7; renamed Design Staff 214; training program of 112–13; *see also* Art and Color Department (General Motors Corporation)
stylists, automobile 50–1, 87, 133–5, 143–51, 160, 199, 213–14; conflict with engineers, 82, 84, 107–8, 113–14, 125, 149, 188, 214; conflict with sales managers 84–5, 108–9; cooperation with engineers 214–15, 221, 222; decline in power 213–15; gender of 84, 86, 87, 166; preference for big cars 154, 188; sexuality of 145; and streamlining 117–19, 125–33; training of 112–13
suburbs 138, 141, 154, 157
surveys *see* consumer surveys
suspension 152, 191, 209
Systeme Panhard 22

Taft–Hartley Act 137
tail fins 159, 165, 199; origins of 135–7; rationale for 162
taillights 129, 130, 172, 176, 201
tape drawings 187
Tara, B. 170, 191
Taylor, F. 17, 40
Teague, W. D. 56–7, 71, 103, 135
teardrop form 116, 117; *see also* streamlining
Technical Center (General Motors Corporation) 148
technological utopianism 100, 134–5, 199, 202, 219
technology, automobile: consumer interest in 22–3, 62, 64; innovations in 23, 62, 75, 97, 107, 118, 142
technology, production 43–6
Telnack, J. 215, 220
through-line 95, 96
Time 145, 207
time and motion study 17, 204–5, 207